THE UZAWA-LUCAS ENDOGENOUS GROWTH MODEL

*To my parents, Giulietta and Pasquale
and to my little twin-nephews,
Alessio and Davide.*

The Uzawa-Lucas Endogenous Growth Model

PAOLO MATTANA
The University of Cagliari, Italy

Routledge
Taylor & Francis Group

LONDON AND NEW YORK

First published 2004 by Ashgate Publishing

Reissued 2018 by Routledge
2 Park Square, Milton Park, Abingdon, Oxon OX14 4RN
605 Third Avenue, New York, NY 10017

First issued in paperback 2021

Routledge is an imprint of the Taylor & Francis Group, an informa business

© Paolo Mattana 2004

Paolo Mattana has asserted his right under the Copyright, Designs and Patents Act, 1988, to be identified as the author of this work.

A Library of Congress record exists under LC control number: 2004049587

Notice:
Product or corporate names may be trademarks or registered trademarks, and are used only for identification and explanation without intent to infringe.

Publisher's Note
The publisher has gone to great lengths to ensure the quality of this reprint but points out that some imperfections in the original copies may be apparent.

Disclaimer
The publisher has made every effort to trace copyright holders and welcomes correspondence from those they have been unable to contact.

ISBN 13: 978-0-815-39835-6 (hbk)
ISBN 13: 978-1-351-14496-4 (ebk)
ISBN 13: 978-1-138-35767-9 (pbk)

DOI: 10.4324/9781351144964

Contents

List of Figures

List of Tables

Preface

At the end of 1999 I began to work at a research project titled "Uniqueness, Indeterminacy and Chaos in a General Two-Sector Model of Endogenous Growth" for which I had received a generous grant from the Autonomous Regional Government of Sardinia (Italy). The project was originally undertaken to determine the conditions under which complicated dynamic phenomena, such as multiple equilibrium paths, instability or even unpredictable chaotic motion, could emerge in the general class of two-sector growth models introduced by Mulligan and Sala-i-Martin [23]. For reasons of analytical tractability, however, the project soon narrowed its attention to the Uzawa-Lucas growth Model (ULM, henceforth), presenting a good balance between the project's scopes and the possibility of actually deriving original results.

A turning point occurred when I started to generalize the analysis to take into consideration the centralized economy; the distinction centralized/decentralized economy is relevant in the ULM on account of the externality associated with human capital in the production of goods and services. As it is well known, the presence of an externality typically determines inefficiency in the market economy and warrants some form of Government interventions. I soon realized that the treatment of these issues by the literature was largely insufficient; in particular, the existing literature was unable to provide a full characterization of the inefficiency and to deliver policy prescriptions of the required nature because of the propensity of the papers to either analyze the properties of the centralized or decentralized economy, but not both. Convinced of the importance of a comprehensive treatment of both economies, I devoted much of my recent research time to the exploration of these issues. This effort has given rise to a lot of original material, temporarily contained in the Working Paper Series of the Department of Economics of the University of Cagliari.

The present book complements the results already obtained in the literature on the standard formulation of the ULM with some parts of the original findings developed for the project; the aim is to provide a comprehensive treatment of the classical descriptive and normative issues typically associated with two-sector economies engaged in the growth process. I thus believe the book is most useful for academics who, confronted with an overwhelmingly vast literature, want to have ready access to a text where a large number of theoretical issues associated with two-sector growth are dealt with in an unified context. Also graduate students, with a solid training in mathematics and willing to become familiar with the possibilities offered by the Maximum Principle might find the text rich of useful insights.

This book would have been impossible to complete without the help and encouragement provided by numerous friends and colleagues. I am particularly indebted to Cuong Le Van: our long and fruitful discussions and his wise and insightful suggestions have greatly improved the quality of the work. I wish also to thank my colleagues of the Department of Economics at the University of Cagliari, especially the director, Professor Beniamino Moro and Carla Massidda for continuous encouragement and help. I would also like to mention Giovanni Bella, Andrea Isoni, Marcello Mereu, Alessio Moro and Romano Piras for providing useful feedbacks on earlier versions of the manuscript. A special thank goes to Stephen Parente who convinced me of the importance of devoting considerable time and effort to the development of the policy implications. Corrado Mocci deserves a particular mention for his continuos assistance with the figures and the editing procedure in the last stages of the composition of the camera-ready copy.

Last but not least, I wish to thank my parents, Giulietta and Pasquale for their caring support. To them and to my little twin-nephews, Alessio and Davide, whose birth has tremendously cheered my family life, I dedicate this work.

Cagliari, December 2003

Introduction and Outline of the Book

1.1   The Uzawa-Lucas Model and the New Growth Theory

The traditional (neoclassical) growth theory, despite being elegant and well formulated, is ultimately stationary and does not satisfactorily explain some aspects of concern of the recorded economic history. In particular, the traditional theory, at least in its strict formulation, has nothing to say when an explanation of the international growth rate differentials is required or when some empirical features of the real world emerge from *growth regressions,* in terms of significant correlation coefficients between the long-run growth rate of the economy and a number of policy and educational-attainment variables.

Motivated by dissatisfaction with this state of affairs, R. Lucas, in the late 1980s, writes a path-breaking paper: by taking some initial intuitions of Uzawa [28] a step further, he proposes a two-sector capital accumulation growth model where human capital plays the role of the key variable through which ongoing growth can be generated. Human capital is understood to refer, in Becker's tradition [3], to the skills and knowledge intensity of the labor force and is accumulated in the learning (or educational) sector *via* a linear constant-returns to scale technology, only requiring older vintages of human capital. The Uzawa-Lucas economy differs in a fundamental way from the standard neoclassical model; since a lower bound to the return of accumulation is implicitly imposed, the long-run growth rate basically reflects an endogenous equilibrium where only the "primitives" of a specific economy (endowments, technology and preferences) are relevant. Other factors, such as increasing population or exogenous technical progress, crucial in the traditional theory, have, conversely, no critical influence.

In order to justify the observed higher wage levels in economies endowed with larger amounts of human capital, Lucas also considers the presence of an externality factor accruing to the final sector of the economy. His choice is rich of powerful consequences; on the one hand, the *natural* result of the traditional growth theory, namely stability/instability in the saddle-point sense, is not automatically achieved. Indeed, the eigenvalues associated with the (modified) canonical system generated by the optimization process can lose their symmetric structure and more complicate dynamic phenomena (such as multiple equilibria, instability or asymptotic convergence to complicated limit sets) can emerge instead. On the other hand, when an externality factor is present, the result of the optimization differs according to whether a hypothetical benevolent Social Planner dictates the choice of the control variables with the aim of maximizing the overall utility of the economic agents or whether decentralized agents follow their optimizing programs in *laissez-faire* conditions. On such premises, the competitive equilibrium is inefficient and authorizes normative discussions on the properties of the most appropriate public actions aimed at raising the growth rate of a market economy.

Soon after its appearance, the Uzawa-Lucas Model (ULM, henceforth) becomes one of the preferred frameworks from which predictions on the growth process of two-sector economies are commonly derived in the literature; indeed, its characteristics, as above detailed, coupled with a simple mathematical structure, offer a particularly appreciated synthesis between complexity of the topics involved and analytical tractability.

Despite the widespread interest shown in the literature, however, there are still wide gaps in the treatment of the model. In particular, whereas the decentralized solution of the model is extensively studied, the optimal benchmark associated with the model has received much less attention. Because of this, the characteristics of the inefficiency in a decentralized equilibrium and the properties of the most appropriate action to be possibly undertaken by the Government have remained largely unexplored.

The next two sections of the Introduction discuss the literature regarding the ULM in its standard formulation[1] and also give a preliminary presentation of the new results achieved in the book. The first part of the discussion distinguishes the contributions according to whether they investigate the balanced-growth properties of the model or the short-run adjustment. A separate section is dedicated to the studies exploring the features of a fiscal policy aimed at reconciling the optimum with the equilibrium. The presentation of the original parts, conversely, groups the extensions of the literature according to whether they refer to the optimal or to the equilibrium properties of the Uzawa-Lucas economy. The new findings integrating the literature in the field of the inefficiency of the market economy are also discussed separately. Very importantly, the extensions of the literature discussed in the book have also found a working paper version which we cite here below and throughout the text as the original source.

The last section of the Introduction presents a brief outline of the Book.

1.2   The Extant Literature

1.2.1   *The BGP Properties of the Economy*

Many of the properties of both the centralized and decentralized economies evolving along balanced paths are described in Lucas's original paper. The crucial finding

---

[1]Many authors have also generalized the original setting of the ULM. Some extension lines deal with: (a) the effects of the inclusion of physical capital as an input in the human capital sector (e.g. Bond *et al* and Ladron-de-Guevara *et al.* [11]); (b) generalizations of the utility function (e.g. Ladron-de-Guevara *et al.* [11], Benhabib and Perli [5] and Faig [9]); (c) implications of the accumulation of human capital in a taxed economy (e.g. Ortiguera [24]). Another related paper is Chamley's [8], where the contribution of an externality factor is extended to the learning sector.

is that in both cases there exist regions in the parameter space where the model supports the existence of non-degenerate BGPs. Along these paths, the economy grows endogenously, according to a positive and constant growth rate. Along these paths, moreover, the growth rates of physical capital, consumption and human capital are also constant and the partition of non-leisure time between production and learning is a positive number lying between 0 and 1. A number of interesting details follows in Lucas's original contribution. In particular, when the economy evolves in a balanced position, the growth rates of physical capital and consumption equal the growth rate of the economy; human capital, conversely, grows at a lower rate.

However, it can be said that Lucas's paper simply obtains and elaborates the necessary first-order conditions from the application of the Maximum Principle without providing formal existence proof of non-degenerate, balanced dynamics, solving the optimization problem from the two (centralized and decentralized) perspectives. Benhabib and Perli [5] are the first to provide arguments in favor of the existence of such, non-degenerate, long-run dynamics in the case of the decentralized economy. Logical arguments in favor of the sufficiency of the first-order conditions in case of the centralized dynamics are proposed in Garcia-Castrillo and Sanso [10].

1.2.2   The Transition along Optimal and Equilibrium Paths

The first authors to become interested in the transition generated by the ULM are Mulligan and Sala-i-Martin [23] and Caballè and Santos [7]. Starting from more general settings, they are able to produce fundamental results on the impact of sudden modifications of the state of the economy on the variables of the model in case of a zero externality factor. Mulligan and Sala-i-Martin show that there are three possible mechanisms that exert a stabilizing influence on an economy characterized by a relative excess of physical capital: a *consumption-smoothing effect,* implying that the relative excess of physical capital can be eliminated through lower savings; a *wage rate effect,* bringing down the high level of physical capital through lower working time; a *Solow effect* by which, even in the hypothesis that the consumption/physical capital ratio and working time do not vary, the economy tends to stabilize simply because of decreasing marginal returns.

Caballè and Santos, again in case of a zero externality factor, prove that three possible growth cases can occur (in a normalized economy) in response to a shock suddenly raising the endowment of physical capital: a *normal case* when the economy asymptotically converges towards a new balanced path where human capital has also increased; a *paradoxical case* when the economy asymptotically converges towards a new balanced path where human capital has, conversely, decreased; an *exogenous case* where the asymptotic value of human capital is left unaffected. Most interestingly, the sole factor discriminating among these growth cases is the size of the inverse of the intertemporal elasticity of substitution *vis-à-vis* with the share of physical capital.

When the externality is not set to zero, the transitional properties of the decentralized solution of the model have been excellently studied by Benhabib and Perli [5]. The authors show that, according to the region of the parameter space, the dimension of the stable manifold changes (in a $\mathbb{R}^3$-reduced space) so that the stability result of saddle-path convergence, multiple equilibria and instability have all a chance to prevail. Their work is complemented by Mattana and Venturi [22] who discuss the emergence of periodic orbits Hopf-bifurcating from the steady state and their stability properties.

Given the complexity of decentralized dynamics, however, all the findings in these contributions are local in nature (i.e. obtained after a linearization of the full dynamics has been performed) and are therefore only valid in a small neighborhood of the steady-state.

The first author to produce valid-in-the-large results on the transitional properties of the ULM, when the decentralized solution of the ULM is considered, is Xie [30]. This author succeeds in achieving the closed-form solution of the model without resorting to the linearization of the dynamics; however, he is able to reach this particular result under conditions in which the inverse of the intertemporal elasticity of substitution is low and equal to the share of physical capital. More detail on the global properties of decentralized dynamics in this critical region of the parameter space is offered in Ruiz-Tamarit [27] where the discussion involves the global behavior of the original variables of the model.

The optimal paths generated by the model when the externality factor is not set to zero and the economy is in transition have received much less attention. Despite the normative interest for developing implications in this specific context, only Garcia-Castrillo and Sanso [10], to our knowledge, pay some attention to the problem. The authors, investigating the properties of a taxed economy, discover some important properties of the optimal transition in a reduced space. In particular, they find that the steady-state is always globally saddle-path stable and that the policy functions are again locally downward (upward) sloping if the coefficient of risk aversion is large (small) with respect to the share of physical capital.

1.2.3   *The Reconciliation of the Equilibrium with the Optimum*

Not unexpectedly, the first-order conditions alternatively proposed by the Maximum Principle to solve the optimization problem associated with the ULM from the centralized and the decentralized viewpoints only differ in the valuation formula for human capital. Starting from this, interesting information on the inefficient dimension of a market economy with respect to its optimal benchmark can be easily obtained. Lucas, again in its original contribution, after setting to one the inverse of the intertemporal elasticity of substitution, finds that the BGP value of the growth rate of the decentralized economy is lower than in a centralized economy, whereas the fraction of total time dedicated to work is higher. As a consequence, also the growth rates of the other primitive variables of the model are lower.

Garcia-Castrillo and Sanso [10] are the first to take interest into the issues related to the desirability of public policies aimed at increasing the growth rates of the market economy in the context of the ULM. In particular, Garcia-Castrillo and Sanso apply the *Path Coincidence Principle* to design an optimal fiscal policy capable of providing the correct incentives for the market economy to behave efficiently. The main characteristics of such a policy is that the return of physical capital has to be left free of taxes and that a combination of a lump-sum tax and taxation on the wage rate provides the resources to subsidize the time devoted to learning by agents.

1.3   The Extensions Proposed in the Book

1.3.1   *BGP and Short-Run Adjustment. The Case of Optimal Paths*

The extensions of the literature proposed in the book in the field of the BGP properties of the centralized dynamics complement Lucas's original discussion. First of all, we go beyond the study of the primitive variables of the model to also take into consideration the long-run properties of the interest rate, the wage rate and the saving rate. The behavior of some crucial stationary combinations of the original variables, such as the average goods production and consumption and the "weighted" ratio between physical and human capital, is also investigated in detail. We also conduct a sensitivity analysis aimed at determining the long-run optimal response of all these variables to shocks modifying technological and preference parameters. The original material for this discussion is contained in [18].

The properties of the optimal transition are also investigated in great detail. We have new results to propose from both the local and global perspectives. From the local point of view, we find that, as in the case of zero externality discussed in Mulligan and Sala-i-Martin [23], the sole factors locally controlling the optimal orientation of the policy functions are the relative sizes of the inverse of the intertemporal elasticity of substitution and the share of physical capital. Moreover, we are also able to show that the two policy functions for working time and average consumption have locally exactly the same elasticity with respect to variations of the state of the economy. The discussion in the book grows out of the material organized in [20].

The global point of view is richer of new results. The possibility of deriving valid-in-the-large information on the evolution of the efficient economy is strictly related to a special transformation of the system of dynamic laws governing the centralized economy. As a matter of fact, even if an externality is present, the Pareto-optimal Hamiltonian dynamics maintains a symmetrical structure which ensures that the motion is contained in the space spanned by the average goods production and the average consumption. This has the following important consequences. On the one hand, we are now able to draw simple phase diagrams providing an immediate visualization of the stable manifold in this reduced dimension. On the other hand, since the dynamics in $\mathbb{R}^2$ becomes very simple, we can prove that the closed-form solution of the differential equations can be obtained by simple analytical methods. In particular, the differential equation optimally governing the average goods production is a technical law which can be easily solved. By fixing the distance between the share of physical capital and the inverse of the elasticity of intertemporal substitution, the law governing the average consumption can be solved as well. Since the evolution of all the variables of the model in the original dimension depends solely on these two laws, the explicit characterization of the entire centralized solution of the ULM can be obtained. The effect of this is that the optimal transition can be studied in global terms without worrying about the distance between the initial position of the economy and the steady-state. Numerical simulations conducted in all regions of the parameter space allow to retrieve a number of further interesting details on the properties of an efficient economy in transition. In particular, many of the results in Mulligan and Sala-i-Martin [23] and Caballè and Santos [7] obtained in absence of the externality factor have a global counterpart in the case of the centralized solution. All these results have in [13] and [14], the original reference.

From another point of view, the availability of valid-in-the-large explicit trajectories gives us a chance of studying the optimal behavior of consumption. In particular, we find that shocks largely increasing (decreasing) the endowment of physical capital (human capital) impose U-shaped trajectories to both consumption and physical capital. Conversely, a shock decreasing (increasing) the endowment of physical capital (human capital) only allows for monotonically increasing levels of consumption and physical capital. The working paper in [15] is the reference for this part.

1.3.2   *BGP and Short-Run Adjustment. The Case of Equilibrium Paths*

Crucial extensions of the literature, again referring to both the BGP and transitional dynamics, are also found for the decentralized solution. As for the centralized economy, we complement Lucas's original investigation of the BGP properties of the model by considering the behavior of other key variables such as the interest rate, the wage rate and the saving rate. The BGP value of some stationary variables such us the average goods production and consumption is considered too. We conclude this part by conducting a sensitivity analysis of the BGP behavior of all these variables with respect to changes of the technological and preference parameters. The reference for these part can be found in [18].

The well-investigated context of the transitional dynamics sees the development of some new findings too. From the local point of view, we study the slopes of the equilibrium functions tying control and *control-like* variables to the state of the economy in the region of the parameter space where the steady-state is saddle-path stable and the eigenvalues are all real. What we have found is interesting: we have not been able to find regions of the parameter space where the optimal orientation of the equilibrium function is not preserved. The elasticity of impact of shocks perturbing the state of the economy, however, now diverges for working time (control variable) and average consumption (control-like variable). The working paper in [16] can be referred to as the original source for these extensions of the literature.

Less general are the new results proposed from the global point of view. As shown by Xie [30] and Ruiz-Tamarit [27], closed-form solutions for the differential equations can only be found in the special region of the parameter space where the share of physical capital equals the inverse of the elasticity of intertemporal substitution (the exogenous growth case). In this context, we have been able to produce a lot of numerical evidence on the global behavior of the variables. In particular, we show that when the economy is characterized by an excess of physical capital, if the shock is large enough, the levels of consumption and physical capital show a U-shaped trajectory. Consider the working paper in [19] as the original source for this discussion.

The availability of the explicit trajectory for consumption in the exogenous growth case also enables us to calculate (again in global terms) the welfare integral over the infinite temporal horizon faced by the representative agent.

1.3.3   *Characteristics of Market Inefficiency*

Another area where we have developed a large number of new findings is in the analysis of the form of the inefficiency of the market economy. As a matter of fact, a by-product of the full characterization of the centralized solution puts us in a good position in this field. The working papers in [18], [19] and [21] can be referred to as the original sources for the extensions of the literature discussed in this field.

We first show that the parameter spaces under which the two solutions, centralized and decentralized, jointly generate meaningful dynamics, do not coincide. We have here a lot of interesting consequences to propose. First of all, very interestingly, only in the intersection of the two parameters spaces the results of a larger growth rate of the centralized economy is guaranteed. Furthermore, in the same region of the parameter space, a common saddle-path stability/instability result holds. Other new crucial findings discussed in the book concern the investigation of the way the market economy distorts the optimal response of the control and *control-like* variables to sudden perturbations of the state of the economy.

Much less general details on the dissimilarities between the two economies can be exposed from the global point of view. Since, as already said, global results on the decentralized dynamics can be only found in the special region of the parameter space where the share of physical capital equals the inverse of the elasticity of intertemporal substitution, the comparison between the properties of the centralized and decentralized dynamics can only occur when the economy evolves along the so-called *exogenous growth case*. We have here some interesting results to propose: we show that the laws driving consumption, human and physical capital in the centralized and decentralized economy have exactly the same explicit forms (even though governed by different constants of control). Numerical simulations coupled with some graphical analysis give an outlook of the differences between the global evolution of the decentralized economy *vis-à-vis* with its optimal counterpart.

The book also extends the extant literature by studying the characteristics of the optimal fiscal policy capable of providing the correct incentives for the market economy to behave efficiently. By combining Garcia-Castrillo and Sanso's *Path Coincidence Principle* [10] and the explicit optimal trajectories we are able to achieve important information on such an optimal fiscal policy when the taxed economy is in transition.

1.4   Outline of the Book

The present book, is aimed, in five Chapters, at complementing the extant literature on the standard formulation of the ULM. The result of this effort is a complete treatment of the normative and descriptive issues emerging in a two-sector economy in presence of an externality factor.

Chapter 1 can be methodologically divided into two distinct parts. The former is devoted to the presentation of the formal structure of the ULM and to the discussion of the general issues concerning the derivation and interpretation of the first order conditions. The latter is involved in a more technical analysis aimed at showing that balanced dynamics can be supported by the model from both the centralized and decentralized perspectives. More in detail, after a brief introduction, section 2 discusses the representative-agent environment, the Cobb-Douglas technology and the CES preferences characterizing the ULM. The utility-maximization problems faced by the centralized and market perspectives are outlined in section 3. In the same section, the solution of both the maximization problems is achieved through the application of the Pontryagin-Hestness's Maximum Principle, in turn requiring the setting-up of the Hamiltonian function and the derivation of the FOCs. The economic interpretation of the first order necessary conditions provides useful insights into the real determinants of macroeconomic growth in presence of a learning sector.

As already discussed, the second part of Chapter 1 is more technical: section 4 studies the second-order conditions associated with both the centralized and decentralized dynamics. Section 5 exploits the proximity between the two allocation sets to derive a four-dimensional system of first-order differential equations, encompassing both the centralized and decentralized dynamics. The availability of the encompassing system allows to address the issues related to the existence proof of non-degenerate asymptotic-consistent balanced dynamics avoiding any duplication of analysis.

Chapter 2 concentrates on the features optimal and equilibrium paths have in common both when the Uzawa-Lucas economy evolves along a non-degenerate BGP and when it is in transition. After a brief introduction on the mathematical tools of utility, the second section undertakes the analysis of the general properties of the BGP. In order to give access to richer details on the dynamic evolution of two-sector economies in presence of a learning sector, the analysis goes beyond the primitive variables of the model, to also take into consideration some interesting combinations of them. A first group of these new variables, labelled as *adjoint variables*, is formed by a broadened configuration of the output of the economy and by the wage rate, the rental price of capital (or interest rate) and the saving rate.

A second group of variables we will find worth separately studying, includes the ratio goods production/physical capital (average goods production), the physical capital/consumption (average consumption) and the *weighted ratio* between the two capital stocks. Abusing the Kaldorian terminology, we label these BGP-stationary combinations of the primitive variables as *Great Ratios*.

Section 3 provides a general context of reference for the analysis of the transitional dynamics in the two economies. First of all, the encompassing system of dynamic laws obtained in Chapter 1 (containing the centralized and decentralized dynamics) is transformed into a much-easier-to-treat stationary system in $\mathbb{R}^3$. This system has an interior fixed point whose properties, by standard arguments, translate into the properties of a balanced trajectory of the economy in the original dimension. There then follows, in the same section, a preparatory work for the local stability analysis of the steady-state in the reduced dimension. Some preliminary results relating to the different stability properties of centralized and decentralized economies are discussed. The final section of the Chapter discusses one of the main original results of the book, namely the possibility of further reducing the effective dimension of the centralized dynamics. It is also shown in the section that this possibility is conversely negated when the decentralized dynamics comes into play.

Chapter 3 assumes that the economy is run by a benevolent Social Planner. Given the propedeutical work of Chapter 2, the characterization of the BGP for such an economy is a relatively simple task and is conducted in section 2. More challenging is the derivation of the properties of the optimal transition. In section 3, again exploiting the work previously done in Chapter 2, the relevant system of dynamic laws governing the centralized economy in the $\mathbb{R}^3$-reduced dimension is easily obtained. From the local point of view, it appears evident that the signs structure of the eigenvalues of the Jacobian matrix associated with the linearized dynamics is fixed and that the explicit value of the negative eigenvalue can be obtained. As a consequence, the analysis can provide a fairly precise picture of the properties of the transition, both in terms of stability analysis and characteristics of the policy functions. The global analysis of the centralized dynamics, developed in section 4, also provides a series of significant results: by exploiting the proof that the centralized dynamics implies a simple system of differential equations in the space spanned by the average goods production and consumption, the section discusses how to obtain the closed-form solution of the dynamics. The same section discusses a lot of numerical evidence, given the parameter space. Section 5 explains how to use the explicit law for consumption to evaluate the welfare integral over the infinity horizon.

Chapter 4 deals with the properties of the decentralized solution. The analysis follows the same logical steps as in Chapter 3. Section 2 provides an assessment of the characteristics of the economy evolving along the BGP. The derivation is greatly simplified by the propedeutical work conducted in Chapter 2. Section 3 proceeds to establish the local stability properties of the fixed point in the $\mathbb{R}^3$-reduced dimension. Unlike what found for the centralized case, the explicit form of the eigenvalues of the Jacobian matrix associated with the linearized dynamics cannot be obtained (unless the share of physical capital equals the inverse of the intertemporal elasticity of substitution). As a consequence the possibility of deriving information on the local stability properties of the fixed point is severely limited. The application of the Routh-Hurvitz criterion here is of great help: according to the region of the parameter space, it is possible to show that saddle-path behavior, indeterminacy or even all-directions instability can be determined. To better understand the local characteristics of the dynamics, the same section sees the results of extensive numerical simulations. The results are interesting. For instance, in the special region of the parameter space where the model is saddle-path stable with real eigenvalues, the decentralized dynamics preserves the orientation of the optimal policy functions. Moreover, it is also shown that there exists a critical boundary (in the parameter space) beyond which the real parts of two complex-conjugate eigenvalues change sign. This is a pre-requisite for the emergence of closed orbits. By using the externality as a bifurcation parameter, it is shown that small amplitude periodic solutions, Hopf bifurcating from a saddle focus, can actually occur.

The last section of the Chapter explores the possibility of deriving valid-in-the-large results. As shown in Xie [30], this can only be done if the inverse of the elasticity of intertemporal substitution matches the share of physical capital. Indeed, in this special region of the parameter space, the dynamics become crystal-clear and the differential equations can be explicitly solved. The discussion on the properties of the global dynamics distinguishes the investigation of the properties of the economy evolving in conditions of exogenous growth (when working time is well adjusted from the beginning) from the analysis of what happens when indeterminacy is present.

Chapter 5 can be divided methodologically into two distinct parts. The first part, in turn divided into three sections, is aimed at discussing the nature of the inefficiency caused by the presence of an externality in the market economy. The nature of the inefficiency is mainly determined by the comparison between the behavior of the centralized and the decentralized economy, given the parameter space. The second part studies the characteristics of public policies capable of providing the correct incentives for the market economy to behave efficiently. More in detail, the second section of the Chapter shows, first of all, that the parameter space under which centralized and decentralized dynamics produce non-degenerate asymptotic results do not coincide since the feasible parameter space for decentralized outcomes is wider in the inverse of the elasticity of intertemporal substitution direction. Therefore, the study of the nature of the inefficiency can be brought successfully to an end only at the intersection of the parameter space, where both dynamics jointly produce meaningful results. In this particular region of the parameter space, the third section of the Chapter proves a number of interesting details characterizing the differences between the market and the centralized economy. In particular, it is shown that the growth rate of the market economy is lower than in the centralized economies, while the fraction of total time dedicated to work is higher.

Evaluating the nature of the inefficiency when the economy is in transition is no easy task. From the local point of view, section 4 describes how, again in the intersection of the parameter spaces where both dynamics jointly produce meaningful results, the possibility of indeterminacy or instability is excluded and how the saddle-path convergence remains the only possible stability result. Other interesting results obtained in the section, concern the comparison between the slopes of the policy functions in the two economies. The global point of view also provides revealing insights into the economic effects of inefficiency. Although the analysis is limited to the special region of the parameter space where the inverse of the intertemporal elasticity of substitution equals the share of physical capital, the comparison between centralized and decentralized dynamics does sketch a clear outline of the effects of such inefficiency.

The last section of the Chapter discusses how the laws of motion under the two regimes can be reconciled through the design of an optimal fiscal policy by means of which the first-best optimum is attained as a market equilibrium.

Chapter 1

The Model and the Existence of Non-Degenerate Balanced Solutions

1.1 Introduction and Plan of the Chapter

This Chapter starts by describing the Uzawa-Lucas capital accumulation growth model (ULM henceforth) in its formal structure. To simplify the analysis, we have chosen to present the per-capita version of the model with constant population size. This means that we need not worrying about population growth rates and/or the contribution of inputs which cannot be accumulated. We also ignore the possibility of capital goods depreciation.

The environment is standard. Infinitely-lived Barro-type workers, all endowed with a unit of non-leisure time and capital, populate the economy. Their total number is normalized to one. Atomistic firms, whose total number is normalized to one too, hire factors of production from workers, paying them rents and salaries.

The productive structure implies the existence of a final goods sector and a learning sector, specialized in the production of new human capital. Both sectors are controlled by Constant-Returns-to-Scale production functions. A crucial point here concerns the role that the model ascribes to the two capital goods: whereas human capital can be intersectorally allocated but cannot be substituted out for consumption, physical capital is a perfect substitute for consumption, but can only be employed in the final goods sector.

Preferences are accommodated in a Constant-Elasticity-of-Substitution context where what matters to consumers is the maximization of the present value of a flow of instantaneous utility, only dependent on consumption.

The whole productive structure is distorted by the existence of extra-gains accruing to the final sector because of a positive externality dependent on the average level of human capital achieved by the economy. Despite not being essential for the generation of self-sustaining growth, the externality raises the social return of the investment in human capital above the private level so that the result of the intertemporal utility maximization differs according to whether the problem is tackled from a centralized or a decentralized perspective.

As shown in Lucas's original paper [12], both versions of the infinite-horizon optimization problems can be solved through the application of Pontryagin-Hestness's Maximum Principle which, in turn, requires setting-up the Hamiltonian function and deriving the necessary first-order conditions (FOCs). .

Not unexpectedly, the two allocation sets proposed by the Maximum Principle only differ in the valuation formula for human capital. Besides this, the FOCs obtained under the two perspectives perfectly overlap and can be seen as providing a particularly useful framework from which deriving rich insights into the very heart of macroeconomic growth in presence of a learning sector.

The second part of the Chapter addresses the technical issues of sufficiency of the FOCs and existence of non-degenerate asymptotically-consistent balanced dynamics. In this regard, if the Maximum Principle proposes a certain number of solution candidates, we can be sure that no others can possibly solve the problem. However, the presence of a distortion in the form of a technological externality implies that sufficiency ought also to be checked. In general terms, several techniques can be employed to study the concavity of the utility-maximization problems. In the case of the ULM, a distinction between the decentralized and centralized viewpoints has to be made; whereas in the decentralized problem the Arrow (weak) concavity condition finds an easy application, the centralized point problem requires a more direct approach.

Another issue is determining whether the necessary conditions can support the existence of non-degenerate, asymptotically-consistent, dynamics. We face here two sets of problems. First, we need to prove that the necessary conditions are actually compatible with the existence of non-degenerate balanced dynamics, where the growth rate of the economy is positive along with the growth rates of consumption and of both kinds of capital.

Secondly, we need showing that a feasibility constraint, implying a positive, asymptotically constant, value of working time, lying between 0 and 1 is satisfied.

Thirdly, the associated trajectories, when existing, have to not violate the transversality condition (TVC). Since we are able to show that there are regions of the parameter space where all these requirements are contemporaneously met in both cases of the centralized and decentralized economy, an existence theorem of optimal and equilibrium balanced dynamics follows. The plan of the Chapter is as follows.

The second section of the Chapter formalizes the structure of the economy. The environment, the technology and preferences are presented in detail.

The third section sets up the centralized and the decentralized optimization problems for analysis. The dynamic laws governing both economies are obtained by applying the Maximum Principle. The question of sufficiency of the FOCs is dealt with in the fourth section.

The fifth and final section broaches the difficult task of elaborating existence theorems for non-degenerate asymptotically-consistent balanced solutions for both the centralized and the decentralized economy.

1.2   The Formal Structure of the Model

1.2.1   *The Environment and the Technology*

For the sake of simplicity, we have decided to base this book on the per-capita version of the ULM. A closed two-sector economic system, with infinite temporal horizon, is populated by a *continuum* (normalized to 1) of identical Barro-type infinitely-lived workers. The representative worker is endowed with a unit of non-leisure time; physical and human capital, respectively k_t and h_t, are also considered to be at his/her full disposal.

The unit of time is partitioned into the fraction u_t representing time spent working and in its complement $(1 - u_t)$ signifying, conversely, time invested in learning. All-identical competitive, atomistic firms borrow labour and capital from agents, paying them rents and salaries.

Production in the final goods sector can be allocated either to consumption or to investment. It is obtained by the representative firm by combining physical capital and skilled labour, $u_t h_t$, according to the following production function:

$$(1.1) \qquad y_t^f = A k_t^\alpha \left(u_t h_t\right)^{1-\alpha} \widehat{h}_t^\gamma$$

where f, at the apex, stands for final and indicates the final sector, A is a technological parameter indicating efficiency in the sector, α is the share of physical capital. $\widehat{h}_t = \frac{1}{t} \int_0^t h_t dt$ is the *average* level reached, at time t, by the accumulation of human capital and γ is a positive externality.

Given the constancy of the total population size, the labour contribution only grows because of improvements in its average quality. Therefore, it is useful to point out from the outset that:

Remark *The per-capita version of the ULM used in the book omits any strict technological progress and does not grant any explicit role to inputs, such as raw labour, which cannot be accumulated.*

Production in the learning or education sector is undertaken by means of the remaining fraction of total non-leisure time. Again the production function is of the Cobb-Douglas constant-returns-to-scale form:

$$(1.2) \qquad y_t^e = B h_t \left(1 - u_t\right)$$

where e, at the apex, stands for education and indicates the human capital production sector. B is an efficiency index. By recalling the characterization of the two-sector growth models given in Mulligan and Sala-i-Martin [23], the technological structure in (1.1) and (1.2) implies that:

Remark *Since the (private) elasticities of production in both sectors with respect to u_t and h_t are equal, the ULM only allows for constant-point-in-time technologies.*

Thus, considering (1.1), (1.2) and the assumptions on consumption, it is evident that the two forms of accumulation have a very different role to play. In particular, we have that:

Remark *Human capital is intersectorally allocated but cannot be substituted out for consumption. On the contrary, physical capital is a perfect substitute for consumption, but can only be employed in the final goods sector.*

1.2.2   *Preferences*

The structure of the preferences considers the representative agent's maximization of a present-valued flow of instantaneous utility depending on consumption, according to the following standard Constant-Elasticity-of-Substitution function:

$$(1.3) \qquad \int_0^\infty \frac{c^{1-\sigma}-1}{1-\sigma} e^{-\rho t} dt$$

where ρ is the subjective rate of time preference and σ is the inverse of the intertemporal elasticity of substitution or coefficient of risk aversion.[2]
    Observe that the form of the utility function to be maximized implies that:

Remark *In the standard formulation of the ULM, agents do not value leisure in their preference structure.*

1.3   The Optimization Problems

1.3.1   *The Optimization Problem from the Planner's Viewpoint*

On several occasions we have defended the idea that, when a positive externality is present, the result of the optimization differs according to whether a central authority has full control of the policy functions or whether, contrariwise, decentralized agents, who operate independently on a private level, follow their optimizing programs.
    We have discussed the implications of this and have also noted that the centralized outcome of the maximization problem leads to a first best solution for the economy whereas the decentralized outcome is sub-optimal.
    This sub-section takes a closer look at the centralized maximization problem. We will therefore imagine that the economy is run by a benevolent Social Planner who, seeking to maximize the utility functions of economic agents, is hypothetically in

---

[2]Of course, given the formulation in (1.3), σ has to be different of one.

charge of taking appropriate decisions on the control variables.

Because the final goods can be either consumed or invested, the constraint to the accumulation of physical capital is:

$$(1.4) \qquad \dot{k_t} = A k_t^\alpha \left(u_t h_t \right)^{1-\alpha} \widehat{h_t^\gamma} - c_t$$

where c_t is per capita consumption. Conversely, since human capital cannot be consumed, the constraint to the accumulation of human capital simply replicates the production function in (1.2):

$$(1.5) \qquad \dot{h_t} = y_t^e = B h_t \left(1 - u_t \right)$$

We now need to give a definition of what in practice is meant by *optimal trajectory*. Following Lucas in his original contribution, an optimal path is taken to mean:

Definition 1.1 *An optimal path is a choice* $\left\{ k_t^*, h_t^*, u_t^*, c_t^* \text{ and } \widehat{h_t^*} \right\}$ *of* k_t, h_t, c_t, u_t *and* $\widehat{h_t}$ *which solves the maximization problem implied by the model, subject to the constraint that* $\widehat{h_t} = h_t \; \forall \; t$.

The critical implication of Definition 1.1 is that, along any optimal path:

Remark *Since* $\widehat{h_t}$ *has to equal* h_t *at each point in time, the relevant elasticity of goods production with respect to human capital has to assume the full value* $1-\alpha+\gamma$.

Therefore, we can represent the optimization problem faced by the Social Planner in the following way:

Definition 1.2 *Given the formal structure of the economy, a benevolent Social Planner faces a continuous-time optimization problem (problem* $\mathbf{P}^c$, *henceforth) which can be expressed as follows:*

$$\text{Max} \int_0^\infty \frac{c^{1-\sigma}-1}{1-\sigma} e^{-\rho t} dt$$

sub:

$$\dot{k_t} = A k_t^\alpha u_t^{1-\alpha} h_t^{1-\alpha+\gamma} - c_t$$

$$\dot{h_t} = B h_t \left(1 - u_t \right).$$

with $k(0) = k_0$ *and* $h(0) = h_0$ *given, and* $u_t \in (0,1) \; \forall \; t$

To solve problem $\mathbf{P}^c$ we can put into practice Pontryagin-Hesteness's Maximum

Principle. The present-value Hamiltonian is:

(1.6) $H^c = \frac{c_t^{1-\sigma}-1}{1-\sigma} + \lambda_{1t}\left[Ak_t^\alpha u_t^{1-\alpha}h_t^{1-\alpha+\gamma} - c_t\right] + \lambda_{2t}\left[Bh_t\left(1 - u_t\right)\right]$

where λ_{1t} and λ_{2t}, the co-state variables, can be interpreted as shadow prices of the accumulation.

Now, let:

(1.7) $\bar{y}_t = Ak_t^\alpha u_t^{1-\alpha}h_t^{1-\alpha+\gamma}$

be the post-optimization production function in the goods sector. Since u_t and c_t are control variables and k_t and h_t are state variables, the solution candidates proposed by the Maximum Principle are:

(1.8a) $H_c^c = 0$ $\Longrightarrow c_t^{-\sigma} = \lambda_{1t}$

(1.8b) $H_u^c = 0$ $\Longrightarrow (1 - \alpha)\lambda_{1t}\frac{\bar{y}_t}{u_t} = Bh_t\lambda_{2t}$

(1.8c) $H_{\lambda_1}^c = \dot{k}_t$ $\Longrightarrow \dot{k}_t = \bar{y}_t - c_t$

(1.8d) $H_{\lambda_2}^c = \dot{h}_t$ $\Longrightarrow \dot{h}_t = Bh_t\left(1 - u_t\right)$

(1.8e) $H_k^c = \rho\lambda_{1t} - \dot{\lambda}_{1t} \Longrightarrow \dot{\lambda}_{1t} = -\alpha\lambda_{1t}\frac{\bar{y}_t}{k_t} + \rho\lambda_{1t}$

(1.8f) $H_h^c = \rho\lambda_{2t} - \dot{\lambda}_{2t} \Longrightarrow \dot{\lambda}_{2t} = -\frac{(1-\alpha+\gamma)\lambda_{1t}\bar{y}_t}{h_t} - \lambda_{2t}\left[B\left(1 - u_t\right)\right] + \rho\lambda_{2t}$

The transversality condition:

(1.9) $\lim_{t\to\infty}\left[e^{-\rho t}\left(\lambda_{1t}k_t + \lambda_{2t}h_t\right)\right] = 0$

rules out explosive paths.

1.3.2 *The Optimization Problem in the Market Economy*

What is, conversely, the nature of the trajectories when agents are left to their private maximization programs? We have already remarked that, in a decentralized economy, agents are unable to fully internalize the contribution of human capital. The decentralized economy, therefore, evolves along equilibrium paths which can be described as follows:

Definition 1.3 *A decentralized equilibrium path is a choice $\{k_t^*, h_t^*, u_t^*, c_t^*\}$ of k_t, h_t, u_t and c_t, which solves the maximization problem after expectations on $\widehat{h}_t$ are formed by the agents. Only in equilibrium market clearing implies $\widehat{h}_t = h_t$ (i.e. expectations coincide with actual values).*

This, in turn, implies that:

Remark *The contribution of human capital to the goods production process, as perceived at the private level, is* $1 - \alpha$.

In accordance with their productive strategies, in a decentralized economy, firms hire factors of production from agents, paying them rents (r_t) and salaries (w_t). The maximization problem faced by the representative agent in a decentralized economy, therefore, is of the following nature:

Definition 1.4 *Given the formal structure of the economy, the representative agent faces a continuous-time optimization problem (problem P^d, henceforth) which can be written as:*

$$\text{Max} \int_0^\infty \frac{c^{1-\sigma}-1}{1-\sigma} e^{-\rho t} dt$$

sub:

$$\dot{k}_t = r_t k_t + w_t \left(uh\right)_t - c_t$$

$$\dot{h}_t = B h_t \left(1 - u_t\right)$$

with $k(0) = k_0$ *and* $h(0) = h_0$ *given and* $u_t \in (0,1) \; \forall \, t$.

To solve problem P^d we can resort again to the Maximum Principle. The present-value Hamiltonian is now:

(1.10) $\quad H^d = \frac{c_t^{1-\sigma}-1}{1-\sigma} + \lambda_{1t} \left[r_t k_t + w_t \left(uh\right)_t - c_t\right] + \lambda_{2t} \left[B h_t \left(1 - u_t\right)\right]$

where λ_{1t} and λ_{2t} are again co-state variables. The solution candidates proposed by the Maximum Principle (given r_t and w_t) are:

(1.11a) $\quad H_c^d = 0 \quad \Longrightarrow c_t^{-\sigma} = \lambda_{1t}$

(1.11b) $\quad H_u^d = 0 \quad \Longrightarrow \lambda_{1t} w_t = B \lambda_{2t}$

(1.11c) $\quad H_{\lambda_1}^d = \dot{k}_t \quad \Longrightarrow \dot{k}_t = r_t k_t + w_t \left(uh\right)_t - c_t$

(1.11d) $\quad H_{\lambda_2}^d = \dot{h}_t \quad \Longrightarrow \dot{h}_t = B h_t \left(1 - u_t\right)$

(1.11e) $\quad H_k^d = \rho \lambda_{1t} - \dot{\lambda}_{1t} \quad \Longrightarrow \dot{\lambda}_{1t} = -\lambda_{1t} r_t + \rho \lambda_{1t}$

(1.11f) $\quad H_h^d = \rho \lambda_{2t} - \dot{\lambda}_{2t} \quad \Longrightarrow \dot{\lambda}_{2t} = -\lambda_{1t} w_t u_t - \lambda_{2t} \left[B \left(1 - u_t\right)\right] + \rho \lambda_{2t}$

plus the transversality condition in (1.9) ruling out explosive paths.

The focus now shifts towards the equilibrium values undertaken in system (1.11i) by r_t and w_t, the rental compensation of physical capital and the wage rate. Let us concentrate on the sequence of static profit maximization problems undertaken by the representative firm at each point in time. Recalling that agents own physical capital and (skilled) labour and rent them to firms, we have that firms operate such that the profit function:

(1.12) $y_t^f - r_t k_t - w_t (u_t h_t)$

is maximized at each point in time.

From the necessary and sufficient necessary conditions for maximization of (1.12), we obtain the following standard result:

Proposition 1.1 *The static profit maximization undertaken by the representative firm implies that the rental price of physical capital and the wage rate are such that:*

(1.13) $r_t = \frac{\partial y_t^f}{\partial k_t} = \alpha \frac{A k_t^\alpha u_t^{1-\alpha} h_t^{1-\alpha} \widehat{h}_t^\gamma}{k_t} = \alpha \frac{y_t^f}{k_t} \equiv MPK$

(1.14) $w_t = \frac{\partial y_t^f}{\partial (uh)_t} = \frac{A(1-\alpha) k_t^\alpha u_t^{1-\alpha} h_t^{1-\alpha} \widehat{h}_t^\gamma}{(uh)_t} = \frac{(1-\alpha) y_t^f}{(uh)_t} \equiv MPL$

where MPK is the Marginal Productivity of Capital and MPL is the Marginal Productivity of (skilled) labour.

Proof By simply taking partial derivatives of the profit function in equation (1.12) with respect to k_t and $(uh)_t$ and equating to zero, it is easy to obtain the results in proposition. $\square$

Therefore, substituting (1.13) and (1.14) into system (1.11i) we have:

(1.15a) $c_t^{-\sigma} = \lambda_{1t}$

(1.15b) $(1-\alpha) \lambda_{1t} \frac{\bar{y}_t}{u_t} = B h_t \lambda_{2t}$

(1.15c) $\dot{k}_t = \bar{y}_t - c_t$

(1.15d) $\dot{h}_t = B h_t (1 - u_t)$

(1.15e) $\dot{\lambda}_{1t} = -\alpha \lambda_{1t} \frac{\bar{y}_t}{k_t} + \rho \lambda_{1t}$

(1.15f) $\dot{\lambda}_{2t} = -\frac{(1-\alpha) \lambda_{1t} \bar{y}_t}{h_t} - \lambda_{2t} [B (1 - u_t)] + \rho \lambda_{2t}$

where, from (1.7), $\bar{y}_t = A k_t^\alpha u_t^{1-\alpha} h_t^{1-\alpha+\gamma}$.

1.3.3   The Properties Shared by Optimal and Equilibrium Paths

All trajectories controlled by systems ($1.8.i$) and ($1.15.i$) (when satisfying the boundary conditions) are *admissible candidates*, for, respectively, the centralized and the decentralized solution of the optimization problem associated with the ULM. In other words, they provide the necessary (but not yet sufficient) allocation sets which are proposed by the Maximum Principle to solve problems $\mathbf{P}^c$ and $\mathbf{P}^d$. The economic interpretation of system ($1.16i$) provides powerful insights into the properties of a two-sector economy evolving in presence of a learning sector.

Notice, preliminarily that:

Remark *The FOCs associated with problems $\mathbf{P}^c$ and $\mathbf{P}^d$ only differ in the instantaneous growth rate of the shadow price of human capital.*

Therefore, if we introduce the new symbol $E_h^{c,d}$ taking the value $E_h^{c,d} = E_h^c = (1 - \alpha + \gamma)$ when the centralized solution is considered and the value $E_h^{c,d} = E_h^d = (1 - \alpha)$ when the decentralized solution of the model is under scrutiny, the two systems in ($1.8i$) and ($1.15i$) can be both represented by the following:

(1.16a) $c_t^{-\sigma} = \lambda_{1t}$

(1.16b) $(1 - \alpha)\,\lambda_{1t}\frac{\bar{y}_t}{u_t} = Bh_t\lambda_{2t}$

(1.16c) $\dot{k}_t = \bar{y}_t - c_t$

(1.16d) $\dot{h}_t = Bh_t\left(1 - u_t\right)$

(1.16e) $\dot{\lambda}_{1t} = -\alpha\lambda_{1t}\frac{\bar{y}_t}{k_t} + \rho\lambda_{1t}$

(1.16f) $\dot{\lambda}_{2t} = -\frac{E_h^{c,d}\lambda_{1t}\bar{y}_t}{h_t} - \lambda_{2t}\left[B\left(1 - u_t\right)\right] + \rho\lambda_{2t}$

Having to deal with system ($1.16i$) will prove very useful here and in the following Chapters; any result which is independent of $E_h^{c,d}$, the actual contribution of human capital to the instantaneous growth rate of λ_{2t}, applies to both the decentralized and centralized dynamics. This avoids the need for studying separately the original systems ($1.8i$) and ($1.15i$) and gives the possibility of isolating the features that optimal and equilibrium paths have in common. Now, let ξ_{λ_2} be the istantaneous growth rate of the shadow price of human capital. A first fundamental result is the following:

Proposition 1.2 *When the decentralized solution is considered, ξ_{λ_2} is constant and equal to $\rho - B$. It is lower and equal to $\rho - B - B\frac{\gamma}{1-\alpha}u_t$ in the case of the centralized solution.*[3]

---

[3]Of course, ξ_{λ_2} is lower in case of decentralized solution because u_t has to be strictly positive. We

Proof Substituting the equilibrium/duality condition (1.16*b*) into the expressions for the growth rates of the shadow price of human capital in (1.16*f*) we obtain $\rho - B -$ $B\frac{E_h^{c,d}-(1-\alpha)}{1-\alpha}u_t$. Alternatively substituting the relevant value of $E_h^{c,d}$, the results in the proposition can be easily retrieved. $\square$

Besides the difference between the centralized and decentralized growth rate of the shadow price of human capital, the admissible candidates for the two solutions have essentially the same form. In particular, both equilibrium and optimal paths are such that:

i)   the final good, at the margin, must be equally valuable in its two uses, consumption and physical capital accumulation (equation 1.16*a*);

ii) non-leisure time, at the margin, must also have the same value in its two uses, production and human capital accumulation (equation 1.16*b*).

Relation *i)* implies that the marginal utility is equal to the shadow price of physical capital accumulation. Relation *ii)* can be interpreted in terms of MPL, or wage rate: what it means is that the wage rate, evaluated in term of goods production, has to equal the (constant) efficacy index *B*.

The equations in (1.16*e*) and (1.16*f*) are also highly interesting. The former means that the growth rate of the shadow price of physical capital accumulation is equal to the difference between the subjective discount rate ρ and the interest rate or MPK. This, in turn, implies that the shadow price of physical capital accumulation decreases only if the subjective discount rate is lower than the MPK.

The latter implies that the growth rate of the shadow price of human capital accumulation is a equal to the difference between the subjective discount rate ρ and the weighted average between the marginal products of human capital (both valued in terms of human capital) in the two sectors. The interpretation is somewhat more complicated: since human capital is intersectorally allocated, the shadow price of human capital accumulation decreases only if the subjective discount rate is lower than the combined value of the marginal products of human capital from the two sectors.

1.4   Sufficiency of the *Admissible Candidates*

As previously emphasized, Pontryagin-Hesteness's Maximum Principle provides a set of admissible candidates for the solution of a generic problem. If the principle proposes a certain number of solution candidates, we can be sure that there are no others that can possibly solve the problem. In general terms, however, the concavity properties of the problem should also be checked to make sure that sufficiency is also met. In the case of the ULM, a particular cautiousness is required because of

will discuss this requirement below.

the presence of a distortion in the form of a technological externality.

Several techniques can be utilized to study the concavity of the optimization problems. We can prove the following:

Proposition 1.3 *The necessary FOCs proposed by the Maximum Principle are also sufficient to solve problem* $\mathbf{P}^d$.

Proof The standard procedure is to resort to the Arrow (weak) sufficient condition which checks whether the maximized Hamiltonian is jointly concave with respect to the state variables.[4] By substituting the equilibrium/duality values $c_t = \lambda_{1t}^{-1/\sigma}$ and $u_t = \frac{Bh_t\lambda_{2t}}{(1-\alpha)\bar{y}_t\lambda_{1t}}$, respectively from (1.8a) and (1.8b), back into the Hamiltonian, we obtain $H_{\max} = C_1 + C_2 k_t \widehat{h}_t^{\gamma/\alpha} + C_3 h_t$ where the C_i terms gather the elements of the maximized Hamiltonian which are independent of k_t and h_t. Since the $\widehat{h}_t^{\gamma/\alpha}$ term is considered exogenous in the decentralized case, the expression becomes linear in k_t and h_t. As a consequence, the problem is concave. $\square$

The situation is different in the case of the centralized solution. Since the Social Planner cannot ignore the $\widehat{h}_t^{\gamma/\alpha}$ term in the Proof above, the maximized Hamiltonian is not concave. Thus, we will be resorting to a more direct approach and follow Asada *et al.* [1], in a similar problem,[5] to prove that:

Proposition 1.4 *Because of constant returns to scale in the final good sector, the necessary FOCs proposed by the Maximum Principle are also sufficient to solve problem* $\mathbf{P}^c$.

Proof Since $H_{cc} = -\sigma c_t^{-\sigma-1}, H_{cu} = H_{uc} = 0$ and $H_{uu} = -\alpha(1-\alpha)\frac{\bar{y}_t}{u^2}\lambda_{1t}$, the Hessian determinant $\begin{vmatrix} H_{cc} & H_{cu} \\ H_{uc} & H_{uu} \end{vmatrix}$ is strictly positive if $\alpha < 1$, which always happens given the constant returns to scale assumption in the production function (1.1). $\square$

1.5   The Possibility for Non-Degenerate Balanced Dynamics

Once it is proven that the FOCs are also sufficient to solve the infinite-horizon optimization problems $\mathbf{P}^c$ and $\mathbf{P}^d$, it becomes interesting to determine whether the resulting motion supports an asymptotically-consistent long-run dynamics. We face here two sets of problems. On the one hand:

---

[4]The other possibility, the Mangasarian (strong) concavity condition (requiring the Hamiltonian to be jointly concave with respect to the state and control variables and $\lambda_{it} > 0 \,\forall t, i = 1, 2$), does not find application here.

[5]Asada *et al.* analyze the second order conditions associated with the centralized solution of Romer's endogenous growth model [26].

i)   we need to preliminarily prove that the FOCs are actually compatible with a form of *ordered* or *balanced* evolution of the economy;

ii) if the dynamics with the characteristics in point *i)* can be actually supported, we also need to check whether it violates the TVC.

On the other, we are interested to check whether the dynamics satisfying points *i)* and *ii)* can be used to provide practical predictions in real cases.

Let us first give a formal definition of what is meant by a non-degenerate Balanced Growth Path (BGP) in the context of the ULM. As discussed above:

Definition 1.5 *Along a BGP*:

a)   *the growth rate of the economy is constant*;

b)   *the growth rates of the variables c_t, k_t, h_t, λ_{1t} and λ_{2t} are constant*;

c)   *the partition of non-leisure time between production and learning is constant and is a positive number lying between 0 and 1*;

The BGP is non-degenerate if the growth rate of the economy is positive and so are the growth rates of c_t, k_t and h_t.

Before proceeding, we find it convenient to compact system (1.16*i*) into a easier-to-treat four dimensional system of first-order differential equations. To this end, we exploit the duality conditions in (1.16*a*) and (1.16*b*) to calculate the growth rates of the two control variables, consumption and working time. We have:

Proposition 1.5 *The candidates proposed by the Maximum Principle to solve the centralized and the decentralized optimization problems associated with the ULM imply the following four-dimension system of first-order differential equations*:

(1.17*a*) $\xi_c = \frac{\dot{c}_t}{c_t} = \frac{\alpha}{\sigma} \frac{\bar{y}_t}{k_t} - \frac{\rho}{\sigma}$

(1.17*b*) $\xi_k = \frac{\dot{k}_t}{k_t} = \frac{\bar{y}_t}{k_t} - \frac{c_t}{k_t}$

(1.17*c*) $\xi_h = \frac{\dot{h}_t}{h_t} = B\left(1 - u_t\right)$

(1.17*d*) $\xi_u = \frac{\dot{u}_t}{u_t} = \frac{B(1-\alpha+\gamma)}{\alpha} - \frac{c_t}{k_t} + B\frac{E_h^{c,d}-(1-\alpha+\gamma)(1-\alpha)}{\alpha(1-\alpha)}u_t$

Proof Taking logarithms and time derivatives of the duality conditions (1.16*a*) and (1.16*b*), the system in the proposition can be easily retrieved after substitution of the relevant growth rates. □

Needless to say, by assigning the appropriate value to $E_h^{c,d}$, the system in Proposition 1.5 can be easily brought to refer either to the decentralized or to the centralized solution of the model. Notice, furthermore:

Remark *All results obtained from system* (1.17i) *when independent of* $E_h^{c,d}$, *are common features, shared by optimal and equilibrium paths.*

1.5.1 Some Preliminary Properties of the Balanced Evolution of the Economy

Let us now verify whether the dynamic system (1.17i) supports the kind of solution trajectories described in Definition 1.5. If ξ_i^* represents the balanced-growth rate of the generic variable i and if we let the new constant $\psi = \frac{1-\alpha+\gamma}{1-\alpha}$ simplify the notation, we obtain the following preliminary result:

Lemma 1.1 *Suppose that both (decentralized and centralized) economies move along the BGP. Then, for both of them*:

$$\xi_c^* = \xi_k^* = \xi_{\bar{y}}^* \equiv \xi^* = \psi\xi_h^* = B\psi\left(1 - u^*\right)$$

Proof
a) The equivalence $\xi_c^* = \xi_k^*$ can be proved by plugging the growth rate of consumption in (1.17a), into the expression for the growth rate of physical capital in (1.17b). We obtain $\xi_k = \frac{\sigma}{\alpha}\xi_c - \frac{c_t}{k_t} + \frac{\rho}{\alpha}$. Since, along a BGP, ξ_c and ξ_k must be constant, the ratio $\frac{c_t}{k_t}$ must be constant as well. The equivalence $\xi_c^* = \xi_k^*$ follows;
b) to prove that the growth rates of consumption and physical capital equal the growth rate of the economy in terms of goods production, equation (1.17b) can again be exploited. Simple calculations of logarithms and time derivatives lead to the BGP relation between the growth rates of physical capital and narrow output $\xi_k^* = \xi_{\bar{y}}^* \equiv \xi^*$. By point a) above, this relation extends to the growth rate of consumption;
c) to prove that $\xi^* = \psi\xi_h^*$ consider that the growth rate of goods production is, by definition, $\xi^* = \alpha\xi_k + (1 - \alpha + \gamma)\xi_h + (1 - \alpha)\xi_u$. Along the BGP, $\xi_u = 0$. Since, from part b), we have that $\xi_k^* = \xi^*$, it follows that $\xi^* = \psi\xi_h^*$;
d) the independence of the results in the proposition from the term $E_h^{c,d}$ implies that they cover both centralized and decentralized dynamics. □

Notice that:

Remark *The positiveness of the growth rates in Lemma* 1.1, *i.e. the non-degeneracy of the BGP according to Definition* 1.5, *is linked to the steady-state value of working time. If* $u^* \in (0, 1)$, *the BGP is non-degenerate.*

Given Lemma 1.1, it is also easy to prove the following:

Lemma 1.2 *Suppose the economy moves along a BGP. Then*:

$$(1.18) \qquad u^* = \frac{\rho(1-\alpha) - B(1-\alpha+\gamma)(1-\sigma)}{B\left[E_h^{c,d} - (1-\alpha+\gamma)(1-\sigma)\right]}$$

In both cases of centralized and decentralized dynamics there exist regions of the parameter space where $u^* \in (0,1)$.

Proof Using Lemma 1.1 to simplify the dynamics of system (1.17i) along the BGP, it is easy to obtain u^*. Since, according to the choice of the parameter values, u^* can be either very large or negative, a simple continuity argument implies that there must exist a region in the parameter space where $u^* \in (0,1)$. The possibility of inverting the sign of (1.18) is independent of the term $E_h^{c,d}$ and therefore applies to both centralized and decentralized economies. $\square$

Notice also that, with equation (1.18) and Lemma 1.1 in hand, the expression for the growth rate of the economy becomes:

$$(1.19) \qquad \xi^* = B\psi(1-u^*) = \psi \frac{BE_h^{c,d} - \rho(1-\alpha)}{E_h^{c,d} - (1-\alpha+\gamma)(1-\sigma)}$$

Of course, if $u^* \in (0,1)$, the BGP is non-degenerate and the growth rate of the economy is positive.

We are now well equipped to prove the main proposition on the existence of a family of non-degenerate BGP solutions to problems $\mathbf{P}^c$ and $\mathbf{P}^d$ satisfying the boundary conditions. We find that:

Proposition 1.6 *Regardless of whether the decentralized or the planner solution are considered, there exist regions in the parameter space where the necessary and sufficient FOCs support the existence of a family of non-degenerate BGPs which, according to Definition 1.5, solve problems $\mathbf{P}^c$ and $\mathbf{P}^d$. All the members of such a family of BGPs do not violate the TVC.*

Proof Lemma 1.2 proves that there exist regions of the parameter space where $u^* \in (0,1)$ for both solutions of the model. From equation (1.17c) this implies that, ξ_h^* is positive and constant. By Lemma 1.1 this property extends to the other variables of the model. Proposition 1.2 guarantees that also the growth rate of the shadow price of human capital is constant. The constancy of the shadow price of physical capital can be seen by applying time derivatives to the equation in (1.16a) to find that $\xi_{\lambda_1}^* = -\sigma\xi_c^* = -\sigma\xi^*$. To prove that the BGPs satisfy the TVC in (1.9), it suffices to demonstrate that the asymptotic values of $-\rho + \xi_{\lambda_{1t}} + \xi_{k_t}$ and $-\rho + \xi_{\lambda_{2t}} + \xi_{h_t}$ are both negative. The first test can be easily performed by substituting the relevant growth rates from system (1.16i); we find the value of $-Bu^*$ which is unambiguously negative for any $u^* \in (0,1)$. For the second test consider the growth rate of the shadow price of human capital accumulation in Proposition 1.2. We find the value of $-B\frac{E_h^{c,d}}{1-\alpha}u^*$ which is also unambiguously negative for $u^* \in (0,1)$. $\square$

Chapter 2

The General Properties of the
Uzawa-Lucas Economy

2.1   Introduction and Plan of the Chapter

When a set of laws of motion governing the economy over time is derived from a specific model, the analysis typically distinguishes two types of conceptually different dynamics. In the first place, the behavior of real economies can be predicted by using the properties of the model when the variables evolve along a Balanced Growth Path (BGP, as in Definition 1.5).

Secondly, if we imagine that *imbalances* can result for a reason whatsoever, the predictions of the model can be investigated when the economy is in *transition*, namely in the special situation in which the economy does not behave, in general terms, as it would along the BGP.

A strictly related issue is determining whether the economy in transition tends to restore its balanced evolution over time. The economic theory finds this possibility extremely interesting: if this is indeed the case, the transition becomes nothing more than the economy's short-run response to events perturbing its ordered evolution and the BGP can be interpreted as the long-run position asymptotically approached by the economy.

This Chapter is aimed at giving a first general assessment of these issues in the case of the dynamics generated by the ULM. In particular, we proceed here to approach the analysis of the behavior of both the centralized and decentralized economies in the long-run. Some preliminary issues concerning the properties of the short-run adjustment are also proposed. As it will be clear in the following Chapters, the results here obtained will drastically simplify the investigation in Chapters 3 and 4 of the *specific* properties of the centralized and decentralized economies. The study of the deformation of the market economy with respect to its efficient benchmark, in Chapter 5, will also take major advantages from these preliminary discussions.

The first section of this Chapter concentrates on the features optimal and equilibrium paths have in common when the Uzawa-Lucas economy evolves along a non-degenerate BGP. In order to give access to richer details on the dynamic evolution of two-sector economies in presence of a learning sector, the analysis goes beyond the primitive variables of the model, to also take into consideration some interesting combinations of them. A first group of these new variables, labelled as *adjoint variables*, is formed by a broadened configuration of the output of the economy and by the wage rate, the rental price of capital (or interest rate) and the saving rate.

A second group of variables we will find worth separately studying, includes the ratio goods production/physical capital (average goods production), the physical capital/consumption (average consumption) and the *weighted ratio* between the two capital stocks. Abusing the Kaldorian terminology, we label these BGP-stationary combinations of the primitive variables as *Great Ratios*.

What we have found is interesting. In addition to the preliminary properties discussed in Chapter 1, we also have that, along the BGP, the Uzawa-Lucas economy (along both optimal and equilibrium paths) behaves such that:

a) the ratio of broad output/goods production is always greater than one;

b) broad output grows at the same rate as goods production;

c) the wage rate grows less than the overall economy and does not grow at all if the externality is set to zero;

d) the saving rate is positive and can never be constant in transition;

e) the interest rate is constant and above the subjective discount rate.

The study of the features of optimal and equilibrium paths when the economy is in transition is much less straightforward. In general terms, the methodologies which can in principle be adopted can be classified into two main types; one type producing *valid-in-the-large* or *global* results, and another producing *local* findings that are only valid in a small neighborhood of the BGP. The former type of analysis has the potential advantage of fully revealing the properties of the transitional paths. However, it can be rarely used, since it requires explicit solutions of the differential equations and/or low dimensions, which are normally very difficult to obtain in the field of two-sector models.

Conversely, the latter type of analysis finds a much more generalized application: by exploiting the Hartman-Grobman[6] theorem on near-BGP topological equivalence between linearized and full dynamics, this methodology greatly simplifies the search for predictive results in specific circumstances. Needless to say, local analysis may also be difficult to implement. In particular, high dimensions and/or numerous control parameters may, in general terms, mean that it will not be possible to solve the characteristic equation associated with linearized dynamics. The effect of this is that both the *economic analysis* of the forces controlling the evolution of the economy in transition and the study of the *propensity* of such an economy to approach the BGP may remain, at least in part, out of reach. However, even in cases in which

---

[6]See, for instance, Wiggings [29] for reference.

the roots of the characteristic equation cannot be found in explicit form, there still exists a number of alternative methodologies which might be used instead to derive (less general) qualitative insights into the properties of trajectories wandering in the neighborhood of the BGP.

To investigate the general properties of the economy in transition and the stability properties of the BGP in our specific case, we only implement here the local analysis. First of all, in order to reduce the degree of complexity of the analysis, we lower the effective dimension of the dynamic laws governing the economy. By exploiting the BGP stationarity of the average consumption and that of the weighted ratio between the two capital stocks, it is possible to transform the four-dimensional system of dynamic laws governing the evolution of the economy into a much-easier-to-treat stationary system in $\mathbb{R}^3$. From among many possible alternatives, the transformation chosen is that used in Benhabib and Perli [5] and has the useful property of isolating the dynamic evolution of the state of the economy. The $\mathbb{R}^3$-reduced motion presents an economically feasible interior fixed point whose properties, by standard arguments, translate into the properties of the BGP in the original dimension.

We proceed by calculating the Jacobian matrix associated with the system of dynamic laws, as well as the related characteristic equation. By assuming that all roots of the Jacobian are real and only one of them is negative, we can solve the linearized dynamics and derive the functions linking any initial state of the economy to the control and control-like variables. Following in the footsteps of Mulligan and Sala-i-Martin [23] and Caballè and Santos [7], we use the knowledge of these functions[7] to provide a descriptive analysis of the economic forces at work in the short-run in the special case of saddle-path stability/instability.

The last sections of the Chapter change the perspective of analysis. We dedicate here some room to a first evaluation of the fundamental differences between the centralized and decentralized dynamics. We are able here to prove a series of crucial findings. In particular, we find that, in the case of efficient dynamics, the characteristic equation can always be factorized to produce a fixed one-negative-two-positive structure of the eigenvalues (in the real axis). As a consequence, the stable manifold associated with the fixed point is always a one-dimensional object in the phase space.

Conversely, the possibility of factorizing the characteristic equation is generally negated in the context of a market economy. Unless the inverse of the intertemporal elasticity of substitution equals the share of physical capital, we are not able to see a fixed structure of the eigenvalues and therefore to infer in general terms the dimension of the stable manifold in the case of the decentralized dynamics. Very interestingly, furthermore, we also prove that the motion associated with the centralized economy admits a further dimensional reduction. As a matter of fact, the motion in $\mathbb{R}^4$ implies a simple system in $\mathbb{R}^2$, in the space opened by the average goods pro-

---

[7]As it will be discussed below, these functions are *policy functions* when the centralized dynamics is considered. They are only *equilibrium functions*, linking the state of the economy to its control part, in the case of decentralized dynamics.

duction and consumption. We also find that this possibility is negated in the case of equilibrium dynamics.

The rest of the Chapter continues as follows.

The second section of the Chapter looks at the common features displayed by a centralized and decentralized economy evolving in a balanced position.

The third section first introduces some basic material on the mathematical tools and concepts used in this Chapter and throughout the rest of the book to infer the local and global properties of the market and efficient dynamics generated by the ULM. In particular, we initiate a discussion on the dynamic possibilities which can be expected from the model. We also show how to reduce the dimension of system (1.17*i*) and how to calculate the Jacobian matrix and the associated characteristic equation. A general form of the functions linking the state of the economy to the control and control-like variables is also determined.

The fourth section deals principally with the motion associated with the centralized optimal dynamics and shows that it can be studied in two dimensions.

2.2   Some General Features of Balanced Growth

2.2.1 *Some BGP-Stationary Useful Variables: the* Great Ratios

We start this section by recalling, for simpler reference, system (1.17*i*) obtained in the preceding Chapter:

$$(2.1a)\qquad \xi_c = \frac{\dot{c}_t}{c_t} = \frac{\alpha}{\sigma}\frac{\bar{y}_t}{k_t} - \frac{\rho}{\sigma}$$

$$(2.1b)\qquad \xi_k = \frac{\dot{k}_t}{k_t} = \frac{\bar{y}_t}{k_t} - \frac{c_t}{k_t}$$

$$(2.1c)\qquad \xi_h = \frac{\dot{h}_t}{h_t} = B\left(1 - u_t\right)$$

$$(2.1d)\qquad \xi_u = \frac{\dot{u}_t}{u_t} = \frac{B(1-\alpha+\gamma)}{\alpha} - \frac{c_t}{k_t} + B\frac{E_h^{c,d}-(1-\alpha+\gamma)(1-\alpha)}{\alpha(1-\alpha)}u_t$$

where, as in (1.7), $\bar{y}_t = Ak^\alpha u^{1-\alpha}h^{1-\alpha+\gamma}$. As already explained, according to the appropriate value of $E_h^{c,d}$, the growth rate of working time either undertakes its optimal or equilibrium value.

Starting from system (2.1*i*) we have proved, in Chapter 1, a number of interesting details on the long-run properties of the Uzawa-Lucas economy. In particular, we have found that, along a non-degenerate BGP, the growth rate of the economy equals the growth rate of consumption and physical capital accumulation. In turn, these growth rates are multiple of the growth rate of human capital.

There is a number of implications following from these results. In particular, along the BGP:

Proposition 2.1 *The average consumption, the average goods production and the* weighted ratio[8] *between the two capital stocks are constant. They respectively equal*:

$$(2.2) \qquad (c/k)^* \equiv m^* = \frac{\rho}{\alpha} - \frac{\alpha - \sigma}{\alpha}\xi^*$$

$$(2.3) \qquad (\bar{y}/k)^* \equiv n^* = \frac{\rho + \sigma\xi^*}{\alpha}$$

$$(2.4) \qquad \left(kh^{-\psi}\right)^* \equiv p^* = \left(\frac{\rho + \sigma\xi^*}{\alpha A}\right)^{\frac{1}{\alpha - 1}} u^*$$

Proof The stationarity of the ratios in the proposition derives from the relationships among the growth rates of the variables involved (cf. Lemma 1.1). To obtain the evaluation of the ratios along the BGP, consider that in the proof of Lemma 1.1 we show that it must be:

$$\xi_k = \frac{\sigma}{\alpha}\xi_c - \frac{c_t}{k_t} + \frac{\rho}{\alpha}.$$

Since, along the BGP, the growth rates of consumption and physical capital are constant and equal to ξ^*, the relation in (2.2) can be easily obtained. By using (2.2) and (2.1b), the stationary values in (2.3) can be obtained. Relation (2.4) follows from the definition for average goods production and (2.3). □

Of course, being the growth rate of the economy as in (1.19), namely equal to:

$$\xi^* = B\psi\left(1 - u^*\right) = \psi\frac{BE_h^{c,d} - \rho(1-\alpha)}{E_h^{c,d} - (1-\alpha+\gamma)(1-\sigma)}$$

the steady-state values is (2.2), (2.3) and (2.4) undertake different values along optimal or equilibrium paths.

2.2.2 *The* Adjoint Variables *along the BGP*

Narrow output is not the only significant measure of the performance of the economy. In particular, a broader configuration of output, y_t^T, where the contribution of both sectors of the economy are taken into consideration, gives a more appropriate indication of the actual evolution of the economy. Of course, to sum the production of goods to the "production" in the learning sector, we need an appropriate context for evaluating human capital. Since a by-product of the application of the Maximum Principle is the derivation of the shadow prices of the accumulation, we can prove that:

Proposition 2.2 *Let λ_2/λ_1 be the relative price of human capital in terms of goods. Then the level of broad output is given by*:

---

[8]Notice that, when the externality is set to zero, this relationship between the two forms of accumulation is the simple $\frac{k_t}{h_t}$ ratio.

(2.5) $y_t^T = \bar{y}_t \frac{1-\alpha(1-u_t)}{u_t}$

Its transitional evolution is governed by the dynamic law:

(2.6) $\frac{\dot{y}_t^T}{y_t^T} \equiv \xi_{y_t^T} = \xi_{\bar{y}_t} - \frac{\dot{u}_t}{u_t} \frac{1-\alpha}{1-\alpha(1-u_t)}$

Proof By definition, $y_t^T = \bar{y}_t + (\lambda_2/\lambda_1)\, y_t^e$. Using the equilibrium-duality condition (1.16b) and equation (1.2), it is easy to obtain the level of broad output. The derivation of the growth rate follows after calculating logarithms and time derivatives. $\square$

An immediate consequence of Proposition 2.2 is the following:

Corollary 2.1 *Let the economy evolve along a non-degenerate BGP. Then, the growth rates of narrow and broad outputs are the same and the index* $\left(\frac{y^T}{\bar{y}_t}\right)^* = \frac{1-\alpha(1-u^*)}{u^*}$ *is always greater than 1.*

Proof Since, along the BGP, $\frac{\dot{u}_t}{u_t} = 0$, equation (2.6) implies $\xi_{y^T}^* = \xi^*$. Furthermore, $\frac{1-\alpha(1-u^*)}{u^*} > 1$ for all $u^* \in (0,1)$. $\square$

Therefore, we also have:

Remark *The BGP contribution of the learning sector to total output is inversely linked to* u_t. *When* $u^* \to 1$, $\left(\frac{y^T}{\bar{y}_t}\right)^* \to 1$.

We can continue the derivation of the analysis of the BGP properties shared by the centralized and decentralized economies by studying the behavior of the interest and wage rates. Recalling from Proposition 1.1 that $r_t \equiv \text{MPK} = \alpha\frac{y_t^f}{k_t}$ and that $w_t \equiv \text{MPL} = (1-\alpha)\frac{y_t^f}{(uh)_t}$ (under the profit maximization hypothesis), we first have:

Proposition 2.3 *The laws of motion of the interest and wage rates can be written as follows:*

(2.7) $\xi_r \equiv \frac{\dot{r}_t}{r_t} = \frac{B(1-\alpha+\gamma)}{\alpha} - \frac{1-\alpha}{\alpha}r_t + Bu_t\frac{E_h^{c,d}-(1-\alpha+\gamma)}{\alpha}$

(2.8) $\xi_w \equiv \frac{\dot{w}_t}{w_t} = r_t - B - Bu_t\frac{E_h^{c,d}-(1-\alpha)}{1-\alpha}$

Proof The laws of evolution in the proposition can be retrieved by calculating logarithms and time derivatives from the definitions $r_t \equiv \text{MPK} = \alpha\frac{y_t^f}{k_t}$ and that $w_t \equiv \text{MPL} = (1-\alpha)\frac{y_t^f}{(uh)_t}$. After substitution of the relevant growth rates from system

(2.1*i*) the laws in the proposition can be obtained. □

Very interestingly, furthermore:

Proposition 2.4 *Let the Uzawa-Lucas economy evolve along a non-degenerate BGP. Then, the interest rate is stationary at the following value:*

(2.9) $r^* = \rho + \sigma\xi^* > 0$

Conversely, along the BGP, the wage rate grows steadily at the rate:

(2.10) $\left(\frac{\dot{w}}{w}\right)^* = \xi_w^* = \frac{\gamma}{1-\alpha+\gamma}\xi^* > 0$

Proof The BGP value of the interest rate can be obtained by evaluating the definition $r_t \equiv MPK = \alpha\frac{\bar{y}_t}{k_t}$ at the BGP. By considering the BGP value of the average goods production in (2.3), we obtain equation (2.9). To derive the BGP growth rate of w_t, consider that from the definition $w_t \equiv MPL = (1-\alpha)\,y_t^f/(uh)_t$ we have $\xi_w = \xi_{\bar{y}} - \xi_h - \xi_u$. Since, along the BGP, $\xi_u^* = 0$ and $\xi_h^* = \frac{\xi^*}{\psi}$, we derive the expression in (2.10). □

Therefore, in the Uzawa-Lucas economy:

Proposition 2.5 *The rental compensation of physical capital can never be constant in transition. The same happens for the level of wages.*

Proof By expression (2.7), the stationarity of r_t is linked to the stationarity of working time. Suppose working time is constant at a given value $\bar{u}$.[9] Only if it happens that $r_t \equiv \bar{r} = B\psi(1-\bar{u}) + B\bar{u}\frac{E_h^{c,d}}{1-\alpha}$ the interest rate is constant in transition. However, by alternatively substituting the optimal or equilibrium values of $E_h^{c,d}$ into the expression for $\bar{r}$ we always obtain $\rho + \sigma\xi^*$. Since, by Proposition 2.4, this value is achieved by the rental compensation of capital only along the BGP, the result in proposition is implied. □

The possibility that the wage rate will grow along the BGP in the Uzawa-Lucas economy depends on the externality. Notice, in fact that:

Remark *The wage rate does not grow along a BGP if the externality is set to zero.*

Notice that, furthermore, for both the centralized and decentralized economies, along a non-degenerate BGP:

Remark *The BGP value of the interest rate is above the subjective discount rate.*

---

[9]We shall prove, in the following Chapters, that this is a concrete possibility in specific regions of the parameter space.

The level of wages grows less than the overall economy.

To complete the picture of the economy, we need to consider the laws governing the saving rate in transition and along the BGP. Since the saving rate is the portion of non-consumed goods production, $s_t = 1 - \frac{c_t}{y_t} = 1 - \frac{c_t/k_t}{y_t/k_t}$, we obtain the following preliminary result:

Proposition 2.6 *The expression*:

$$(2.11) \quad \dot{s}_t = \frac{\rho}{\sigma} + (1-\alpha)B\left(\frac{(1-\alpha+\gamma)-E_h^{c,d}}{\alpha}\right)(1-u_t) +$$

$$+\frac{B}{\alpha}E_h^{c,d} + \frac{\bar{y}_t}{k_t}\left(s_t + \alpha\frac{1-\sigma}{\sigma} - 1\right)$$

governs the motion of the saving rate.

Proof The expression in the proposition can be retrieved by calculating logarithms and time derivatives from the definition of the saving rate, $s_t = 1 - \frac{c_t}{y_t}$. A simple substitution of the relevant growth rates from system (2.1i) brings to the growth rate in (2.11). □

Interestingly, it is possible to prove here that, again in both cases of centralized and decentralized dynamics:

Corollary 2.2 *The Uzawa-Lucas economy can never support a constant-in-transition saving rate.*

Proof Suppose $s_t = 1 - \alpha\frac{1-\sigma}{\sigma}$. Since the rest of the second hand side of the equation in (2.11) is always positive, the saving rate can never be constant in transition.[10] □

Now, we have that:

Proposition 2.7 *Let the Uzawa-Lucas economy evolve along the BGP. Then the saving rate is constant and equal to*:

$$(2.12) \quad s^* = \frac{\alpha}{\rho/\xi^* + \sigma}$$

Proof Consider the definition of the saving rate $s_t = 1 - \frac{c_t/k_t}{y_t/k_t}$. Since, as proved in Proposition 2.3, both $\frac{c_t}{k_t}$ and $\frac{\bar{y}_t}{k_t}$ are constant along the BGP, simple substitution of the values in (2.4) and (2.5) imply that the saving rate has the stationary value in the proposition. □

---

[10]Mullighan and Sala-i-Martin [23] find a possibility of a constant saving rate in transition when the externality factor is set to zero and depreciation rates are explicitly taken into consideration.

2.3 The Transition along Optimal and Equilibrium Paths

2.3.1 *Some Principles for Mathematical Analysis*

In the preceding section, we have sketched some properties of the relevant variables which are shared by the centralized or decentralized economies evolving along the BGP. Are there, conversely, general features which are displayed by both optimal and equilibrium paths when the Uzawa-Lucas economy in an off-balanced position?

As already discussed in the introduction to this Chapter, the methodologies which can in principle be adopted to study these issues, in a generic autonomous vector field of the form:

$$(2.13) \quad \dot{x}_t = f(x_t) \qquad x \in \mathbb{R}^n$$

having a fixed point x^* such that $f(x^*) = 0$, can be classified into two main types; one producing *valid-in-the-large* or *global* results, and another type producing *local* findings, only valid in a small neighborhood of x^*.

Given the complexity of our general system (1.17i), we will proceed by using the tools of the local analysis which considerably simplify the analysis.[11] In particular, the Hartman-Grobman theorem[12] proves that system (2.13) is topologically equivalent, in the neighborhood of the fixed point x^*, to the associated linearized:

$$(2.14) \quad \dot{x}_t = J(x^*)[x_t - x^*]$$

where $J(x^*) = Df(x^*)$ is the Jacobian matrix associated with system (2.13), evaluated at the steady-state.

When governed by the flow of the linearized system (2.14), the motion is much easier to treat than in the original full setting (2.13). In particular, simple linear algebra arguments can be used to show that if the roots of $J(x^*)$ are available, (2.14) can be solved by standard methods to produce a number of useful details on the mechanisms at work behind the transition in the neighborhood of the steady-state. Information on the (approximate) local speed of convergence towards the fixed point can also be obtained.

The tools of the local analysis are also precious from the viewpoint of the stability analysis: as a matter of fact, it can be shown that the form and signs of the real parts of the κ_n roots of $J(x^*)$ can also be used to detect the local dimension of the stable manifold of the fixed point associated with system (2.13) as well as to assess the modality of convergence/divergence towards/from the steady state. In particular, the number of roots with negative real parts will determine the local dimension of the stable manifold of the fixed point whereas the real/complex nature of the eigenvalues will have an effect on the modality (oscillating/non oscillating) of

---

[11] Only in the following Chapters, devoted to the analysis of the specific properties of the optimal and equilibrium paths, we will be able to use the arguments of the global analysis.

[12] See, for instance Wiggins [29] for a thorough discussion on these issues.

the convergence/divergence towards/from the steady-state.[13]

2.3.2 *A Dimensional-Reducing Transformation of the Variables*

Needless to say, also the local analysis is difficult to undertake when the set of laws of motion is large. In these circumstances, any possibility of reducing the effective dimension of a generic dynamic system is welcome.

In the case of the ULM, there is a wide range of suitable transformed variables which are stationary along the BGP.

We choose to keep the already-stationary control variable u_t plus the $\frac{c_t}{k_t} = m_t$ and $k_t h_t^{-\psi} = p_t$ ratios, which, according to the terminology used by Mulligan and Sala-i-Martin in [23], are, respectively a *control-like* and a *state-like* variable. The reason for this choice, as it will become clear in the following Chapters, is because it allows us to maintain a critical separation between the state of the economy, represented by the variable p_t, and its control part, the variables m_t and u_t.

The following can be easily proven:

Proposition 2.8 *The motion in* (2.1*i*) *implies a three-dimensional system of first order differential equations of the form*:

$$(2.15a) \qquad \frac{\dot{p}_t}{p_t} = Au_t^{1-\alpha}p_t^{\alpha-1} - m_t - B\psi\left(1 - u_t\right)$$

$$(2.15b) \qquad \frac{\dot{u}_t}{u_t} = B\frac{1-\alpha+\gamma}{\alpha} - m_t + B\frac{E_h^{c,d}-(1-\alpha)(1-\alpha+\gamma)}{\alpha(1-\alpha)}u_t$$

$$(2.15c) \qquad \frac{\dot{m}_t}{m_t} = A\frac{\alpha-\sigma}{\sigma}u_t^{1-\alpha}p_t^{\alpha-1} + m_t - \frac{\rho}{\sigma}$$

The system possesses an interior steady state characterized by the stationary values in (2.6), (1.18) *and* (2.4).

Proof By calculating logarithms and time derivatives of the new variables, the system in proposition can be easily obtained after substitution of the relevant growth rates from the original system. □

Notice that, in this reduced dimension:

Remark *The lack of full internalization of the contribution of human capital in equilibrium only matters for the growth rate of working time.*

---

[13]It appears evident that, in order to understand the properties of the linearized dynamics, it is important that the roots of the Jacobian matrix are readily available. The easiest case is met when the explicit form of the eigenvalues can be retrieved by simply solving the characteristic equation associated with $J(x^*)$. However, when the dynamics are too intricate and the characteristic equation cannot be factorized, qualitative information on the form of the eigenvalues can still be obtained by a number of alternative methods. In this respect, a powerful tool we will be using in Chapter 4 is the Routh-Hurwitz criterion. This criterion allows to detect the sign path of the (real parts) of the eigenvalues without deriving them explicitly.

By standard arguments, the steady-state in the lower dimension corresponds to the unique family of BGPs generated by the model according to Proposition (1.6).

A first glance at system (2.15i) reveals the following property, applying to both centralized and decentralized dynamics:

Corollary 2.3 *The origin cannot be a fixed point of system* (2.15i).

Proof Since the variable p_t is raised to a negative power in (2.15a) and (2.15c), the origin in this reduce dimension cannot be a fixed point. $\square$

In the following discussions, therefore, we shall concentrate on the investigation of the system's interior solutions

2.3.3 The Jacobian and the Characteristic Equation

As discussed above with regard to generic systems of differential equations, the linear dominance in the neighborhood of the steady-state can be used to infer the properties of the transition in a simplified context.

We need initially to compute the Jacobian matrix for system (2.15i). Using the calculations in the Appendix of this Chapter (part a), we have that the Jacobian matrix evaluated at the steady-state, J^*, can be written as follows:

$$(2.16) \qquad J^* = \begin{bmatrix} J_{11}^* & \frac{p^*}{u^*}\left(B\psi u^* - J_{11}^*\right) & -p^* \\ 0 & B\eta u^* & -u^* \\ \phi\frac{J_{11}^* m^*}{p^*} & -\phi\frac{J_{11}^* m^*}{u^*} & m^* \end{bmatrix}$$

where the new constants $\eta = \frac{E_h^{c,d}-(1-\alpha+\gamma)(1-\alpha)}{(1-\alpha)\alpha}$ and $\phi = \frac{\alpha-\sigma}{\sigma}$ simplify the notation. Recalling the steady-state values of p_t and n_t from equations (2.4) and (2.3), the upper-left element of the Jacobian matrix has the following general form:

$$(2.17) \qquad J_{11}^* = -A\left(1-\alpha\right)\left(\frac{u^*}{p^*}\right)^{1-\alpha} = -\left(1-\alpha\right)n^* = -\frac{1-\alpha}{\alpha}\left(\rho+\sigma\xi^*\right) < 0$$

The explicit value of J_{11}^* in terms of the parameters, can be found by substituting the expression for ξ^*.

After simple calculations, the characteristic equation associated with the Jacobian in (2.16) can then be put in the form:

$$(2.18) \qquad \left(\kappa - J_{11}^*\right)\left(\kappa - B\eta u^*\right)\left(\kappa - m^*\right) - \phi B J_{11}^* m^* u^*\left(\psi - \eta\right) = 0$$

Notice the following:

Remark *When $\phi = 0$ (namely when the inverse of the intertemporal elasticity of substitution equals the share of physical capital) or when $\psi = \eta$, the characteristic* *equation in (2.18) can be factorized.*

We find here a very interesting result: since $\eta = \frac{E_h^{c,d} - (1-\alpha+\gamma)(1-\alpha)}{(1-\alpha)\alpha}$ always equals $\psi = \frac{1-\alpha+\gamma}{1-\alpha}$ in the case of the centralized solution,[14] we have that:

Proposition 2.9 *The Jacobian associated with the centralized dynamics is always characterized by a fixed one-negative-two-positive structure of the eigenvalues.*

Proof When the centralized dynamics is involved, $\psi = \eta$. As a consequence, the characteristic equation in (2.18) can be factorized; the eigenvalues are $\kappa_1 = J_{11}^* < 0$, $\kappa_2 = B\psi u^* > 0$, $\kappa_3 = m^* > 0$. $\square$

Consider, furthermore that:

Remark *The equivalence $\eta = \psi$ also occurs for equilibrium paths when the externality is set to zero.*

2.3.4 The Potential for non Saddle-Path Behavior in the Dynamics of the Model

Given the results in the preceding section, what can we expect from the stability analysis of the ULM?[15]

Let us first consider system (2.15*i*) in the case of optimal dynamics. As proved in Proposition 2.9, even in presence of a distorting factor in the form of a positive externality factor we can only have a fixed one-negative-two-positive sign patter for the eigenvalues associated with the Jacobian in (2.16). The saddle-path stability result (as it will be formally proved in Chapter 3) is therefore the only possible outcome: the stable manifold of the fixed point is a one-dimensional object and the asymptotic position of the economy, in terms of the *scaled* variables, will converge to the rest point if the initial conditions of the controls are accurately chosen to belong to the stable manifold of the fixed point itself. This has further implications. In particular, an economy beginning with lower levels of human and physical capital (determining the same initial state of the economy), will remain permanently below an initially better endowed economy.

Potentially richer are the dynamic possibilities offered when the decentralized economy is considered. Since the sign structure of the eigenvalues is not fixed, non saddle-path behavior may occur. In particular, let us suppose that the Jacobian associated with the decentralized version of system (2.15*i*) implies the existence of three eigenvalues with a positive real part. In this case, there will be asymptotic instability of the fixed point in $\mathbb{R}^3$. In this case, there are no equilibrium paths converging

---

[14]Simply substitute $E_h^{c,d} = (1 - \alpha + \gamma)$ in the definition for η.

[15]We shall only give here a brief introduction of the dynamic possibilities related to the signs of the real parts of the eigenvalues, which will be relevant for the following Chapters. A complete treatment of these issues remains well beyond the scope of the book.

to the steady-state and the control variables have to be chosen so that the economy is already initially set at the steady-state (in terms of the original $\mathbb{R}^4$ dimension, this means that the economy evolves along the BGP from the very beginning). Since no transition towards the fixed point is possible, any perturbation of the state of the economy implies a progressively increasing distance from the steady-state as $t \to \infty$.

Consider now the more interesting case in which the real parts of the three eigenvalues are positive in one case and negative in the others. The stable manifold of the fixed point now has dimension 2. This possibility results in a *continuum* of equilibria, giving rise to *indeterminacy of the BGP*. Also, since there is an infinite number of equilibrium paths which can be followed by an economy starting from any given initial position, the characteristic of the BGP in terms of the long-run levels of the original non-stationary variables, will be directly dependent on the specific history of a generic economic system. Provided that technology and preferences are the same, the very underlying implication of the indeterminacy result is that cultural, institutional and political factors are key variables in selecting one particular equilibrium path and therefore the long-run levels of welfare. Indeed, in cases where indeterminacy of the BGP is present, some countries might well end up better off than others, even though initially similar in wealth and endowments.[16]

2.3.5 *The Functions Linking the State of the Economy to its Control Part*

We try now to infer more information on the economic mechanism at work when the economy wanders in the neighborhood of the steady state. To this end, we undertake in the Appendix to this Chapter (part *b*) the solving procedure of the linearized version of system (2.15*i*) in the special case in which all eigenvalues are real and one of them is negative.[17]

The result of these calculations is in the following equations:

(2.19*a*) $\dfrac{u^*-u(0)}{u^*} = \phi\delta_1 \dfrac{p^*-p(0)}{p^*}$

(2.19*b*) $\dfrac{m^*-m(0)}{m^*} = \phi\delta_2 \dfrac{p^*-p(0)}{p^*}$

where $\delta_1 = \dfrac{J_{11}^* m^*}{\Gamma(\eta B u^*-\kappa_1)}$, $\delta_2 = \dfrac{J_{11}^*}{\Gamma}$ and $\Gamma = \left(\dfrac{J_{11}^* m^* \phi}{B\eta u^*-\kappa_1} - m^* + \kappa_1\right)$. Notice that the equations above link the initial values of the control variables to the state of the economy. The values of $\phi\delta_1$ and $\phi\delta_2$ can be interpreted as impact elasticities giving information of the percent variation of, respectively, working time and average consumption in response to a percent variation of the state of the economy in terms of weighted ratio between physical and human capital. Indeed, with the state of the

---

[16]Of course, recalling from the preceding Chapter that, given the parameter space, the BGP is unique (both when the decentralized and the centralized economy are taken into consideration), this possibility is called *local indeterminacy*, not to be confused with the possibility of *global indeterminacy* which can only happen when more than one non-degenerate BGP can be determined for the same parameter space.

[17]The original reference for this sub-section is in [16].

economy known, the signs of $\phi\delta_1$ and $\phi\delta_2$ provide information on the initial position of the control variable $u(0)$ and of the control-like variable $m(0)$. For instance, for a positive ϕ, if $Sign(\delta_1) = Sign(\delta_2) > 0$, a higher-than-BGP level of the $p(0)$ ratio implies higher-than-BGP initial levels for both consumption and working time. The contrary happens if $Sign(\delta_1) = Sign(\delta_2) < 0$. A symmetric argument applies if ϕ is known to be negative.

We will show in the following Chapters that expressions (2.19i) have a very important role to play in giving information on the behavior of both the centralized and decentralized economies in the neighborhood of the steady-state. Notice however that, since in the centralized economy the Planner has the full control of the decision variables, equations (2.19i) can be interpreted as (modified) linearized *policy functions* (MPF); conversely, in the decentralized economy, the equations in (2.19) are only generic functions linking the state of the economy to $u(0)$ and $m(0)$. As a consequence we will be referring to equations (2.19i) as to (modified) linearized *equilibrium functions* (MEF). The term "modified" applies since the standard way of representing the functions linking the control variables and the state of the economy is through the *level* of the control variable and the *level* of the state variable.[18]

2.3.6   *The Mechanisms Driving the Adjustment of the Economy*

Having obtained the functions tying together the control part of the economy to its state (in the case of only one real negative root), we now turn our attention to the economic interpretation of the forces possibly involved in the transition from a given initial state of the economy (in terms of $p(0)$) to its asymptotic position.

Let us consider, without any loss of generality, a case where there is an initial relative excess of physical capital. The opposite situation, i.e. one in which the economy presents a relative lack of physical capital, would produce symmetric results. The control variables which are in charge in the Lucas economy to restore the balanced evolution are consumption and working time.

A first crucial point to consider is that, as discussed in the first section of Chapter 1, the structure of the model implies that k_t is readily transformed into consumption. Therefore, a relative excess of physical capital decreases the shadow price of the physical good through equation (1.16b) determining, by equation (1.16a), a pressure for higher levels of consumption. Such effect will depend on σ. At the same time, a relative excess of physical capital raises the MPL, namely the prevailing wage rate of the economy (or *opportunity cost of schooling*). In such conditions agents are stimulated to increase the time dedicated to work and consequently, to study less. This effect is directly proportional to the share of physical capital.

A third effect is that, even in the hypothesis that the m^* and u^* are well adjusted from the very beginning, the economy tends to stabilize by decreasing the accumulation of physical capital through equation (2.15a).

---

[18]In the case of the ULM, the policy functions can be defined as projections of the stable manifold into the $[u, p]$ and $[m, p]$ planes.

Therefore, following the trail set by Mulligan and Sala-i-Martin [23], we give the following Definition:

Definition 2.1 *Let an economy be characterized by a relative excess of physical capital. Then, the economy sees a prevalence of*:

i) *the* Consumption-Smoothing Effect, *if the relative excess of physical capital is eliminated because of lower savings*;

ii) *the* Wage Rate Effect, *if the relative excess of physical capital is eliminated because of diminished working time*;

iii) *the* Solow Effect, *if the relative excess of physical capital is eliminated because of decreasing returns*;

Of course which effect prevails is determined by the signs of the impact elasticity in (2.19i). In particular, case i) requires high consumption in transition; therefore, again considering, without any loss of generality, a case where there is an initial relative excess of physical capital, $\phi\delta_2$ has to be positive. Conversely, case ii) requires a negative value for $\delta_1\phi$. The third case occurs when $\delta_1\phi = \delta_2\phi = 0$.

These aspects will be investigated in depth in the following Chapters, for both the centralized and decentralized economies.

2.3.7 Growth Cases

The above discussion has given us a preliminary outline of the behavior of the economy in response to shocks modifying the state of the economy in terms of the reaction of the control variables, consumption and working time, in the special situation in which both the centralized and decentralized economies are characterized by saddle-path stability/instability. The implications for the asymptotic values of the variables when any one of the effects above discussed prevails are also well worth investigating.

Let us first define as $\tilde{x} = \lim_{t\to\infty} x_t e^{-\xi_x^* t}$ the asymptotic normalized level of a generic variable x_t with asymptotic growth rate ξ_x^*. Let us again concentrate in the case in which the economy is characterized by an excess of physical capital. Following in the tracks laid by Caballè and Santos [7], we have:

Definition 2.2 *Convergence towards the BGP implies*:

i) *a normal case if* $\tilde{h} > h(0)$;

ii) *a paradoxical case if* $\tilde{h} < h(0)$;

iii) *an exogenous growth case if* $\tilde{h} = h(0)$.[19]

---

[19]This possibility rests on a constant-in-transition value of working time. If we call the constant growth rate of the economy g, the production function of the first sector can then be written as $\bar{y}_t = \pi k_t^\alpha e^{gt}$,

Notice that an implication of Definition 2.2 which is worth pointing out is that:

Remark *In the case of exogenous growth, the asymptotic value of human capital does not depend on the initial value of physical capital.*

Given Definition 2.2, and again supposing convergence towards the BGP, we are now in a position to prove the following crucial result:

Proposition 2.10 *Let the parameters imply a prevalence of the Consumption Smoothing Effect (Wage Rate Effect). Let, furthermore, Sign($\delta_1\phi$) = Sign($\delta_2\phi$). Then the economy belongs to the paradoxical (normal) case. The prevalence of the Solow Effect means that there will be exogenous growth.*

Proof As discussed above, the prevalence of the Consumption-Smoothing Effect implies a jump in $c(0)$. By assumption, it also implies a jump in $u(0)$ and transitional lower-than-BGP values of working time. This, in turn, leads to low transitional growth rates of human capital. Therefore, a relative abundance of physical capital is necessarily associated with a $\tilde{h} < h(0)$. The opposite occurs when it is the Wage Rate Effect that prevails. Constant control and control-like variables in transition imply that we are dealing with an exogenous growth case. $\square$

From the stationarity of average consumption and of the weighted ratio between the two state variables, we can further say that:

Remark *Low (high) values of $\tilde{h}$ with respect to $h(0)$ also imply low (high) values of $\tilde{k}$ and $\tilde{c}$ with respect to $k(0)$ and $c(0)$.*

2.4   The Possibility of a Further Dimensional Reduction

We find here that the alternative possibility of stationarizing the dynamic system in (2.1*i*) using the average goods production instead of the weighted ratio between physical and human capital will have a number of surprising consequences.
We can prove the following:

Lemma 2.1 *The motion in system (2.1i) implies the following:*

$$(2.20a) \quad \frac{\dot{n}_t}{n_t} = B\frac{(1-\alpha+\gamma)}{\alpha} + B\frac{E_h^{c,d}-(1-\alpha+\gamma)}{\alpha}u_t - (1-\alpha)\,n_t$$

$$(2.20b) \quad \frac{\dot{m}_t}{m_t} = \frac{\alpha-\sigma}{\sigma}n_t - \frac{\rho}{\sigma} + m_t$$

Proof Simple application of logarithms and time derivatives to the definitions of

---

where π is a generic constant. This formulation replicates the neoclassical production function with an exogenous growth rate of the productivity level.

average goods production and consumption leads to the dynamic system (2.20i) after substitution of the relevant growth rates from system (2.1i). $\square$

Now, given Lemma 2.1, the following critical result can be made available:

Proposition 2.11 *Regardless of the externality, the motion along optimal paths can always be contained in* $\mathbb{R}^2$. *The same happens for equilibrium paths when working time is constant in transition.*

Proof When the centralized economy is considered, $E_h^{c,d} = 1 - \alpha + \gamma$. Thus system (2.20$i$) is no longer dependent on the law of evolution of working time and can be studied as a independent simple system in $\mathbb{R}^2$. The same happens when $u_t = u^*$. $\square$

Of course, from Proposition 2.11 it follows that:

Corollary 2.4 *The competitive dynamics can also be studied in* $\mathbb{R}^2$ *when the externality is set to zero.*

Proof When the externality is set to zero, system (2.20i) again becomes independent of the motion of working time and can be studied as a simple system in $\mathbb{R}^2$. $\square$

As we will discuss in the following Chapters, the simple form of the optimal version of the differential equations in system (2.20i) will be crucial for many of the extensions of the literature discussed in the book. In particular, we will prove that Corollary 2.4 implies that the complex arguments used, for instance, in [23] and [7], to infer the properties of the transition generated by the ULM in the absence of an externality, can be avoided, since we find that it can be solved in explicit form if we know the distance between the inverse of the intertemporal elasticity of substitution and the share of physical capital.

2.5   *Appendix*

a)   *Elements of the Jacobian Associated with the General System*

$J_{11} = \frac{\partial \dot{p}_t}{\partial p_t} = \alpha A p_t^{\alpha-1} u_t^{1-\alpha} - m_t - B\psi(1-u_t) = \frac{\dot{p}_t}{p_t} - A(1-\alpha) p_t^{\alpha-1} u_t^{1-\alpha}$

$J_{12} = \frac{\partial \dot{p}_t}{\partial u_t} = A(1-\alpha) p_t^{\alpha} u_t^{-\alpha} + B\psi p_t$

$J_{13} = \frac{\partial \dot{p}_t}{\partial m_t} = -p_t$

$J_{21} = \frac{\partial \dot{u}_t}{\partial p_t} = 0$

$J_{22} = \frac{\partial \dot{u}_t}{\partial u_t} = \frac{\dot{u}_t}{u_t} + B\frac{E_h^{c,d}-(1-\alpha+\gamma)(1-\alpha)}{(1-\alpha)\alpha} u_t$

$J_{23} = \frac{\partial \dot{u}_t}{\partial m_t} = -u_t$

$J_{31} = \frac{\partial \dot{m}_t}{\partial p_t} = -\frac{\alpha-\sigma}{\sigma}(1-\alpha) A p_t^{\alpha-1} u_t^{1-\alpha} m_t$

$J_{32} = \frac{\partial \dot{m}_t}{\partial u_t} = \frac{\alpha-\sigma}{\sigma}(1-\alpha) A p_t^{\alpha} u_t^{-\alpha} m_t$

$J_{33} = \frac{\partial \dot{m}_t}{\partial m_t} = 2m_t + \frac{\alpha-\sigma}{\sigma} A p_t^{\alpha-1} u_t^{\alpha-1} - \frac{\rho}{\sigma} = \frac{\dot{m}_t}{m_t} + m_t$

b)   *Solution of the Linearized General Dynamic System*

Taking up the thread of the discussion in sub-section 2.3.1, we know that the full dynamics of system (2.15i):

(A2b.1a) $\frac{\dot{p}_t}{p_t} = A u_t^{1-\alpha} p_t^{\alpha-1} - m_t - B\psi (1 - u_t)$

(A2b.1b) $\frac{\dot{u}_t}{u_t} = B\frac{1-\alpha+\gamma}{\alpha} - m_t + B\frac{E_h^{c,d}-(1-\alpha)(1-\alpha+\gamma)}{\alpha(1-\alpha)}u_t$

(A2b.1c) $\frac{\dot{m}_t}{m_t} = A\frac{\alpha-\sigma}{\sigma}u_t^{1-\alpha}p_t^{\alpha-1} + m_t - \frac{\ell}{\sigma}$

can be approximated (in a small neighborhood of the steady-state), by the following:

(A2b.2) $\begin{bmatrix} \dot{p}_t \\ \dot{u}_t \\ \dot{m}_t \end{bmatrix} = J^* \left(p^*, u^*, m^* \right) \begin{bmatrix} p_t - p^* \\ u_t - u^* \\ m_t - m^* \end{bmatrix}$

We suppose here that all roots of the characteristic equation in (2.18) are real and only one is negative. By standard arguments, we know that, if this is the case, the two positive roots of the characteristic equation of J^* would asymptotically drive the system towards unlimited growth unless the arbitrary constants associated with them are set to zero.

Let us now find the eigenvector associated with the negative root, say κ_1.[20] This means that we are interested in the following system:

(A2b.3) $\begin{bmatrix} J_{11}^* - \kappa_1 & \frac{p^*}{u^*}(B\psi u^* - J_{11}^*) & -p^* \\ 0 & B\eta u^* - \kappa_1 & -u^* \\ \phi\frac{J_{11}^* m^*}{p^*} & -\phi\frac{J_{11}^* m^*}{u^*} & m^* - \kappa_1 \end{bmatrix} \begin{bmatrix} \theta_1 \\ \theta_2 \\ \theta_3 \end{bmatrix} = \begin{bmatrix} 0 \\ 0 \\ 0 \end{bmatrix}$

where the θ_i elements are the (still unknown) components of the eigenvector associated with the negative root. After normalizing with respect to θ_3, an eigenvector solving (A2b.3) is:

(A2b.4) $m^T = \left[\left(\frac{J_{11}^* m^* \phi}{B\eta u^* - \kappa_1} - m^* + \kappa_1 \right) \frac{p^*}{\phi J_{11}^* m^*}\theta_3, \ \frac{u^*}{\eta u^* - \kappa_1}\theta_3, \theta_3 \right]$

The solution of system (A2b.3), if only one negative root is present, is therefore:

---

[20] A similar solving procedure for the case of a zero externality factor is also used in Piras [25].

$$\text{(A2b.5)} \quad \begin{bmatrix} p_t \\ u_t \\ m_t \end{bmatrix} = \begin{bmatrix} \left(\dfrac{J_{11}^* m^* \phi}{B\eta u^* - \kappa_1} - m^* + \kappa_1\right) \dfrac{p^*}{\phi J_{11}^* m^*} \theta_3 \\ \dfrac{u^*}{\eta B u^* - \kappa_1} \theta_3 \\ \theta_3 \end{bmatrix} e^{\kappa_1 t} + \begin{bmatrix} p^* \\ u^* \\ m^* \end{bmatrix}$$

where, asymptotically, the first term of the right hand side vanishes and the three variables tend to their stationary values.

Now, to determine the value of θ_3, recall that at time zero $p(0)$ is given. Therefore, from the first equation of system (A2b.5) we have the following:

$$p(0) = \left(\frac{J_{11}^* m^* \phi}{\eta B u^* - \kappa_1} - m^* + \kappa\right) \frac{p^*}{\phi J_{11}^* m^*} \theta_3 + p^*$$

$$\Rightarrow \theta_3 = \frac{p(0) - p^*}{p^*} \phi J_{11}^* m^* \left(\frac{J_{11}^* m^* \phi}{\eta B u^* - \kappa_1} - m^* + \kappa\right)^{-1}$$

Finally, by substituting θ_3 into (A2b.5), we obtain:

$$\text{(A2b.6)} \quad \begin{bmatrix} p_t \\ u_t \\ m_t \end{bmatrix} = \begin{bmatrix} \dfrac{p^*}{\phi J_{11}^* m^*} \Gamma \\ \dfrac{u^*}{\eta B u^* - \kappa_1} \\ 1 \end{bmatrix} \frac{p(0) - p^*}{p^*} \frac{\phi J_{11}^* m^*}{\Gamma} e^{\kappa_1 t} + \begin{bmatrix} p^* \\ u^* \\ m^* \end{bmatrix}$$

where $\Gamma = \left(\dfrac{J_{11}^* m^* \phi}{B\eta u^* - \kappa_1} - m^* + \kappa_1\right)$. At time zero, therefore:

$$\text{(A2b.7)} \quad \begin{bmatrix} p(0) \\ u(0) \\ m(0) \end{bmatrix} = \begin{bmatrix} p(0) \\ \dfrac{p(0) - p^*}{p^*} \dfrac{u^*}{\eta B u^* - \kappa_1} \dfrac{\phi J_{11}^* m^*}{\Gamma} \\ \dfrac{p(0) - p^*}{p^*} \dfrac{\phi J_{11}^* m^*}{\Gamma} \end{bmatrix} + \begin{bmatrix} 0 \\ u^* \\ m^* \end{bmatrix}$$

Now, after simple algebra, the system in (A2b.7) implies:

$$\text{(A2b.8)} \quad \begin{bmatrix} \dfrac{u(0) - u^*}{u^*} \\ \dfrac{m(0) - m^*}{m^*} \end{bmatrix} = \frac{p(0) - p^*}{p^*} \begin{bmatrix} \dfrac{\phi J_{11}^* m^*}{\Gamma(\eta B u^* - \kappa_1)} \\ \dfrac{\phi J_{11}^*}{\Gamma} \end{bmatrix}$$

which can be considered as functions linking the state of the economy. The form presented in (2.19*i*) in the text:

$$\text{(A2b.9a)} \quad \frac{u^* - u(0)}{u^*} = \phi \delta_1 \frac{p^* - p(0)}{p^*}$$

$$\text{(A2b.9b)} \quad \frac{m^* - m(0)}{m^*} = \phi \delta_2 \frac{p^* - p(0)}{p^*}$$

therefore implies:

(A2b.10) $\delta_1 = \frac{J_{11}^* m^*}{\Gamma(\eta B u^* - \kappa_1)}$

(A2b.11) $\delta_2 = \frac{J_{11}^*}{\Gamma}$

Chapter 3

The Centralized Economy

3.1 Introduction and Plan of the Chapter

In this Chapter we shall investigate the properties of the BGP and of the transitional dynamics generated by the ULM in the case of a centralized economy.

Given the preliminary work done in Chapters 1 and 2, the determination of the BGP-stationary values and growth rates of all the relevant variables is a fairly straightforward task. We are simply required to:

a) substitute the appropriate value of the contribution of human capital into the general expression for working time obtained in Chapter 1;

b) determine, according to Definition 1.5, in which regions of the parameter space the BGP is non-degenerate;

c) substitute the correct value of the contribution of human capital into the general expression for the growth rate of the economy obtained in Chapter 1;

d) exploit Lemma 1.1 to obtain the positive growth rates of the primitive variables of the economy;

e) substitute the efficient growth rate of the economy into the general expressions for the *Great Ratios* in Chapter 2;

f) substitute the efficient growth rate of the economy into the general expressions for the *adjoint variables*, again in Chapter 2.

A crucial finding is that, in the case of a centralized economy, the non-degeneracy of the BGP can only be achieved if an upper bound for the subjective discount rate and a lower bound for the inverse of the intertemporal elasticity of substitution are imposed. As a consequence the ULM is able to give useful prediction of the efficient behavior of real two-sector economies only when the subjective discount rate is low and the inverse of the intertemporal elasticity of substitution is high.

The analysis of the signs of the partial derivatives of the stationary values or growth rates of each variables w.r.t. the parameters (inside this restricted region of the parameter space) reveals details on the long-run efficient response of a two-sector economy facing a structural modification. In particular, we find that larger preference (technological) parameters imply a lower (higher) growth rate of the economy and, by Lemma 1.1, of the other primitive variables of the model, consumption, physical capital and human capital.

Furthermore, the technological (preference) parameters have a positive (negative) influence on the BGP value of the saving rate and on the BGP growth rate of wages. The preference parameters have no influence on the efficient BGP value of the interest rate. Evaluating the impact of the size of the parameters on the BGP stationary values of the Great Ratios is somewhat less straightforward, owing to the fact that the impact is ambiguous in some cases. For instance, variations of the share of physical capital have a positive impact on average goods production when small, and a negative effect when high. The inverse of the intertemporal elasticity of substitution has a role in inverting the sign of the partial derivatives of the average consumption with respect to the externality and the efficacy index in the accumulation of human capital.

The level of technology in the final goods sector confirms its nature of scale parameter, not affecting the average variables.

Deriving the optimal properties of the economy in transition is more challenging.

From the local point of view, we have already proved in Chapter 2 that the characteristic equation associated with the $\mathbb{R}^3$-transformed system can always be factorized to reveal a fixed one-negative-two-positive sign pattern for the eigenvalues (in the real axis). Consequently, the only possible stability result which can be expected from the optimal dynamics is saddle-path stability, without oscillating motion: given the initial state of the economy, there is only one pair of initial values of the control variables (consumption and working time) which implies convergence towards the steady-state in the lower dimension.

Since the explicit form of the eigenvalues is known in all regions of the relevant parameter space, the analysis can provide a highly accurate picture of the local characteristics of the transition. In particular, we can explicitly derive the elasticities which optimally link the controls to the state variables of the economy. In this respect, we are able to extend the results in Mulligan and Sala-i-Martin [23] and prove that the policy functions are both locally downward (upward) sloping if the inverse of the intertemporal elasticity of substitution is large (small) with respect to the share of physical capital.[21]

This information has further implications: according to Definition 2.1, the slopes of the policy functions imply that, when the inverse of the intertemporal elasticity of substitution is large (small) with respect to the share of physical capital, imbalances in the economy are corrected by a prevalence of the Consumption-Smoothing Effect (Wage Rate Effect). In the critical case of the inverse of the intertemporal elasticity of substitution being equal to the share of physical capital, we find that the *consumption-smoothing effect* and the *wage rate effect* offset each other and that the

---

[21]Recall that Interesting Result 7 in Mulligan and Sala-i-Martin [23] is obtained for the model without externality factor.

imbalance is corrected by means of the *Solow effect*.

From Definition 2.2 and Proposition 2.10, furthermore, we also find that the efficient economy belongs to what Caballè and Santos [7] have termed the *paradoxical growth case* if the inverse of the intertemporal elasticity of substitution is small and to the *normal growth case* if the inverse of the intertemporal elasticity of substitution is high (with respect to the share of physical capital). The possibility of an *exogenous growth case* can also arise if the inverse of the intertemporal elasticity of substitution exactly matches the share of physical capital.

The global point is also rich with interesting results.

The opportunity of deriving valid-in-the-large information on the evolution of the efficient economy is strictly related to the further reduction of the relevant dimension of the system of dynamic laws governing the efficient economy achieved in Chapter 2, at Proposition 2.11. As a matter of fact, even if an externality is present, the Pareto-optimal Hamiltonian dynamics maintains a symmetrical structure which ensures that the motion can be contained in the space spanned by the average goods production and the average consumption. This has the following important consequences. On the one hand, we are now able to draw simple phase diagrams providing an immediate visualization of the stable manifold in this reduced dimension. On the other hand, since the motion in $\mathbb{R}^2$ becomes very easy to treat, we can prove that the explicit solution of the differential equations can be obtained by simple analytical methods. In particular, the differential equation optimally governing the average goods production is a technical law which can be easily solved. By fixing the distance between the share of physical capital and the inverse of the elasticity of intertemporal substitution, the law governing the average consumption can be solved as well. Since the evolution of all the variables of the model in the original dimension depends solely on these two laws, the explicit characterization of the entire centralized solution of the ULM can be obtained. The effect of this is that the optimal transition can be studied in global terms without worrying about the distance between the initial position of the economy and the steady-state. The possibility of deriving the sequences for the variables in the original dimension is also exploited to numerically investigate the valid-in-the-large properties of the optimal transition.

As a by-product, the availability of the explicit trajectory for consumption also enables us to calculate (again in global terms) the welfare integral over the infinite temporal horizon faced by the representative agent.

The plan of the Chapter is as follows. The second section discusses the properties of the efficient economy evolving along the BGP. The issue of the non-degeneracy of the BGP is first discussed. The determination of the efficient growth rates and stationary values of all the variables considered follow.

The third section is concerned with the local analysis of the transition in $\mathbb{R}^3$. By studying the dynamics in the transformed three-dimensional space, we gain some insight into the stability properties of the steady-state. We also provide a positive analysis of the economics behind the behavior of the variables in a small neighborhood of the steady-state.

The fourth section investigates the implications of the second dimensional reduction of the dynamic system. 5 sub-sections are dedicated to the analysis of the global properties of the efficient economy.

In the fifth and final section, we use the explicit trajectory of consumption to calculate the welfare integral over the infinite temporal horizon faced by the representative agent.

3.2   Optimal BGP Evolution of the Variables

3.2.1   *The Relevant System of Differential Equations*

We start this section by obtaining the set of dynamic laws governing the optimal evolution of the economy. By simply imposing $E_h^{c,d} \equiv E_h^c = 1 - \alpha + \gamma$ in system (2.1*i*), it is quite straightforward to obtain:

(3.1*a*) $\xi_c = \frac{\dot{c}_t}{c_t} = \frac{\alpha}{\sigma}\frac{\bar{y}_t}{k_t} - \frac{\rho}{\sigma}$

(3.1*b*) $\xi_k = \frac{\dot{k}_t}{k_t} = \frac{\bar{y}_t}{k_t} - \frac{c_t}{k_t}$

(3.1*c*) $\xi_h = \frac{\dot{h}_t}{h_t} = B\left(1 - u_t\right)$

(3.1*d*) $\xi_u = \frac{\dot{u}_t}{u_t} = \frac{B(1-\alpha+\gamma)}{\alpha} - \frac{c_t}{k_t} + B\psi u_t$

where $\bar{y}_t = Ak_t^{\alpha-1}u_t^{1-\alpha}h_t^{1-\alpha+\gamma}$ and $\psi = \frac{1-\alpha+\gamma}{1-\alpha}$ is the already-used notation-simplifying constant.

3.2.2   *The Optimal Allocation of Time along the BGP*

Now, before actually beginning the analysis of the BGP properties of a decentralized economy, we find useful to preliminarily characterize the unrestricted parameter space. To keep notation simple, we define as $\omega \equiv (A, B, \alpha, \rho, \sigma, \gamma)$ where $\omega \in \Delta = \mathbb{R}_{++}^2 \times (0,1) \times \mathbb{R}_{++}^2 \times \mathbb{R}_+$ the parameter space.

Given the expression for u^* in (1.18), we have:

Proposition 3.1 *The optimal BGP-constant fraction of total non-leisure time dedicated to work is equal to:*

(3.2) $u^* = 1 - \frac{(1-\alpha)(B-\rho)+B\gamma}{B\sigma(1-\alpha+\gamma)}$

If the parameters are restricted such that:

(3.3) $\bar{\Delta}^c = \{\omega \in \Delta : \rho \in (0, B\psi), \sigma > 1 - \rho/(B\psi)\}$

u^* *is economically meaningful and the BGP is non-degenerate.*

Proof By imposing $E_h^{c,d} \equiv E_h^c = 1 - \alpha + \gamma$ in the expression for u^* obtained in Lemma 1.2 (equation 1.18), it is possible to derive the stationary value in proposition. In order to have $u^* \in (0,1)$, that is to guarantee that the BGP is non-degenerate, we must make sure that $\frac{(1-\alpha)(B-\rho)+B\gamma}{B\sigma(1-\alpha+\gamma)} < 1$ (for u^* to be positive), and $\frac{(1-\alpha)(B-\rho)+B\gamma}{B\sigma(1-\alpha+\gamma)} > 0$ (for u^* to be less than one). By jointly solving the two inequalities, we see that $u^* \in (0,1)$ if and only if the parameters lie in the subset of Δ identified in (3.3). $\square$

In relation to the $\bar{\Delta}^c$ subset of the feasible parameter space, observe that:

Remark *The existence of a non-degenerate BGP, when associated with the centralized solution, requires an upper bound for the subjective discount rate and a lower bound for the inverse of the intertemporal elasticity of substitution (less and less binding, the closer ρ is to $B\psi$).*

Visual representation of the region in the parameter space where $u^* \in (0,1)$ in the (ρ, B) space is given in Figure 3.1:

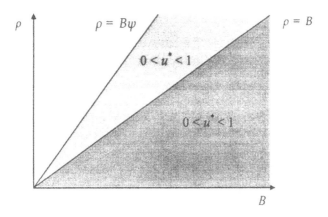

Figure 3.1 A characterization of the (ρ, B) space where $u^* \in (0, 1)$

Another interesting point of view is revealed by plotting the values of u^* against σ and γ for given values of the other parameters. Figure 3.2a shows the values of u^* for growing σ. As required in equation (3.3), the threshold value of σ for u^* to be in its feasible range is $1 - \rho/(B\psi)$. Figure 3.2b does the same for growing values of the externality, in case of a value of $\sigma - 1 > 0$.

Table 3.1 below evaluates the impact of parameter changes on the BGP value of working time.

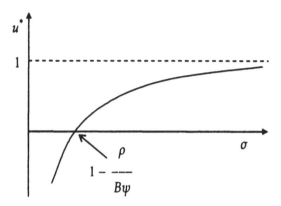

Figure 3.2a Steady-state values of working time for growing σ

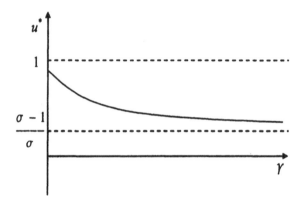

Figure 3.2b Steady-state values of working time for growing γ

3.2.3 *The BGP Growth Rate of the Centralized Economy*

We are now in a position to determine the optimal BGP growth rates of the ULM's non-stationary primitive variables. We have:

Proposition 3.2 *Let $\omega \in \bar{\Delta}^c$. Then the growth rate of the economy, in terms of goods production, ξ^*, is positive and equal to:*

$$(3.4) \qquad \xi^* = B\psi\,(1 - u^*) = \tfrac{1}{\sigma}\,(B\psi - \rho) > 0$$

Proof We have already proved in Lemma 1.1 that the growth rate of the economy along the BGP is equal to $\xi^* = B\psi\,(1 - u^*)$. By substituting out u^* from (3.2), we obtain the growth rate of the economy shown in proposition. ξ^* is obviously positive when $\omega \in \bar{\Delta}^c$. $\square$

A direct consequence of Proposition 3.2 is the following:

Corollary 3.1 *Recall Lemma* 1.1 *and let* $\omega \in \bar{\Delta}^c$. *Then, the BGP growth rates of consumption, physical capital and human capital are linked through the following:*

$$\xi_c^* = \xi_k^* = \psi\xi_h^* = \xi^* = \frac{B\psi-\rho}{\sigma} > 0$$

Proof Given Lemma 1.1, the extension of the results in Proposition 3.2 to the growth rates of k_t, c_t and h_t is immediate. $\square$

Given the expressions for the stationary values of working time and growth rate of the economy, respectively in (3.2) and (3.4), it becomes interesting to evaluate the impact of variations of the structure of the economy implying larger or lower values for the parameters. Consider Table 3.1, where the signs of the partial derivatives of u^* and ξ^* with respect to the parameters are reported. The following is evident:

Remark *Higher preference (technological) parameters determine a lower (higher) BGP growth rate for the economy. The contrary happens to the BGP value of working time.*

Table 3.1 Signs of partial derivatives of u^* and ξ^* w.r.t. the parameters

Parameters	u^*	ξ^*
A	NR	NR
B	-	+
α	-	+
γ	-	+
ρ	+	-
σ	+	-

NR = Not Relevant

3.2.4 *The BGP Values of the* Great Ratios

As shown in Chapter 2, the balanced evolution of the economy implies the stationarity of the *Great Ratios*, a collective term by which we have indicated in Chapter 2 the average consumption $(c/k)^* = m^*$, the average production $(\bar{y}/k)^* = n^*$ and the weighted ratio between the two forms of accumulation $(kh^{-\psi})^* = p^*$.

Given the results in Chapter 2, tying the BGP values of these ratios to the efficient growth rate of the economy, we get:

Proposition 3.3 *Let the centralized economy evolve along a non-degenerate BGP. Then, the* Great Ratios *are all positive and respectively equal to:*

$$(3.5) \quad \left(\frac{c}{k}\right)^* = m^* = B\frac{\psi}{\alpha} - \frac{1}{\sigma}(B\psi - \rho) > 0$$

$$(3.6) \quad \left(\frac{\bar{y}}{k}\right)^* = n^* = \frac{B}{\alpha}\psi > 0$$

(3.7) $\left(\frac{k}{h\psi}\right)^* = p^* = \left(\frac{\alpha A}{B\psi}\right)^{\frac{1}{1-\alpha}}$ $u^* = \left(\frac{\alpha A}{B\psi}\right)^{\frac{1}{1-\alpha}} \left[1 - \frac{(1-\alpha)(B-\rho)+B\gamma}{B\sigma(1-\alpha+\gamma)}\right] > 0$

Proof By substituting the efficient growth rate of the economy and the efficient value of u^* from (3.2) and (3.4) into (2.2), (2.3) and (2.4), the expressions in the proposition are easily obtained. The positiveness of the expressions, when $\omega \in \bar{\Delta}^c$, is clearly evident for (3.6) and (3.6). To evaluate the sign of (3.5), substitute the minimum feasible value of σ in the right hand side; the unambiguously positive value $\frac{1-\alpha}{\alpha} B\psi$ can be obtained. $\square$

Given the steady-state values in Proposition 3.3, as for u^* and ξ^*, it becomes interesting to evaluate the impact of a modification of the structure of the economy implying lower or larger values for the technological and preference parameters. Consider Table 3.2, where the sign evaluation of the partial derivatives of the stationary values of the Great Ratios with respect to all the parameters is presented.

Table 3.2 Signs of partial derivatives of p^*, n^* and m^* w.r.t. the parameters

Paramet.	p^*	n^*		m^*	
		$\alpha < 1/2$	$\alpha > 1/2$	$\sigma < \alpha$	$\sigma > \alpha$
A	$+$	NR	NR	NR	NR
B	$-$	$+$	$+$	$-$	$+$
α	$+$	$+$	$-$	NO	NO
γ	$-$	$+$	$+$	$-$	$+$
ρ	$-$	NR	NR	$+$	$+$
σ	$+$	NR	NR	$-$	$-$

NR = Not Relevant
NO = Not Obvious

A number of interesting details can be learned. In particular, besides the indeterminate role of the share of physical capital in determining the size of average consumption (without further parameter restrictions), observe that:

Remark *The effect of the parameters on the BGP optimal values of the* Great Ratios *is ambiguous in some cases. In particular, the share of physical capital has a positive impact on the average goods production when small, and a negative effect when high. There is also a role for the inverse of the intertemporal elasticity of substitution in inverting the sign of the partial derivatives of m^* with respect to γ and B. Parameter A confirms its nature of scale coefficient, not affecting the average variables. The average goods production does not depend on preference parameters.*

3.2.5   *The* Adjoint Variables *Along the BGP*

Having obtained the BGP growth rates and stationary values of both the primitive variables and *Great Ratios*, we can now complete the representation of the centralized economy by analyzing the behavior of the *Adjoint Variables*, namely broad output, the rental compensation of capital, the level of wages and the saving rate.

We start by considering the evolution of broad output. In Chapter 2 we have already discussed some properties this variable displays along both equilibrium and optimal paths. In particular, in Corollary 2.1 we have proved that broad output, along the BGP, always grows at the same rate as the (narrow) economy. We have also shown, in the same corollary, that the ratio $y_t^T/\bar{y}_t$ is constant and greater than one along a non-degenerate BGP.

By substituting the BGP value for working time into the expression (2.5), we are now able to determine the efficient value of $y_t^T/\bar{y}_t$. The resulting formulation:

$$(3.8) \qquad \left(\frac{y^T}{\bar{y}}\right)^* = \frac{B\psi(\sigma-\alpha)+\alpha\rho}{B\psi(\sigma-1)+\rho} > 1$$

offers information on the relative size of the learning sector with respect to the goods production when the efficient economy is evolving along the BGP. Table 3.3, at the end of the section, contains a sign evaluation of the partial derivative of the index in relation with the parameter space.

Let us now continue the description of the optimal BGP behavior of the adjoint variables by studying the interest rate (or rental compensation of physical capital) r_t. As shown in Chapter 1, this variable equals the marginal productivity of capital, $MPK = \partial y_t^f/\partial k_t = \alpha y_t^f/k_t$. We have already discussed in Chapter 2 (Proposition 2.5) that r_t, in both cases of equilibrium or optimal paths, is constant and positive along a non-degenerate BGP. In the case of the centralized solution, we also have:

Proposition 3.4 *Let the centralized economy evolve along a non-degenerate BGP. Then, the value of the rental price of capital is*:

$$(3.9) \qquad r^* = B\psi > 0$$

Proof By substituting the efficient growth rate of the economy in (3.4) in the expression in (2.9), the positive value of r^* can be easily obtained. $\square$

Notice that, very interestingly, if $\omega \in \bar{\Delta}^c$:

Remark *The efficient BGP value of the rental price of capital (interest rate) is always above the subjective discount rate $\rho \in (0, B\psi)$. It is unaffected by the preference parameters.*

Let us now investigate the BGP properties of the wage rate. We know already, as proved in Proposition 2.5, that the presence of a positive externality makes the wage rate grow along the BGP. In the case of the optimal dynamics, we also have:

Proposition 3.5 *Let the centralized economy evolve along a non-degenerate BGP. Then, the wages grow according to the following positive rate*:

(3.10) $\left(\frac{\dot{w}}{w}\right)^* = \frac{\gamma}{\sigma(1-\alpha+\gamma)}\left(B\psi - \rho\right) > 0$

Proof By substituting the optimal growth rate of the economy in (3.4) into the expression (2.10), we obtain the result in proposition. The positiveness of (3.10) is evident when $\omega \in \bar{\Delta}^c$. □

The relation in (3.10) implies that, in the efficient economy, given a parameter configuration $\omega \in \bar{\Delta}^c$:

Remark *Small BGP growth rates of wages,* ceteris paribus, *are either associated with small externalities or with large discount factors.*

We complete the picture of the economy determining the BGP properties of the saving rate. From Proposition 2.7 we already know that the saving rate is constant along the BGP. We also have, in case of optimal paths:

Proposition 3.6 *Let the centralized economy evolve along a non-degenerate BGP. Then, the value of the saving rate is between 0 and 1 and has the following value:*

(3.11) $s^* = \frac{\alpha}{\sigma}\left(\frac{B\psi - \rho}{B\psi}\right)$

Proof By substituting the optimal growth rate of the economy in the expression (2.12) we obtain the result in proposition which is positive when $\omega \in \bar{\Delta}^c$. To see that the maximum value of s^* is lower than 1, substitute the minimum value of σ. □

It is interesting here to notice that, as for the efficient growth rate of wages, the saving rate tends to zero when ρ approaches its upper bound $B\psi$.

Table 3.3 Partial derivatives of the *adjoint variables* w.r.t. the parameters

Parameters	$\left(y^T/\bar{y}\right)^*$	r^*	ξ_w^*	s^*
A	NR	NR	NR	NR
B	$+$	$+$	$+$	$+$
α	NO	$+$	$+$	$+$
γ	$+$	$+$	$+$	$+$
ρ	$-$	NR	$-$	$-$
σ	$-$	NR	$-$	$-$

NR = Not Relevant
NO = Not Obvious

To conclude the analysis of the properties of the efficient economy in a balanced position, we present in Table 3.3 the evaluation of how the adjoint variables are affected by the parameters. Interesting information emerge from Table 3.3. In particular, it can be pointed out that:

Remark *The technological (preference) parameters have a positive (negative) impact on the adjoint variables. A confirms its nature of scale parameter. As already remarked, the preference parameters have no influence in determining the interest rate.*

3.3 Transitional Dynamics. The Local Point of View

3.3.1 *A First Stationarizing Transformation of the Variables*

Before starting to derive information on the properties of the centralized economy evolving along off-balanced trajectories, let us consider the possibility of reducing the dimension of the relevant system of dynamic laws through the stationarizing transformation used in Chapter 2.

Recalling that p_t and m_t respectively indicate the "weighted" ratio between the two capital goods, $\frac{k_t}{h_t^\psi}$, and the average consumption, $\frac{c_t}{k_t}$, we first prove that:

Proposition 3.7 *The motion generated by the centralized solution of the ULM implies the following three-dimensional system of first-order differential equations:*

$(3.12a)$ $\quad \frac{\dot{p}_t}{p_t} = A u_t^{1-\alpha} p_t^{\alpha-1} - m_t - B\psi\left(1 - u_t\right)$

$(3.12b)$ $\quad \frac{\dot{u}_t}{u_t} = B\frac{1-\alpha+\gamma}{\alpha} - m_t + B\psi u_t$

$(3.12c)$ $\quad \frac{\dot{m}_t}{m_t} = A\frac{\alpha-\sigma}{\sigma} u_t^{1-\alpha} p_t^{\alpha-1} + m_t - \frac{\rho}{\sigma}$

The system possesses an interior steady-state characterized by the stationary values in (3.7), (3.2) and (3.5).

Proof By substituting $E_h^{c,d} \equiv E_h^c = 1 - \alpha + \gamma$ in the reduced system in (2.15i), the dynamic laws in (3.12i) can be easily retrieved. The fixed point is obtained solving the system for $\frac{\dot{p}_t}{p_t} = \frac{\dot{u}_t}{u_t} = \frac{\dot{m}_t}{m_t} = 0$. The steady-state values of the transformed variables are in (3.7), (3.2) and (3.5). We have already shown them to be unambiguously positive under $\omega \in \bar{\Delta}^c$. $\square$

The fixed point in the reduced dimension corresponds to the unique family of BGPs in the original dimension and standard arguments can be used to translate its properties into properties of the BGP in the original system.

3.3.2 *The Local Stability Properties*

Let us now consider the stability properties of the optimal dynamics in the reduced dimension.[22] In Lemma 2.4 we have already proved that it is possible to factorize the

---

[22]The original material for this sub-section is in [20].

characteristic equation associated with the Jacobian of the linearized dynamics. We thereby obtain the explicit forms of the eigenvalues for the region in the parameter space where the BGP is non-degenerate. We have the following:

Proposition 3.8 *Let* $\omega \in \bar{\Delta}^c$. *Then, the Jacobian matrix associated with system* (3.12i) *has one negative and two positive real eigenvalues, respectively equal to* $\kappa_1 = J_{11}^* = -B\frac{1-\alpha+\gamma}{\alpha} < 0$, $\kappa_2 = B\psi u^* > 0$ *and* $\kappa_3 = m^* > 0$. *The steady-state of the reduced system* (3.12i) *is thus saddle-path stable and the corresponding BGP is determinate.*

Proof If $\omega \in \bar{\Delta}^c$, $E_h^{c,d} = 1 - \alpha + \gamma$ and $\psi = \eta$. Then the characteristic equation in (2.18) has the roots in proposition. In the case of the centralized solution, J_{11}^* in (2.17) has the value $-B\frac{1-\alpha+\gamma}{\alpha} < 0$. Considering that when $\omega \in \bar{\Delta}^c$ both $B\psi u^*$ and m^* are positive, the sign pattern of the eigenvalues is as stated in the proposition. Standard arguments can be called upon to obtain the stability results (see also the discussion in sub-section 2.3.4). $\square$

The result in Proposition 3.8 is somewhat surprising in the context of the most recent growth literature, where a fixed saddle-path stability property is considered as a "natural" outcome of two-sector infinite-horizon growth models only in cases where there are no distortions. The proof that saddle-path stability is here the only possible outcome also extends this natural result to centralized economies (at least of the Uzawa-Lucas type), regardless of whether distorting factors are present or not.

An obvious Corollary of Proposition 3.8 is the following:

Corollary 3.2 *Neither indeterminacy nor oscillating or periodic solutions can characterize optimal paths in the ULM with externality.*

Proof The result in Corollary follows again from the fixed one-negative-two-positive structure of the eigenvalues (in the real axis). $\square$

The availability of the explicit form for the negative eigenvalue makes it possible to derive a number of interesting details on the optimal evolution of the variables.

Corollary 3.3 *The* (approximate) *optimal speed of convergence in the neighborhood of the steady-state is equal to* $B\frac{1-\alpha+\gamma}{\alpha}$. *It is a "technical" law, not influenced by preference parameters.*

Proof Standard arguments state that it is the absolute value of the negative eigenvalue that governs the speed of convergence in the neighborhood of the steady-state. Since, by Proposition 3.8 the absolute value of the negative eigenvalues equals $B\frac{1-\alpha+\gamma}{\alpha}$ the result in the Corollary follows. $\square$

Of course, the fact that the optimal convergent path is unique does not mean that we can only have one asymptotic optimum level of the primitive variables in $\mathbb{R}^4$. The same ratios can in fact be obtained with infinite combinations of the primitive variables. Therefore, contrarily to what we will show occurs in the case of equilibrium dynamics for special regions of the parameter space, we invariably find that:

Remark *Countries with the same (different) initial endowments in terms of physical and human capital are bound to end up with the same (different) levels of the original variables.*

3.3.3 Some Local Characteristics of the Transition

The knowledge of the exact form of the roots associated with the linearized dynamics enables us to infer detailed information on the adjustment mechanisms activated by the centralized economy.[23]

In particular, we are now in the position to evaluate which of the three stabilization mechanisms isolated in [23] and presented in Definition 2.1 will prevail in specific circumstances. The prevalence of one or other of these stabilization mechanisms, in turn, also determines, in the light of Definition 2.2, to which growth case, *paradoxical*, *exogenous* or *normal*, the economy belongs.

Recall the general form of the (modified) policy functions in equations (2.19i):

(3.13) $\frac{u^*-u(0)}{u^*} = \delta_1 \phi \frac{p^*-p(0)}{p^*}$

(3.14) $\frac{m^*-m(0)}{m^*} = \delta_2 \phi \frac{p^*-p(0)}{p^*}$

where $\delta_1 = \frac{J_{11}^* m^*}{\Gamma(\eta Bu^* - \kappa_1)}$ and $\delta_2 = \frac{J_{11}^*}{\Gamma}$. Recall also that, in this general formulation we have:

$$\Gamma = \left(\frac{J_{11}^* m^* \phi}{B\eta u^* - \kappa_1} - m^* + \kappa_1 \right)$$

where $\eta = \frac{E_h^{c,d} - (1-\alpha+\gamma)(1-\alpha)}{(1-\alpha)\alpha}$ and $\phi = \frac{\alpha-\sigma}{\sigma}$ simplify the notation. We can prove the following preliminary results:

Lemma 3.1 *Let $\omega \in \bar{\Delta}^c$. Then $\eta = \psi$ and $B\eta u^* - \kappa_1 = B\psi u^* - J_{11}^* = m^* > 0$.*

Proof When $\omega \in \bar{\Delta}^c$, $E_h^{c,d} = (1 - \alpha + \gamma)$. By substituting this value in the general formulation for η we obtain the value $\eta = \frac{1-\alpha+\gamma}{1-\alpha} = \psi$. Now, from Proposition 3.8 we have that that $\kappa_1 = J_{11}^* = -B\frac{1-\alpha+\gamma}{\alpha} < 0$. With a few algebraic calculations, therefore, $B\eta u^* - \kappa_1 = B\psi u^* - J_{11}^* = m^*$. $\square$

As a consequence:

---
[23]The original material for this sub-section is in [20].

Corollary 3.4 *Let Lemma* 3.1 *apply. Then working time and average consumption react with the same response elasticity to variations of the state of the economy (expressed in terms of the p_t ratio).*

Proof In Lemma 3.1 we have shown that $B\eta u^* - \kappa_1 = m^*$. Therefore, $\delta_1 = \frac{J_{11}^* m^*}{\Gamma(B\eta u^* - \kappa_1)} = \frac{J_{11}^*}{\Gamma} = \delta_2 \equiv \delta$. Furthermore, Γ can be simplified to give the negative value of $\Gamma = \frac{\alpha}{\sigma} J_{11}^* - m^*$. As a consequence, being J_{11}^* negative, δ is positive. $\square$

Therefore, given a deviation in the state of the economy from its balanced position:

Proposition 3.9 *The policy functions are locally upward (downward) sloping if the inverse of the intertemporal elasticity of substitution is small (large) with respect to the share of physical capital.*

Proof Let us prove the case with $p^* - p(0) > 0$. From the proof of Corollary 3.4 we know that $\delta_1 = \delta_2 = \delta > 0$. Therefore, if $\alpha > \sigma$, $\phi > 0$ and $Sign(u^* - u(0)) = Sign(m^* - m(0)) > 0$: the policy functions are upward sloping. The opposite occurs if $\alpha < \sigma$. A symmetric argument apply in case of $p^* - p(0) < 0$. $\square$

Let now $D_x = \frac{x^* - x(0)}{x^*}$ represent the deviation of the generic variable x from its steady-state position. Figures 3.3i depict the modified policy functions (MPF) in the two cases of low and high inverse of the intertemporal elasticity of substitution. Of course, the two possible trends of the policy functions are separated by the following critical case:

Corollary 3.5 *When $\alpha = \sigma$, the optimal policy functions are horizontal at the zero value.*

Proof From (3.13) and (3.14), it appears evident that if $\phi = 0$, $m^* - m(0) = u^* - u(0) = 0$. $\square$

The above discussed findings can be further elaborated. As a matter of fact, in the light of Definition 2.1, we also have the following interesting result:

Corollary 3.6 *Let Proposition* 3.9 *apply. Let furthermore $p^* - p(0) < 0$. Then, if the inverse of the intertemporal elasticity of substitution is small ($\phi > 0$), the consumption-smoothing effect dominates and the excess of physical capital is eliminated through higher consumption. Conversely, if the inverse of the intertemporal elasticity of substitution is large ($\phi < 0$), the wage rate effect dominates and the excess of physical capital is eliminated through lower work effort. Symmetric results apply for transitions starting from a low $p(0)$.*

Proof Let us prove the case with $p^* - p(0) < 0$ when the inverse of the intertemporal elasticity of substitution is small ($\phi > 0$). In this case we know, by Proposition 3.9, that a negative $p^* - p(0)$ implies that both $u(0)$ and $m(0)$ are low in transition. By Definition 2.1, this implies that the consumption-smoothing effect has to prevail. Again by Definition 2.1, the wage rate effect has to prevail in the opposite case of a negative ϕ. $\square$

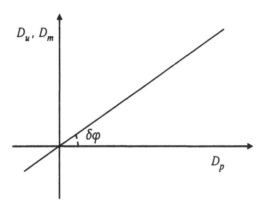

Figure 3.3a MPF when σ is small

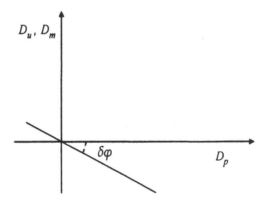

Figure 3.3b MPF when σ is large

The results in Proposition 3.9 are interesting by themselves. However, they merely give an idea of the qualitative behavior of the economy in the $\mathbb{R}^3$ reduced space, without unveiling the dynamic evolution of the primitive variables of the model in response to a perturbation in the economy.

The connection between the signs of the initial values of the variables and ϕ enable us to investigate some further implications regarding the way the variables in the original dimension respond to a shock. Recalling Definition 2.2, which characterizes the possible outcomes of an adjustment in terms of paradoxical, normal or exogenous cases, we can prove that:

Proposition 3.10 *Let $\alpha > \sigma$. Then the economy belongs to the paradoxical case. Contrariwise, the economy will belong to the normal case if $\alpha < \sigma$. If $\alpha = \sigma$ human capital behaves as an exogenous variable.*

Proof Let us first prove the case of $\alpha > \sigma$. High (low) values of $p(0)$ imply, by Proposition 3.9, a jump (fall) in $u(0)$. As a consequence, the transitional growth rate of human capital is below (above) its BGP level and so is its asymptotic normalized level. Thus we have an example of a paradoxical case. As stated in the proposition, the contrary happens when $\alpha < \sigma$ (normal case). When $\alpha = \sigma$ human capital behaves as an exogenous variable. □

3.4   Transitional Dynamics. The Global Point of View

3.4.1   *The Dynamics in $\mathbb{R}^2$*

Let us now go back to the results in the last section of Chapter 2. We have shown there that the centralized regime preserves a critical symmetry in the Hamiltonian dynamics meaning that the motion can be contained in a $\mathbb{R}^2$–reduced space.[24] Recalling that $n_t = \frac{y_t}{k_t}$ and $\frac{c_t}{k_t} = m_t$, we arrive at showing that:

Proposition 3.11 *The motion generated by the optimal solution of the ULM implies the following two-dimensional system of first-order differential equations*:

$$(3.15a) \qquad \dot{n}_t = (1 - \alpha)\left(\frac{B\psi}{\alpha} - n_t\right) n_t$$

$$(3.15b) \qquad \dot{m}_t = \frac{\alpha - \sigma}{\sigma} n_t m_t - \frac{\rho}{\sigma} m_t + m_t^2$$

The system possesses an isolated interior steady-state in correspondence with the stationary values in (3.6) *and* (3.5).

Proof By considering that $E_h^{c,d}$ in case of centralized dynamics equals $1 - \alpha + \gamma$, the system (2.20i) reduces to that in the proposition. The fixed point is obtained by solving the system under $\frac{\dot{n}_t}{n_t} = \frac{\dot{m}_t}{m_t} = 0$. In (3.6) and (3.5) we have already reported the results of these calculations. □

3.4.2   *The Logistic Path of the Average Goods Production*

As already discussed, the steady-state in the proposition corresponds to the unique

---

[24]The original material for this sub-section is in [13] and [14].

family of BGPs in the original dimension. The cost of the transformation is relevant: the "visibility" of the original variables is lost and the distinction between state-like and control-like variables also vanishes. However, the simple form of the bi-dimensional system (3.15i) is certainly striking and will be a crucial point of reference for the rest of the section.

By letting $\mu = \frac{n^* - n(0)}{n(0)}$, we first prove that:

Proposition 3.12 *The optimal time evolution of the average goods production is governed by the law*:

$$(3.16) \qquad n_t = n^* \left(1 + \mu e^{-(1-\alpha)n^* t}\right)^{-1}$$

Proof The equation defining the motion for average goods production can be written as $\dot{n}_t = (1 - \alpha)(n^* - n_t) n_t$. It is a simple differential equation, easy to solve by means of standard methods. $\square$

As a first interesting global result, we find that the average production adjusts according to a simple technical law (not depending on preference parameters) in logistic form. The logistic adjustment of the average goods production has important implications in terms of the properties of its convergence towards the stationary state (at least in the reduced space).

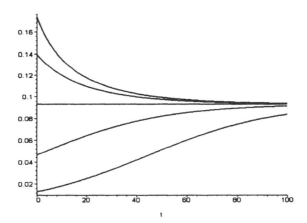

Figure 3.4 Optimal convergence paths of average production

Consider Figure 3.4 showing generic paths converging towards the steady-state value of the average goods-production. The following interesting property can be proved:

Corollary 3.7 *Let $\epsilon = n(0) - n^*$. Then the halving time of transition is lower in the* *case of a positive ϵ than in the symmetric case of a negative ϵ.*

Proof The result in the corollary is evident in Figure 3.4. Formal proof can be obtained from the well-known properties of equation (3.16). $\square$

The result in Corollary 3.7 seems to imply a form of asymmetric convergence towards the steady-state according to whether n_t is above or below its BGP value.

Now, since $n(0) = A \left[u(0)h(0)^\psi / k(0) \right]^{1-\alpha}$, a confirmation of this asymmetric timing in the original dimension, would lead to the interesting result that an efficient economy gets rid faster of a relative excess of human capital than of a relative excess of physical capital. We will examine this point in more detail later on.

3.4.3   The Global Behavior of the Average Consumption

Let us now characterize the explicit law of the average consumption. We start by proving that:

Proposition 3.13 *The optimal evolution of the average consumption follows the law*:

$$(3.17) \qquad m_t = \frac{e^{-\rho t/\sigma} \left[e^{(1-\alpha)n^* t} + \mu \right]^\varsigma}{\int_t^\infty e^{-\rho \theta/\sigma} \left[e^{(1-\alpha)n^* \theta} + \mu \right]^\varsigma d\theta}$$

where $\varsigma = \frac{\alpha - \sigma}{\sigma(1-\alpha)}$. Asymptotically, the average consumption converges to its steady-state value m^*.

Proof (See the Appendix to the Chapter, part a). The evolution of m_t, after the explicit trajectory of n_t is substituted out, is governed by a Bernoulli differential equation whose solution is as in proposition. Since, as shown in the Appendix, part a), $\lim\limits_{t \to \infty} m_t = m^*$, the second part of the proposition is implied. $\square$

Given Propositions 3.12 and 3.13, we also have the following counterpart in $\mathbb{R}^2$ of the stability property proved in [10] for the centralized dynamics generated by the ULM:

Corollary 3.8 *The steady-state in $\mathbb{R}^2$ is globally stable.*

Proof This result follows from the convergence properties towards the steady-state of both m_t and n_t.

Notice also that the relative sizes of the coefficient of risk aversion and the share of physical capital, already known to be crucial for the model without externality (see [7] and [23]) and for the model with externality, along equilibrium paths (see [30]), also dictate the global qualitative properties of the optimal transition. In particular, in the critical case of $\alpha = \sigma$, the following global counterpart, in presence of an externality factor, of Interesting Result 7 in [23] can be proved:

Corollary 3.9 *Let* $\varsigma = 0$ ($\alpha = \sigma$). *Then the policy functions for consumption and working time are globally horizontal, respectively at the value of* $m(0) = m_t = m^* = \frac{\varrho}{\alpha}$ *and* $u(0) = u_t = u^*$.

Proof If $\varsigma = 0$ ($\alpha = \sigma$) the law of evolution of the average consumption in Proposition 3.11 can be obtained in closed form; we have $m(0) = m_t = m^* = \frac{\varrho}{\alpha}$. This implies that the dynamic equation for u_t in (3.12b) becomes $\dot{u}_t = \left[\frac{B(1-\alpha+\gamma)}{\alpha} - \frac{\varrho}{\alpha} \right] u_t + B\psi u_t^2 = -B\psi u_t (u^* - u_t)$. This is a simple differential equation which, solved, gives $u_t = \frac{u^*}{1 + \_C2 u^* e^{B\psi u^* \tau}}$, where $\_C2$ is a constant of integration. Since $B\psi u^*$ is always positive, the constant of integration has to be fixed to zero to prevent u_t from asymptotically vanishing. Therefore $u_t = u(0) = u^*$. $\square$

Given the result in Corollary 3.9, also the following extension of the "exogenous growth case" obtained in [7] for the model without externality factor can be achieved:

Corollary 3.10 *Let* $\varsigma = 0$ ($\alpha = \sigma$). *Then human capital behaves globally as an exogenous variable.*

Proof Given the always-constant value of working time, the solution of the differential equation for human capital in (3.1c), brings to the simple $h_t = h(0)e^{B(1-u^*)t} = h(0)e^{\varsigma_h t}$ $\forall t$. $\square$

In the remaining regions of the parameter space, equation (3.17) still offers valuable general information on the properties of the transition in the reduced dimension. In particular, we have:

Corollary 3.11 *Let* $\sigma < \alpha$. *Then, a shock suddenly increasing (decreasing) the average goods production implies low (high) values of the average consumption. The opposite occurs if* $\sigma > \alpha$.[25]

Proof Recall that $\mu = \frac{n^* - n(0)}{n(0)}$ and consider again the solution for m_t in (3.17). Since, as shown in Appendix, part b), $Sign(\frac{dm_t}{dn(0)}) = -Sign(\frac{dm_t}{d\mu}) = -Sign(\varsigma) = Sign(\frac{\sigma - \alpha}{\sigma(1-\alpha)})$ the result in the Corollary follows. $\square$

A visualization of the impact of variations in the average goods production on the average consumption is in Fig. 3.5 in the following section for specific parameter choices.

---

[25]Notice that, given the slopes of the policy functions derived in [10], this result implies that the policy function for the average goods production is always negatively sloped regardless of the relative sizes of the share of physical capital and coefficient of risk aversion. We will numerically derive the policy function for the average goods production in the following sub-section for specific parameter configurations.

3.4.4   Time Paths in the Original Dimension

Since we know the explicit path of n_t, we can try to solve the differential equation for consumption.[26] We thus have:

Proposition 3.14 *The optimal evolution of consumption is governed by the law:*

$$(3.18) \qquad c_t = c(0)e^{\xi^* t} \left[\frac{1 + \mu e^{-(1-\alpha)n^* t}}{1+\mu} \right]^{\frac{\alpha}{\sigma(1-\alpha)}}$$

The initial value $c(0)$ has to be chosen to be consistent with $c(0)$ from $m(0)k(0)$ in (3.17).

Proof By substituting equation (3.16) into the equation for motion of consumption, we can easily determine the explicit law in the proposition. Of course, the initial value of consumption has to be equalized in the two formulations (3.17) and (3.18). $\square$

Notice that, when the economy belongs to the exogenous growth case, the initial value of consumption in (3.18) can be retrieved without further information. As a matter of fact, if $\Sigma = \left(\frac{A(u^*)^{1-\alpha} h(0)^{1-\alpha+\gamma}}{n^*} \right)^{\frac{1}{1-\alpha}}$ simplifies the notation, we have:

Corollary 3.12 *In the exogenous growth case, the laws of evolution of physical capital and consumption can be fully identified without further information. They are equal to:*

$$(3.19a) \qquad c_t = \frac{\rho}{\alpha} \Sigma e^{\xi^* t} \left[1 + \mu e^{-(1-\alpha)n^* t} \right]^{\frac{1}{1-\alpha}}$$

$$(3.19b) \qquad k_t = \Sigma e^{\xi^* t} \left[1 + \mu e^{-(1-\alpha)n^* t} \right]^{\frac{1}{1-\alpha}}$$

Proof In the case of exogenous growth, we know from Corollary 3.9 that $m(0) = m^* = \frac{\rho}{\alpha}$. From this, $c(0) = \frac{\rho}{\alpha} k(0)$. Furthermore, again for Corollary 3.9, $u(0) = u^*$. After some algebraic calculations, therefore, the time path for consumption can then be put in the form given in the corollary (consider also that $\mu = \frac{n^*}{n(0)} - 1$ where $n(0) = A (u^*)^{1-\alpha} h(0)^{1-\alpha+\gamma} k(0)^{\alpha-1}$). $\square$

As a further by-product of this exogenous growth case consider also that:

Corollary 3.13 *The asymptotic levels of human capital, physical capital (and consumption) will only depend on $h(0)$ [and not on $k(0)$].*

Proof To see this consider the explicit time paths in (3.19i). $\square$

---

[26]The original reference for this sub-section is [15].

In the more general case, since the explicit value of $m(0)$ in (3.17) cannot be obtained without fixing ς, we do not have general information on the value of $c(0)$.

Regardless of the initial condition, however, a further interesting detail relating to the time path of consumption is as follows:

Corollary 3.14 *Let a shock increase the endowment of physical capital present in the economy (or decrease human capital). Then, if $n(0) < \frac{\rho}{\alpha}$, the level of consumption initially decreases, reaches a minimum at $t = -\frac{\ln[\sigma\xi^*/(\rho\mu)]}{(1-\alpha)n^*}$ and then starts growing again. A shock decreasing the endowment of physical capital (or increasing human capital) only allows for monotonically increasing levels of consumption.*

Proof The time derivative of the explicit law for consumption changes sign at $\xi^* = \mu e^{-(1-\alpha)n^*t}\left[\frac{\alpha}{\sigma}n^* - \xi^*\right]$. Since $n^* = \frac{\sigma\xi^* + \rho}{\alpha}$, the term inside the square brackets becomes $\frac{\rho}{\sigma} > 0$. By taking logarithms, the value of t at which the derivative changes sign can be retrieved. Since the sign change of the derivatives must occur in positive time, in order to actually observe a reduction in the level of consumption, the shock needs to be large enough so that $\sigma\xi^*/(\rho\mu) < 1$. Considering that $\mu = \frac{n^*}{n(0)} - 1 = \frac{(\sigma\xi^* + \rho)/\alpha}{n(0)} - 1$, this further implies that $n(0) < \frac{\rho}{\alpha}$. $\square$

We proceed now to achieve the main goal of the paper, by showing that the solution of system $(3.15i)$ allows for the explicit characterization of the trajectories of the variables in the original dimension. We have:

Proposition 3.15 *Let $\tilde{\Delta}^c$ be the region of the parameter space where the differential equation for the average consumption can be actually solved. Then there exists a non empty $\hat{\Delta}^c \subseteq \tilde{\Delta}^c$ such that if the parameters are inside $\hat{\Delta}^c$ it is possible to compute explicit optimal paths for all the variables in the original dimension.*

Proof Once the explicit paths for n_t and m_t are known, obtaining the explicit trajectories of the primitive variables of the economy is a simple matter of solving differential equations which, by assumption, happens if the parameters are inside $\hat{\Delta}^c$. The proof is completed here below, where we show that $\hat{\Delta}^c$ is not empty. $\square$

Proposition 3.15 further implies:

Corollary 3.15 *Once determined the optimal sequences for the variables, setting time to zero, the unique optimal pair of initial conditions for the control variables associated with the stable manifold can be obtained as well.*

Proof The initial value for the fraction of non-leisure time dedicated to work can be found by setting time to zero in the explicit law for u_t and obtaining $u(0)$ from $u(0) = u(0)\left[\mu\left(u(0), k(0), h(0), Z\right), Z\right]$, where Z is a vector of known parameters and $k(0)$ and $h(0)$ are given. Once determined $u(0)$ it also becomes possible to find

$c(0)$ by setting time to zero in the explicit solution of the average consumption. □

3.4.5 The Explicit Transition Simulated

In the above section, we have shown how it is possible to solve the system of dynamic laws associated with the Pareto-optimal Hamiltonian dynamics generated by the ULM. The methodology is a simple four-step procedure which we have detailed in the Appendix to the Chapter (part c). Its main advantage, with respect to other methodologies which could be used instead,[27] is that it does not require sophisticated computer programs; indeed, in simplified sections of the parameter space, it does not require computers at all, since the differential equations can be easily solved by hand. Moreover, for at least one variable in the original dimension, consumption, we can analytically obtain the general solution of the variable without any restriction of the parameter space.[28]

In this section,[29] in order to complete the proof of Proposition 3.15 by showing that $\hat{\Delta}^c$ is not empty and also to infer more properties of the optimal transition. in the reduced and in the original dimension, we will investigate two parameter-specific cases, one where the coefficient of risk aversion is lower than the share of physical capital and the other where it is higher. As in the other parts of the book containing numerical simulations, the results are presented through a sequence of *Interesting Results*.

Furthermore:

Remark *The qualitative results here retrieved have always been obtained in a large number of simulations conducted in all regions of the feasible parameter space.*

To allow for easy to solve equations, the parameters are chosen such that $B = 0.04$, $\alpha = 0.4$, $\gamma = 0.15$, $\sigma = 0.25$ and $\rho = 0.046875$ for the case of a small σ and $B = 0.04$, $\alpha \simeq 0.571$, $\gamma \simeq 0.142$, $\sigma = 1.6$ and $\rho \simeq 0.032$ for the case of a large σ. This implies $\varsigma = 1$ when σ is small and $\varsigma = -(3/2)$. when σ is large. Given the parameter choices, the stationary values of n_t and m_t are, respectively, 0.125 and 0.1125 when σ is small and 0.0932 and 0.08 when σ is large. In both cases $u^* = 0.75$ and the growth rate of human capital is 0.01. The growth rate of the economy is 0.0125 in the case of small σ and approximately 0.0133 in case of large σ.

Recall now that $p_t = \frac{k_t}{h_t^\psi}$ is a stationary variable representing the state of the economy. In the simulations, the economy is normalized at a value of $p^* = \left(\frac{k}{h^\psi}\right)^* = 5$. We will also suppose that the shocks always affect physical capital and that $h(0) = 1$.[30]

---

[27] Consider, for instance, the time-elimination algorithm deviced by Mulligan and Sala-i-Martin in [23].
[28] See Proposition 3.14.
[29] The original reference for this sub-section is [13] and [14].
[30] To this end, A is chosen at around 0.39 in case of $\varsigma > 0$ and 0.21 for the case of $\varsigma < 0$.

By applying our solving procedure as detailed in the Appendix to the Chapter (part c), we first obtain the set of explicit trajectories of the original variables and the initial conditions for the controls (as functions of μ). The shock modifying the initial state of the economy is imagined very large such that the resulting deviation of the economy from the steady-state n^* is of size $\pm\frac{n^*}{2}$. μ, therefore, takes alternatively the values of 1 and -1/3.[31]

We start by inferring more information on the properties of the optimal transition in the reduced dimension.

Consider Figures 3.5i, where numerical simulations of the convergence paths of the average consumption in response to shocks affecting the state of the economy such that n_t is symmetrically increased or decreased are depicted in both cases of a positive and negative ς.

The dashed lines are associated with shocks lowering the average goods production ($\mu > 0$); the solid lines to shocks increasing the average goods production ($\mu < 0$).

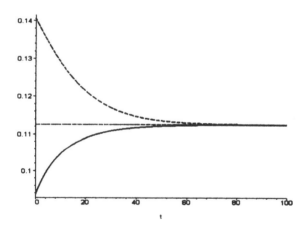

Figure 3.5a Optimal convergence paths of average consumption when $\varsigma > 0$

Combining the information in the two graphs, in addition to what proved in Corollary 3.11, we also find that:

Interesting Result 3.1 *The impact on m_t of a shock decreasing the average production of a given size is more intense than a shock increasing n_t of the same size. The halving time of transition is also longer. The opposite occurs if $\varsigma < 0$.*

---

[31]The implied values of $k(0)$ in case of normalization $h(0) = 1$ are approximately 21.15 and 2.18 when $\varsigma > 0$ and approximately 17.76 and 2.36 in case of $\varsigma < 0$.

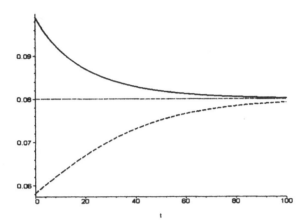

Figure 3.5b Optimal convergence paths of average consumption when $\varsigma < 0$

A different perspective is given in Fig. 3.6, where the phase diagrams for system (3.15i) are presented for the specific regions of the parameter space. The global convergence property proved in Corollary 3.8 for the general case is made evident.

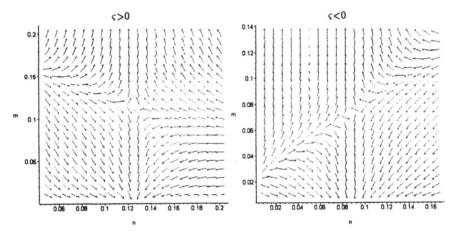

Figure 3.6 The stable manifold in $\mathbb{R}^2$

We present now, in Figures 3.7 and 3.8, the optimal trajectories obtained for the original variables of the model in case of $\varsigma = 1$ and $\varsigma = -3/2$. To save space only the normalization with $h(0) = 1$ is reported. As before, the dashed lines are trajectories implied by a shock such that $\mu = 1$. The solid lines represent the trajectories in case of a shock such that $\mu = -1/3$. The dot lines represent the unperturbed evolution of the economy.

The visualization of the transitional paths offers further qualitative insights into the optimal response to shocks perturbing the state of the economy. Consider that, as already proved in Corollary 3.14, since the shock largely increases the relative

amount of physical capital in the economy, consumption and physical capital follow
U-shaped paths. Furthermore, as made evident in the graphs:

Interesting Result 3.2 *The decreasing period occurs both when $\varsigma > 0$ and when
$\varsigma < 0$, but it is much more intense and long lasting in case of a positive ς.*

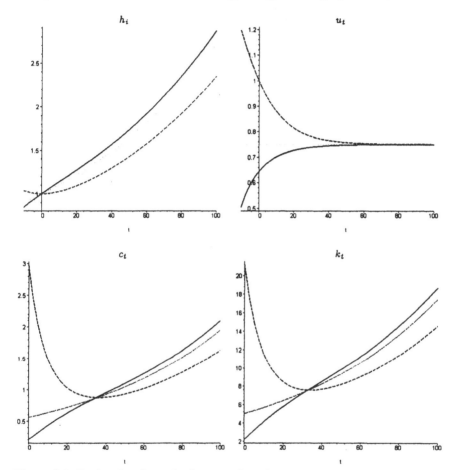

Figure 3.7 Optimal trajectories in case of $\varsigma = 1$

It is also clear from the visualization of the trajectories that the local results obtained
in [7] for the model without externality factor find an interesting extension to the
large, at least in the specific regions of the parameter space under investigation. In
fact, we find that:

Interesting Result 3.3 *If $\varsigma > 0$, the optimal response of the economy to a shock
reducing (increasing) the endowment of physical capital of the economy implies
asymptotically higher (lower) levels of both physical and human capital (the para-*

doxical case). The opposite occurs (the normal case) if $\varsigma < 0$.

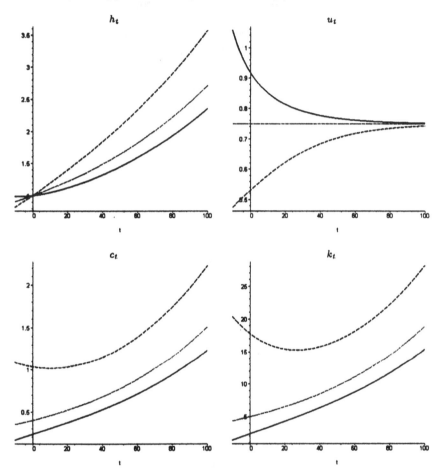

Figure 3.8 Optimal trajectories in case of $\varsigma = -3/2$

Since we now have the explicit trajectories of the two capital goods, it becomes easy to find the optimal policy functions.

Consider the visualization offered in Figures 3.9 and 3.10 where the optimal policy functions are plotted given the choices in the parameter space. As it is made clear in the Figures, the global results obtained in [10] concerning the sign of the slopes of the policy functions are confirmed: in particular:

Interesting Result 3.4 *The optimal policy functions for working time and average consumption are globally downward (upward) sloping if the coefficient of risk aversion is large (small) with respect to the share of physical capital.*

The rest of this section develops the implications in the original dimension of the asymmetric convergence in $\mathbb{R}^2$ implied by the logistic behavior of the average goods production in Fig. 3.4. We consider two aspects: on the one hand, we calculate the elasticity of the average goods production with respect to p_t. On the other hand, we study the timing of the convergence in relation to the initial state of the economy. What we have found is interesting. As already argued in footnote 25:

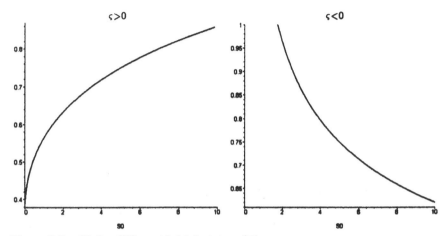

Figure 3.9 $u(0)$ **for different initial states of the economy**

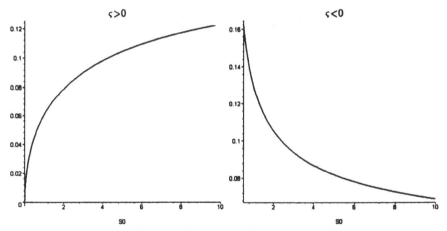

Figure 3.10 $m(0)$ **for different initial states of the economy**

Interesting Result 3.5 *The slopes of the policy function for the average goods production is always negative, regardless of the relative sizes of the coefficient of risk aversion and share of physical capital.*

We have plotted in Fig. 3.11 the policy functions for the average goods production.

We then calculate the elasticity of n_t with respect to p_t; in all regions of the parameter space, this elasticity is either constant or shows very small variations even for large deviation of p_t from its steady-state value. Therefore, in terms of Corollary 2, positive or negative variations of the state of the economy of a given size tend to produce a symmetric deviation of the average goods production from its steady-state value (see also Fig. 1).[32]

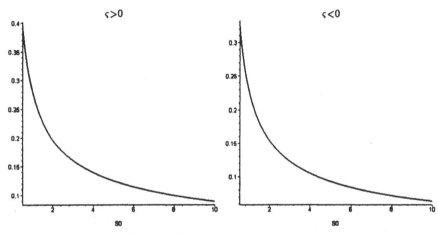

Figure 3.11 $n(0)$ for different initial states of the economy

Not quite the same for the timing of convergence. We have calculated and plotted in Fig. 3.12 the halving times of the transition for working time as functions of $p(0)$.

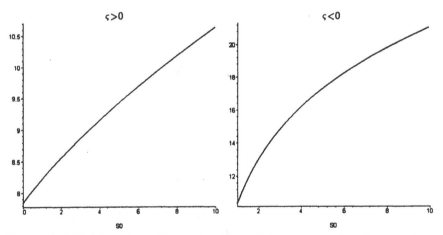

Figure 3.12 Halving time of transition for working time as a function of $p(0)$

Very interestingly, the numerical simulations bring to the following:

---

[32]Recall from Fig. 3.5, however, that the impact is not symmetric in terms of the average consumption.

Interesting Result 3.6 *The halving time of the transition is a positive function of the initial level of the variable p_t regardless of whether ς is positive or negative.*[33]

This means that a shock increasing human capital implies a shorter halving time of the transition than a shock symmetrically decreasing the same capital good.

Of course, the contrary happens if the shock symmetrically increases or decreases the endowment of physical capital of the economy.

3.5   Global Welfare Analysis

The availability of the trajectory for consumption also implies that it is possible to solve the welfare integral in explicit form.[34] Recall the explicit law of evolution of consumption in (3.19a) and the general form for the welfare integral in (1.3):

$$W = \tfrac{1}{1-\sigma} \int_0^\infty \left(c_t^{1-\sigma} - 1 \right) e^{-\rho t} dt$$

Let, furthermore, $\frac{\alpha(1-\sigma)}{\sigma(1-\alpha)} = z$. We can obtain the following preliminary result:[35]

Lemma 3.2 *The welfare integral in the case of a centralized regime has the form*:

$$(3.20) \qquad W = \tfrac{1}{(1-\sigma)} \left[-\tfrac{1}{\rho} + \tfrac{c(0)^{1-\sigma}}{(1+\mu)^z} \int_0^\infty e^{-\frac{\rho}{\sigma} t} \left[e^{(1-\alpha)n^* t} + \mu \right]^z dx \right]$$

Proof Using (3.18) and recalling from (2.3) that $n^* = \tfrac{1}{\alpha}(\rho + \sigma \xi^*)$, the general form of the welfare integral in the proposition can be retrieved by using a little algebra. □

Notice that:

Remark *Since, in general terms, we cannot ascribe an explicit value to $c(0)$,[36] the initial value of consumption in (3.20) remains unidentified.*

Now, to have an explicit indication of the welfare over the infinite horizon, we shall consider two cases:

i)   the general unperturbed case $\mu = 0$;

ii)   the exogenous growth case ($\sigma = \alpha$) in the general case of a $\mu \neq 0$.

---

[33]Notice also that the halving time of the transition is always longer in case of negative ς for any given value of $p(0)$.

[34]Of course, even without the availability of the closed form solution for consumption, it is still possible to solve the welfare integral by using its linear approximation.

[35]The original reference for this section is [15].

[36]In particular, as proved above, we cannot solve the explicit law for average consumption without fixing the distance between σ and α and therefore identifying $c(0)$ through the relation $c(0) = m(0)k(0)$.

The unperturbed case is easy to deal with. Recalling that, from (3.5), $m^* = B\frac{\psi}{\alpha} - \frac{1}{\sigma}(B\psi - \rho)$, we have:

Proposition 3.16 *In the unperturbed case, the welfare integral in Lemma 3.2 is equal to:*

$$(3.21) \quad W = \frac{1}{(1-\sigma)}\left[-\frac{1}{\rho} + \frac{[m^*k(0)]^{1-\sigma}}{\rho/\sigma - zn^*(1-\alpha)}\right] =$$

$$= \frac{1}{(1-\sigma)}\left[-\frac{1}{\rho} + \frac{\sigma[m^*k(0)]^{1-\sigma}}{B\psi(\rho/B\psi - 1 + \sigma)}\right].$$

For all parameter configurations inside $\hat{\Delta}^c$ there exists a threshold value of $k(0)$ such that W is positive.

Proof In the unperturbed case, $\mu = 0$ and the integral can be solved. Furthermore, since $m(0) = \frac{c(0)}{k(0)} = m^*$, the initial position of consumption can be identified at the value:

$$c(0) = m^*k(0).$$

Since, $(\rho/B\psi - 1 + \sigma)$ is always positive (see the parameter space in 3.3), the rest of the proposition follows. $\square$

Let us now consider the exogenous growth case in the more general situation of $\mu \neq 0$. Since in this case, the exponent $z = \frac{\alpha(1-\sigma)}{\sigma(1-\alpha)}$ boils down to 1, the integral can again be solved to give:

$$(3.22) \quad W = \frac{1}{(1-\alpha)}\left[-\frac{1}{\rho} + \frac{1}{\rho}\frac{[c(0)]^{1-\alpha}}{(1+\mu)}\left(\mu + \frac{\rho}{\rho/\alpha - n^*(1-\alpha)}\right)\right]$$

Therefore:

Proposition 3.17 *In the exogenous growth case the welfare integral in Lemma 3.2 has the following form:*

$$(3.23) \quad W = \frac{1}{(1-\alpha)}\left[-\frac{1}{\rho} + \frac{\alpha}{\rho}A\frac{[(\rho/\alpha)u^*h(0)^\psi]^{1-\alpha}}{B\psi}\left(\mu + \frac{\alpha\rho}{B\psi(\rho/B\psi - 1 + \alpha)}\right)\right]$$

Proof Starting from (3.22), it is an easy task to obtain (3.23) by considering that $m(0) = \frac{c(0)}{k(0)} = m^* = \frac{\rho}{\alpha}$, $\mu = \frac{n^* - n(0)}{n(0)}$ and $n^* = \frac{B\psi}{\alpha}$. The result in the proposition is thus easily obtained. Recall also that, in the case of exogenous growth, $n(0) = A\left(\frac{u^*h(0)^\psi}{k(0)}\right)^{1-\alpha}$. $\square$

It is interesting to note that:

Corollary 3.16 *Let the economy belong to the exogenous growth case. Sudden increases (decreases) of both physical and human capital always lead to higher (lower) welfare levels.*

Proof Studying the signs of the partial derivatives of W w.r.t the initial values of the state variables we obtain the result in the corollary quite easily. □

3.6   Appendix

a) The explicit path of the average consumption

The solution of the Bernoulli differential equation in (3.15b), after the explicit value for n_t has been substituted, is:

$$(A3a.1) \qquad m_t = \frac{e^{-\rho t/\sigma} \left[e^{(1-\alpha)n^* t} + \mu \right]^\varsigma}{C1 - \int_0^t e^{-\rho\theta/\sigma} \left[e^{(1-\alpha)n^* \theta} + \mu \right]^\varsigma d\theta}$$

Notice first that $-\rho/\sigma + (1-\alpha)\varsigma n^* = -m^*$; this means that the numerator vanishes for $t \to \infty$. For m_t to be meaningful, therefore, also the denominator, asymptotically, has to vanish. This happens only if:

$$(A3a.2) \qquad \_C1 = \int_0^\infty e^{-\rho\theta/\sigma} \left[e^{(1-\alpha)n^* \theta} + \mu \right]^\varsigma d\theta$$

By substituting the value of $\_C1$, we obtain the value in expression (3.17) in Proposition 3.13.

Now, to prove that the average consumption converges to m^*, recall first that $-\rho/\sigma + \varsigma(1-\alpha)n^* = -m^*$. Therefore, for $\forall \epsilon > 0$, $\exists A$, such that for $\forall t \geq T$:

$$(A3a.3) \qquad (1-\epsilon)e^{-m^* t} \leq e^{-\rho t/\sigma} \left(e^{(1-\alpha)n^* t} + \mu \right)^\varsigma \leq (1+\epsilon)e^{-m^* t}$$

This implies that:

$$(A3a.4) \qquad (1-\epsilon)\int_t^\infty e^{-m^* \theta} d\theta \leq \int_t^\infty \frac{\left[e^{(1-\alpha)n^* \theta} + \mu \right]^\varsigma}{e^{\rho\theta/\sigma}} d\theta \leq (1+\epsilon)\int_t^\infty e^{-m^* \theta} d\theta$$

As a consequence, since:

$$(A3a.5) \qquad \int_t^\infty e^{-m^* \theta} d\theta = -\frac{1}{m^*} \left[e^{-m^* \theta} \right]_t^\infty = \frac{1}{m^*} e_t^{-m^* t}$$

we have:

$$(A3a.6) \qquad \frac{1+\epsilon}{m^*} e^{-m^* t} \geq \int_t^\infty \frac{\left[e^{(1-\alpha)n^* \theta} + \mu \right]^\varsigma}{e^{\rho\theta/\sigma}} d\theta \geq \frac{1-\epsilon}{m^*} e^{-m^* t}$$

Thus, taking limits, from the explicit solution for m_t we have:

$$(A3a.7) \qquad \frac{m^*}{1+\epsilon} \leq \lim_{t\to\infty} m_t \leq \frac{m^*}{1-\epsilon}$$

which implies $\lim_{t\to\infty} m_t = m^*$

b) *The Study of the Sign of* $\frac{dm_t}{d\tau}$

Since the integral in the explicit solution for m_t respects the conditions for uniform convergence, we have:

$$(A3b.1) \qquad \frac{dm_t}{d\tau} = \varsigma \frac{\int_t^\infty e^{-\rho\theta/\sigma}\left[e^{(1-\alpha)n^*\theta}+\mu\right]^\varsigma d\theta -}{e^{\rho t/\sigma}\left[e^{(1-\alpha)n^*t}+\mu\right]^{1-\varsigma}\left[\int_t^\infty e^{-\rho\theta/\sigma}\left[e^{(1-\alpha)n^*\theta}+\mu\right]^\varsigma d\theta\right]^2} +$$

$$-\varsigma \frac{\left[e^{(1-\alpha)n^*t}+\mu\right]\int_t^\infty e^{-\rho\theta/\sigma}\left[e^{(1-\alpha)n^*\theta}+\mu\right]^{\varsigma-1}d\theta}{e^{\rho t/\sigma}\left[e^{(1-\alpha)n^*t}+\mu\right]^{1-\varsigma}\left[\int_t^\infty e^{-\rho\theta/\sigma}\left[e^{(1-\alpha)n^*\theta}+\mu\right]^\varsigma d\theta\right]^2}$$

Now, putting everything under the same sign of integral, we obtain:

$$(A3b.2) \qquad \frac{dm_t}{d\tau} = \varsigma \frac{\int_t^\infty e^{-\rho\theta/\sigma}\left[e^{(1-\alpha)n^*\theta}+\mu\right]^{\varsigma-1}\left[e^{(1-\alpha)n^*\theta}-e^{(1-\alpha)n^*t}\right]d\theta}{e^{\rho t/\sigma}\left[e^{(1-\alpha)n^*t}+\mu\right]^{1-\varsigma}\left[\int_t^\infty e^{-\rho\theta/\sigma}\left[e^{(1-\alpha)n^*\theta}+\mu\right]^\varsigma d\theta\right]^2}$$

Therefore, being $\theta > t$, the sign of the derivative only depends on ς.

c) The Methodology for Solving the Centralized Dynamics

The procedure developed in the Chapter to solve the dynamics generated by the centralized solution of the ULM is a four-step methodology where we are required to:

1) Transform the four-dimensional system (3.1*i*) (for which there exists a BGP) into a bi-dimensional one (for which there exists a stationary point) of the form:

(A3c.1) $\dot{n}_t = f(n_t, Z)$

(A3c.2) $\dot{m}_t = g(n_t, m_t, Z)$

where $n_t = \frac{y_t}{k_t}$ is the average production, $m_t = \frac{c_t}{k_t}$ is the average consumption and Z is a vector of parameters.

2) Obtain the explicit trajectory of n_t:

(A3c.3) $n_t = n(\mu(n(0), Z), Z, t)$

Then, given ς, obtain the explicit trajectory of m_t:

(A3c.4) $m_t = m(m(0)(\mu(n(0), Z), Z), Z, t)$

The only unknown is $n(0)$.

3) Given the explicit trajectories of n_t and m_t, solve the system in the original dimension:

(A3c.5) $u_t = u(\mu(n(0), Z), Z, t)$

(A3c.6) $c_t = c(\mu(n(0), Z), Z, t)$

(A3c.7) $k_t = k(\mu(n(0), Z), Z, t)$

(A3c.8) $h_t = h(\mu(n(0), Z), Z, t)$

$n(0)$ is still unknown.

4) Set time to zero in equation (A3c.5). Obtain:

(A3c.9) $u(0) = F(\mu(n(0), Z), Z)$.

Now, since:

$$n(0) = A \left(\frac{u(0)h(0)^\psi}{k(0)} \right)^{1-\alpha}$$

where $k(0)$ and $h(0)$ are known, solve (A3c.9) for $u(0)$.

Once the (unique) initial value of working time is known, obtain $c(0)$ from (A3c.4) (after setting time to zero).

Chapter 4

The Properties of the
Competitive Equilibrium

4.1 Introduction and Plan of the Chapter

The aim of this Chapter is to investigate the properties of the Uzawa-Lucas economy evolving along competitive equilibrium paths. As explained in Chapter 1, competitive equilibrium paths, when a distorting factor is present, typically arise in case of decentralized or market solution of the optimization problem.

The characterization of the long-run properties (the BGP) is a fairly straightforward task. Given the preliminary work done in Chapters 1 and 2, we are simply required to:

a) substitute the appropriate value of the contribution of human capital into the general expression for working time obtained in Chapter 1;

b) determine, according to Definition 1.5, in which regions of the parameter space the BGP is non-degenerate;

c) substitute the correct value of the contribution of human capital into the general expression for the growth rate of the economy obtained in Chapter 1;

d) exploit Lemma 1.1 to obtain the positive growth rates of the primitive variables of the economy;

e) substitute the efficient growth rate of the economy into the general expressions for the *Great Ratios* in Chapter 2;

f) substitute the efficient growth rate of the economy into the general expressions for the adjoint variables, again in Chapter 2.

A fundamental result, first achieved by Benhabib and Perli in [5], shows that the non-degeneracy of the BGP can be obtained in two non-connected regions of the parameter space; one where the subjective discount rate is low and the inverse of the intertemporal elasticity of substitution is high and the other where the contrary happens.

The relationship between size of the parameters and BGP levels or growth rates of the variables in these regions of the parameter space provides useful details on the behavior of two-sector market economies facing modification of their preference or technological structure. We find that, only in the former region of the parameter space, will larger technological parameters and lower preference parameters mean higher economic growth. The contrary happens when the decentralized economy is characterized by high discount rates and low elasticities of intertemporal substitution. Moreover, the size of the technological parameters (preference parameters) has a positive (negative) impact on the rental compensation of capital, on the saving rate and on the growth rate of wages only when the inverse of the intertemporal elasticity of substitution is high.

The impact is negative when the intertemporal elasticity of substitution is low.

The impact of the size of the parameters is more mixed when the BGP-stationary values of the *Great Ratios* are taken into consideration. Consider first the region of the parameter space where the discount rate is low and the inverse of the intertemporal elasticity of substitution is high. In this case, besides the difficult-to-read impact of the size of the share of physical capital, we find that the level of technology in the final good sector only matters for the "weighted" ratio between the two capital stocks.[37]

Furthermore, economies with larger preference parameters are characterized by lower BGP levels of the average product and higher values of the "weighted ratio" between the two forms of accumulation. In the same region of the parameter space, we also show that a higher level of the efficacy index in the learning sector implies higher values of both the average product and consumption but lower values of the weighted ratio between physical and human capital. The other feasible region of the parameter space generally implies an inverted impact of the size of all the parameters bar the externality.

Detecting the properties of the decentralized equilibrium when the economy is in transition is much more complicated. From the local point of view, we have already seen in Chapter 2 that the characteristic equation cannot be factorized, unless the share of physical capital equals the inverse of the intertemporal elasticity of substitution. Consequently, any possibility of obtaining general qualitative information on the stability properties of the BGP and on the economics around the fixed point is now severely limited. Nonetheless, the application of the Routh-Hurvitz theorem to the $\mathbb{R}^3$-transformed dynamics, coupled with some tools of the bifurcation theory does work here admirably well in enabling us to detect some interesting facts.

A first crucial result we find here is that saddle-path stability is not the only possible outcome associated with the decentralized solution of the ULM: indeed, when the parameters belong to the region of the parameter space in which the discount rate is high and the inverse of the intertemporal elasticity of substitution is low, indeterminacy, or even instability of the equilibrium, can emerge instead.

---

[37]This means that parameter A in the production function (1.1) is a scale parameter, not affecting the average variables.

In order to extract more details on the local properties of the dynamics, we conduct intense numerical work with the intention of partitioning the parameter space into regions where different stability conditions (in terms of different dimensions of the stable manifold) will prevail. The results of this work allows us to draw an (approximate) map showing where there emerges, in a simplified parameter space, the conditions of total instability, indeterminacy or uniqueness of the equilibrium in both cases of real and complex-conjugate eigenvalues.

An interesting border whose existence we are able to prove is that between the regions of the parameter space where instability and indeterminacy prevail in the presence of complex-conjugate eigenvalues. As we know from the bifurcation theory, this is a pre-requisite for the existence of Hopf cycling in the neighborhood of the steady-state (in $\mathbb{R}^3$). Since the other pre-requisites are also satisfied, we find that deterministic cycling is actually viable for the decentralized economy. The economic interpretation of this mathematical result is interesting and worthy of note: as the bifurcation parameter (we choose the externality) crosses a critical value either from the right or from the left, an invariant cycle emerges around the steady-state, forcing the variables associated with the complex conjugate eigenvalues to oscillate around a constant value.

Further relevant information on the behavior of trajectories wandering in the neighborhood of the steady state in the case of Hopf cycling can be derived from a stability analysis of the orbits themselves. These, in general, can either attract or repel. If there is an attracting orbit, trajectories on the centre manifold are locally attracted by the orbit which thus becomes a limit set. In this so-called *sub-critical case*, the stationary point is an unstable solution which is meaningless from an economic point of view (unless the initial conditions happen to coincide with the stationary value). Conversely, if the cycle is unstable in the dynamics of the center manifold, the steady state is attracting. In this *super-critical* case, the cycle is only economically relevant if the initial conditions are such that the economy fluctuates from the beginning. There exist standard analytical procedures which can be used to unveil the stability properties of the orbits in specific cases: in particular, it can be proved that the orbit structure near the bifurcation point (on the vector field restricted to the centre manifold) depends on up-to-third order derivatives on the non-linear terms. According to the numerical work in [22], the orbits can be either super-critical or sub-critical, according to whether the inverse of the intertemporal elasticity of substitution is high or low (inside the region of the parameter space where the Hopf theorem finds application).

The numerical work done to establish the form and size of the eigenvalues in different regions of the parameter space can also be used to study (again from the local point of view) the slopes of the functions linking the control and control-like variables to the state of the economy in the specific case in which the steady-state is saddle-path stable in presence of only real eigenvalues. Most interestingly, as in the case of optimal paths, we are able to show that these functions are locally downward (upward) sloping if the inverse of the intertemporal elasticity of substitution is large (small) with respect to the share of physical capital. This implies that, according to Definition 2.1, imbalances in the economy are corrected by a prevalence of the Consumption-Smoothing Effect (Wage Rate Effect). In the critical case of an inverse of the intertemporal elasticity of substitution being equal to the share of physical capital, we find that the Consumption-Smoothing Effect and the Wage Rate Effect compensate each other and that the imbalance is corrected by means of the Solow Effect.

In connection with these results, Definition 2.2 tells us that the decentralized economy belongs to the *paradoxical growth case* if the inverse of the intertemporal elasticity of substitution is small and to the *normal growth case* if the inverse of the intertemporal elasticity of substitution is high (with respect to the share of physical capital). An *exogenous growth case* can also arise if the inverse of the intertemporal elasticity of substitution equals the share of physical capital.

The global point of view finds a much less general application. As shown in Chapter 2, the symmetry of the Hamiltonian dynamics breaks down in the case of the decentralized solution. The $\mathbb{R}^4 \rightarrow \mathbb{R}^2$ dimensional reduction becomes unworkable and there is no possibility of explicitly solving, in general terms, the differential equations (unless the inverse of the intertemporal elasticity of substitution has the same size as the share of physical capital). As a consequence, although this region of the parameter space is not particularly relevant from an empirical point of view (the inverse of the elasticity of substitution is too low and it seems not to match the empirical findings), the simplification derived is quite substantial and the transition can now also be studied from the global point of view.

We shall develop here two sets of considerations. On the one hand, we follow Xie [30] and investigate the implications of multiple equilibria for the global properties of the decentralized economy. On the other, we solve the differential equations when working time and average consumption are constant, in order to explore the properties of the equilibrium transition along the exogenous growth case. Since, in the latter case we can obtain the explicit trajectory for consumption, we also obtain a global evaluation of the welfare integral.

The plan of the Chapter is as follows.

The second section discusses the equilibrium properties of the decentralized economy as it evolves along a non-degenerate BGP. We thereby determine the long-run growth rate of the economy, along with the equilibrium behavior of the primitive and adjoint variables of the model. The analysis also elaborates the equilibrium BGP values of the *Great Ratios* in the long-run and their sensitivity to variations in the parameters.

The third section starts the local analysis of the transition in $\mathbb{R}^3$. Applying the Routh-Hurvitz theorem, we discuss the stability properties of the fixed point. In the same section, furthermore, we employ the tools of the bifurcation theory to investigate the emergence of deterministic cycles and their stability properties.

The fourth section examines the possibility of drastically simplifying the system of differential equations by imposing the extreme assumption that the inverse of the intertemporal elasticity of substitution equals the share of physical capital. As already said, although this assumption is at odds with the empirical evidence, it does allow us to analyze the global behavior of the variables in the case of a competitive solution and to draw some interesting conjectures on global transition in other regions of the parameter space.

Some interesting hints on the present value of the welfare integral, in this specific region of the parameter space, are also discussed.

4.2 Equilibrium Dynamics Along the BGP

4.2.1 The Relevant System of Differential Equations

We start this section by obtaining the set of dynamic laws governing the equilibrium evolution of the economy. By simply imposing $E_h^{c,d} \equiv E_h^c = 1 - \alpha$ in system (2.1i), it is easy to obtain:

$$(4.1a) \qquad \xi_c = \frac{\dot{c}_t}{c_t} = \frac{\alpha}{\sigma}\frac{\bar{y}_t}{k_t} - \frac{\rho}{\sigma}$$

$$(4.1b) \qquad \xi_k = \frac{\dot{k}_t}{k_t} = \frac{\bar{y}_t}{k_t} - \frac{c_t}{k_t}$$

$$(4.1c) \qquad \xi_h = \frac{\dot{h}_t}{h_t} = B(1 - u_t)$$

$$(4.1d) \qquad \xi_u = \frac{\dot{u}_t}{u_t} = \frac{B(1-\alpha+\gamma)}{\alpha} - \frac{c_t}{k_t} + B\frac{\alpha-\gamma}{\alpha}u_t$$

where $\bar{y}_t = Ak_t^{\alpha-1}u_t^{1-\alpha}h_t^{1-\alpha+\gamma}$ is the usual post-optimization production function.

4.2.2 The Equilibrium Allocation of Time along the BGP

Let us now start the analysis of the main characteristics of the BGP. As in the preceding Chapter, to keep notation simple, we first define the unrestricted parameter space as $\omega \equiv (A, B, \alpha, \rho, \sigma, \gamma)$ where $\omega \in \Delta = \mathbb{R}_{++}^2 \times (0,1) \times \mathbb{R}_{++}^2 \times \mathbb{R}_+$.

Recalling the expression for u^* obtained in Chapter 1 and letting $\psi = \frac{1-\alpha+\gamma}{1-\alpha}$ again simplify the notation, we have:

Proposition 4.1 *Let the decentralized economy evolve along the BGP. Then the fraction of total non-leisure time dedicated to work is equal to:*

$$(4.2) \qquad u^* = 1 - \frac{(1-\alpha)(B-\rho)}{B[\sigma(1-\alpha+\gamma)-\gamma]}$$

Only if the parameters are restricted to the following subsets of Δ:

$$\bar{\Delta}_a^d \equiv \left\{ \omega \in \Delta^d : \rho \in (0,B), \sigma > 1 - \frac{\rho}{B\psi} \right\}$$

$$\bar{\Delta}_b^d \equiv \{\omega \in \Delta^d : \rho \in (B, B\psi), \sigma < 1 - \frac{\rho}{B\psi}, \gamma \in (\frac{(1-\alpha)(\rho-B)}{B}, \infty)\}$$

is u^* economically meaningful and is the BGP non-degenerate.

Proof By imposing $E_h^{c,d} \equiv E_h^d = 1 - \alpha$ in the general expression for working time in (1.18), it is simple to obtain the stationary value in the proposition. In order to guarantee that $u^* \in (0, 1)$, we need to jointly study the inequalities:

$$\frac{(1-\alpha)(B-\rho)}{B[\sigma(1-\alpha+\gamma)-\gamma]} < 1 \text{ (for } u^* \text{ to be positive) and:}$$

$$\frac{(1-\alpha)(B-\rho)}{B[\sigma(1-\alpha+\gamma)-\gamma]} > 0 \text{ (for } u^* \text{ to be less than one).}$$

By combining the two inequalities, we see that $u^* \in (0, 1)$ if and only if the parameters lie in the subsets identified above. By Definition 1.5, this also implies that the BGP is non-degenerate. $\square$

A first interesting feature of the decentralized solution of the ULM is, therefore, the splitting of the parameter space into two regions. In this regard, note that:

Remark *When associated with the decentralized economy, the existence of a non-degenerate BGP implies that when the subjective discount rate is low (high), the inverse of the intertemporal elasticity of substitution is high (low). Furthermore, in $\bar{\Delta}_b^d$, σ cannot be made larger than 1. The lower floor for the externality in $\bar{\Delta}_b^d$ prevents σ from becoming negative.*

The two subsets $\bar{\Delta}_a^d$ and $\bar{\Delta}_b^d$ are not connected, but are separated by the surface:

$$\bar{\Delta}_s^d \equiv \left\{\omega \in \Delta^d : \rho = B, \sigma = 1 - \frac{\rho}{B\psi}, \gamma \in (\frac{(1-\alpha)(\rho-B)}{B}, \infty)\right\}$$

such that if $\omega \in \bar{\Delta}_s^d$ there are infinitely many BGPs.

To simplify the notation, henceforth, we will jointly indicate as $\bar{\Delta}^d = \bar{\Delta}_a^d \cup \bar{\Delta}_b^d$ the union of the two relevant sub-sets of Δ^d guaranteeing the non-degeneracy of the BGP.

Another important characteristic of the partitioned parameter space (particularly useful later on in the Chapter) is the following:

Corollary 4.1 *Since $1 - \rho/(B\psi)$ can be either larger or smaller than α, $\alpha - \sigma$ can be either positive or negative in both subsets $\bar{\Delta}_b^d$ and $\bar{\Delta}_a^d$. However, for $\alpha - \sigma > 0$ in $\bar{\Delta}_a^d$, γ must be lower than α.*

Proof To allow for $\alpha - \sigma > 0$, it must be that $1 - \rho/(B\psi) < \alpha$. This, in turn, implies $\rho > B(1 - \alpha + \gamma)$ which, in turn, is possible inside $\bar{\Delta}_a^d$ only when $\gamma < \alpha$.
$\square$

Consider, furthermore, Table 4.1, which determines in which direction u^* changes in response to variations in the parameters.

Table 4.1 Signs of partial derivatives of u^* w.r.t. the parameters

$Parameters$	$\omega \in \Delta_a^d$		$\omega \in \Delta_b^d$
	$\sigma < 1$	$\sigma > 1$	
A	NR	NR	NR
B	-	-	+
α	-	+	+
γ	-	+	+
ρ	+	+	-
σ	+	+	-

NR = Not Relevant

It appears evident from table 4.1 that:

Remark *Let $\sigma < 1$. Then the BGP value of working time is negatively (positively) affected by the preference parameters if $\omega \in \bar{\Delta}_a^d$ ($\bar{\Delta}_b^d$). There is also a role for the size of σ (when larger than 1) in determining the impact of the preference parameters on u^*. Notice that the size of σ is not important when $\omega \in \bar{\Delta}_b^d$.*

A visualization of the region in the parameter space where $u^* \in (0,1)$ in the (ρ, B) space is shown in figure 4.1 below:

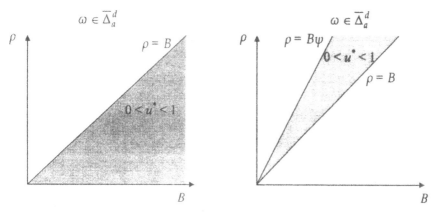

Figure 4.1 A characterization of the (ρ, B) space where $u^* \in (0, 1)$

Another interesting point of view is offered in Figure 4.2, where the values of u^* are plotted against σ, for given values of the other parameters. The vertical asymptote is at $\sigma = \frac{\gamma}{1-\alpha+\gamma}$.

A qualitatively similar behavior is obtained if we plot u^* with respect to the externality (Figure 4.3). The vertical asymptote is now at $\gamma = \frac{\sigma(1-\alpha)}{1-\sigma}$.

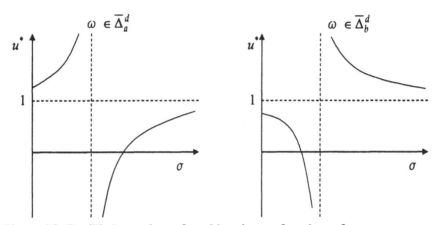

Figure 4.2 Equilibrium values of working time as functions of σ

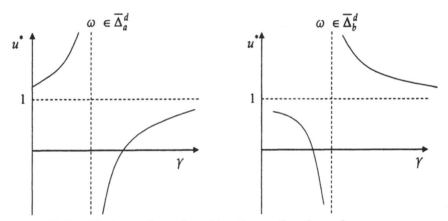

Figure 4.3 Equilibrium values of working time as functions of γ

4.2.3   *The BGP Growth Rates of the Primitive Variables*

Given u^* it becomes possible to characterize the BGP behavior of the other primitive variables of the economy.

Let us first obtain the non-degenerate BGP growth rate of the economy (in terms of goods production). We have:

Proposition 4.2 *Let $\omega \in \bar{\Delta}^d$. Then the growth rate of the economy, in terms of goods production, is positive and equal to:*

(4.3) $\xi_{\bar{y}} \equiv \xi^* = B\psi(1 - u^*) = \frac{(B-\rho)(1-\alpha+\gamma)}{\sigma(1-\alpha+\gamma)-\gamma}$

Proof Either by imposing $E_h^{c,d} = 1 - \alpha$ in the expression in (1.19) or substituting the equilibrium value of u^* from (4.2) the result in the proposition is easily obtained. ξ^* is positive by definition if $\omega \in \bar{\Delta}^d$. $\square$

Table 4.2 contains the signs of the partial derivatives of the growth rate of the economy with respect to all parameters in the two relevant subsets of $\bar{\Delta}^d$. The results in the Table are such that, in the case of a decentralized regime, the ULM implies:

Remark *Market economies characterized by larger technological parameters and lower preference parameters than other market economies enjoy higher growth rates only when $\omega \in \bar{\Delta}_a^d$. The contrary happens when $\omega \in \bar{\Delta}_b^d$.*

Table 4.2 Signs of partial derivatives of ξ^* w.r.t. the parameters

Parameters	$\omega \in \Delta_a^d$	$\omega \in \Delta_b^d$
A	NR	NR
B	$+$	$-$
α	$+$	$-$
γ	$+$	$-$
ρ	$-$	$+$
σ	$-$	$+$

NR = Not Relevant

Jointly taking into consideration Tables 1 and 2, notice also that:

Remark *There is a region of the parameter space where increases of u^* due to larger values of α and γ do not translate into a lower BGP growth rate of the economy. Such a region can be characterized as $\{\omega \in \bar{\Delta}_a^d : \sigma > 1\}$.*

The identification of the growth rate of the market economy opens the doors to a number of other crucial results. In particular, recalling Lemma 1.1, we have:

Corollary 4.2 *Let $\omega \in \bar{\Delta}^d$. Then, the BGP growth rates of consumption, physical capital and human capital in the market economy are linked by the following*:

$$(4.4) \qquad \xi_c^* = \xi_k^* = \psi\xi_h^* = \xi^* = \frac{(B-\rho)(1-\alpha+\gamma)}{\sigma(1-\alpha+\gamma)-\gamma} > 0$$

Proof Given Lemma 1.1, the extension of the results in Proposition 4.2 to the growth rates of k_t, c_t and h_t is straightforward. $\square$

4.2.4 *The Stationary Values of the* Great Ratios

As shown in Chapter 2, another easy-to-characterize implication of the economy evolving along the BGP, in both cases of the centralized and decentralized solution of the ULM, is the stationarity of the average consumption $(c/k)^* = m^*$, of the average production $(\bar{y}/k)^* = n^*$ and of the weighted ratio between the stocks of the two capital goods $(kh^{-\psi})^* = p^*$ (the *Great Ratios*, in our terminology).

We can now add that, in the case of the market economy:

Proposition 4.3 *Let* $\omega \in \bar{\Delta}^d$. *Then the average consumption, the average goods production and the weighted ratio between physical and human capital are positive and respectively equal to:*

(4.5) $\left(\frac{c}{k}\right)^* = m^* = \frac{(1-\alpha)}{\alpha}\left[\frac{B\psi(\sigma-\alpha)+\rho(\alpha-\gamma)}{\sigma(1-\alpha+\gamma)-\gamma}\right] > 0$

(4.6) $\left(\frac{\bar{y}}{k}\right)^* = n^* = \frac{1}{\alpha}\left[\frac{B\sigma(1-\alpha+\gamma)-\gamma\rho}{\sigma(1-\alpha+\gamma)-\gamma}\right] > 0$

(4.7) $\left(\frac{k}{h^\psi}\right)^* = p^* = \left(\frac{A\alpha}{\rho+\sigma\xi^*}\right)^{\frac{1}{1-\alpha}} u^* > 0$

Proof The values in proposition can be obtained by substituting the expressions for the decentralized growth rate of the economy and for u^* [in (4.3) and (4.2)] into the general expression for m^*, n^* and p^* in (2.2), (2.3) and (2.4). The positiveness of the ratios along a non-degenerate BGP is obvious for (4.7) when $\omega \in \bar{\Delta}^d$. The signs of (4.5) and (4.6) is also obvious after a little algebra. $\square$

The evaluation of the signs of the partial derivative of the Great Ratios with respect of the parameters is shown in Table 4.3.

Table 4.3 Signs of partial derivatives of m^*, n^* and p^* w.r.t. the parameters

	m^*				n^*		p^*	
	$\bar{\Delta}^d_a$		$\bar{\Delta}^d_b$		$\bar{\Delta}^d_a$	$\bar{\Delta}^d_b$	$\bar{\Delta}^d_a$	$\bar{\Delta}^d_b$
	$\gamma > \alpha$	$\gamma < \alpha$	$\gamma > \alpha$	$\gamma < \alpha$				
A	NR	NR	NR	NR	NR	NR	$+$	$+$
B	$+$	$+$	$-$	$-$	$+$	$-$	$-$	$+$
α	NO	NO	NO	NO	NO	$-$	NO	NO
γ	$+$	$+$	$+$	$+$	$-$	$+$	$+$	$+$
ρ	$-$	$+$	$+$	$-$	$-$	$+$	$+$	$-$
σ	$-$	$+$	$+$	$-$	$-$	$+$	$+$	$-$

NR = Not Relevant;
NO = Not Obvious.

From Table 4.3, a number of useful details on the BGP properties of the decentralized economy can be learnt. Besides the difficult-to-read effects of variations of the share of physical capital and the relevance of the size of A only for the p^* ratio, what we have found is that, if $\omega \in \bar{\Delta}^d_a$, economies with larger preference parameters are characterized by lower BGP levels of the average product and higher values of the "weighted" ratio between the two forms of accumulation.

The effect of higher preference parameters on the level of average consumption depends on the relative size of the externality with respect to the share of physical capital. Moreover, in the same region of the parameter space, a higher level of the efficacy index in the learning sector implies higher values of the average product and consumption but lower values of the weighted ratios between physical and human capital. The externality always has a positive effect on the BGP values of the Great Ratios except for the n^* ratio.

The $\omega \in \bar{\Delta}_b^d$ case shows the usual sign inversion for all the parameters, bar the externality.

4.2.5 *The BGP Behavior of the* Adjoint Variables

We can now proceed to complete the characterization of the long-run properties of the decentralized economy by investigating the BGP behavior of the adjoint variables, namely broad output, the interest rate, the level of wages and the saving rate.

We start the analysis by the study of the BGP behavior of broad output. In Chapter 2, we have already discussed some general features of this variable applying to both the centralized and decentralized economy. In particular, we have found that, along a non-degenerate BGP, broad output's growth rate asymptotically equates the growth rate of the (narrow) economy. We have also found that the $\left(\frac{y^T}{\bar{y}}\right)^*$ index is larger than one and inversely related to u^*.

Let us now complete the knowledge of this variables by studying its decentralized-economy specific properties. We start by considering the BGP value of the $\left(\frac{y^T}{\bar{y}}\right)^*$ index. We thus arrive at the following:

Proposition 4.4 *In a decentralized economy, the BGP ratio between broad output/goods production is equal to*:

$$(4.8) \qquad \left(\frac{y^T}{\bar{y}}\right)^* = \frac{B\psi(\sigma-\alpha)+\alpha\rho}{B\psi(\sigma-1)+\rho}$$

Proof The stationary value of the ratio is obtained by substituting the BGP value of working time in (4.2) into the general formula obtained in Corollary 2.1. After little algebra we find the value in proposition. □

Let us now continue the description of the specific BGP properties of the adjoint variables for the market economy by studying the behavior of the interest rate (or rental compensation of physical capital) r_t. We already know, from Proposition 1.1, that the interest rate equals the marginal productivity of capital, $MPK = \partial y^f/\partial k_t = \alpha\bar{y}/k_t$. We also know from Proposition 2.5 that the interest rate is positive and stationary along a non-degenerate BGP.

In the case of a decentralized economy, we also have the following:

Proposition 4.5 *Let the decentralized economy evolve along a non-degenerate BGP. Then, the rental price of capital equals*:

(4.9) $r^* = \frac{\gamma\rho - B\sigma(1-\alpha+\gamma)}{\gamma-\sigma(1-\alpha+\gamma)}$

Proof The value of the interest rate in proposition can be easily obtained by substituting the growth rate of the decentralized economy (equation 4.3) in the expression (2.9). $\square$

Let us now investigate the BGP market-economy specific properties of the wage rate. We already know, from Chapter 2, that for the level of wages to display a positive BGP growth, there must be a positive externality. We also know that the wages growth rate is "small" with respect to the overall growth rate of the economy. In this particular case of the decentralized economy, we also obtain:

Proposition 4.6 *Let the market economy evolve along a non degenerate BGP. The wage rate will then grow according to the following*:

(4.10) $\left(\frac{\dot{w}}{w}\right)^* = \gamma\frac{(\rho-B)}{\gamma-\sigma(1-\alpha+\gamma)} > 0$

Proof By substituting the growth rate of the decentralized economy (equation 4.3) in the expression (2.10) and re-arranging terms, we obtain the result in the proposition. $\square$

To complete the picture of the economy, we need now to determine the BGP properties of the saving rate. We can state that, in a decentralized economy:

Proposition 4.7 *Let the market economy evolve along a non-degenerate BGP. Then, the saving rate has the following stationary value*:

(4.11) $s^* = \frac{\alpha(\rho-B)(1-\alpha+\gamma)}{\gamma\rho-\sigma B(1-\alpha+\gamma)}$

and remains between 0 and 1.

Proof By substituting the growth rate of the market economy in the expression (2.12), the result in the proposition is obtained with some straightforward algebra. The boundaries of s^* can be obtained by studying the limits of $\frac{\alpha(\rho-B)(1-\alpha+\gamma)}{\gamma\rho-\sigma B(1-\alpha+\gamma)}$ in the parameter space, under $\omega \in \bar{\Delta}^d$. $\square$

We conclude the analysis of the BGP properties of a decentralized economy with Table 4.4, showing the effect of parameter variations on the BGP behavior of the adjoint variables.

Many interesting details emerge from this analysis. First of all, we find that, besides the transversal irrelevance of A and the difficulty (in same cases) of determining the general effect of variations of α without restricting the other parameters, the technological parameters have a positive impact and the preference parameters a negative impact on the rental compensation of capital, the saving rate and the growth rate of wages only when $\omega \in \bar{\Delta}_a^d$. Signs are inverted if we cross the boundaries between the $\bar{\Delta}_a^d$ and $\bar{\Delta}_b^d$ regions of the parameter space. Signs are much more mixed for the $\left(y^T/\bar{y}\right)^*$ index, where the inverse of the intertemporal elasticity of substitution plays a role in determining the impact of the externality.

Table 4.4 Signs of partial derivatives of the *adjoint variables* w.r.t parameters

	$\left(y^T/\bar{y}\right)^*$			r^*		ξ_w^*		s^*	
	Δ_a^d		Δ_b^d	Δ_a^d	Δ_b^d	Δ_a^d	Δ_b^d	Δ_a^d	Δ_b^d
	$\sigma < 1$	$\sigma > 1$							
A	NR	NR	NR	NR	NR	NR	NR	NR	NR
B	-	-	+	+	-	+	-	+	-
α	NO	+	-	+	-	+	-	NO	NO
γ	-	+	+	+	-	+	-	+	-
ρ	-	-	+	-	+	-	+	-	+
σ	+	+	-	-	+	-	+	-	+

NR = Not Relevant
NO = Not Obvious

4.3 Transitional Dynamics from the Local Point of View

4.3.1 *A Stationarizing Transformation of the Dynamic Laws*

To derive information on the properties of the decentralized economy evolving along off-balanced trajectories, let us first consider the possibility of reducing the actual dimension of the relevant system of dynamic laws through the stationarizing transformation already introduced in general terms in Chapter 2. Recalling that p_t and m_t respectively indicate the "weighted ratio" between the two capital goods and the average consumption, we first prove that:

Proposition 4.8 *The motion generated by the decentralized solution of the ULM implies the following three-dimensional system of first-order differential equations*:

$$(4.12a) \qquad \frac{\dot{p}_t}{p_t} = A u_t^{1-\alpha} p_t^{\alpha-1} - m_t - B\psi\,(1 - u_t)$$

$$(4.12b) \qquad \frac{\dot{u}_t}{u_t} = B\frac{1-\alpha+\gamma}{\alpha} - m_t + B\frac{\alpha-\gamma}{\alpha}u_t$$

$$(4.12c) \qquad \frac{\dot{m}_t}{m_t} = A\phi u_t^{1-\alpha} p_t^{\alpha-1} + m_t - \frac{\rho}{\sigma}$$

where $\phi = \frac{\alpha - \sigma}{\sigma}$. The system possesses an interior steady-state characterized by the stationary values in (4.7), (4.2) and (4.5).

Proof By substituting $E_h^{c,d} = 1 - \alpha$ in the system in (2.15i), the laws driving the equilibrium dynamics are as stated in Proposition. Solving the system when $\frac{\dot{m}_t}{m_t} = \frac{\dot{u}_t}{u_t} = \frac{\dot{p}_t}{p_t} = 0$, we obtain the steady-state values in (4.7), (4.2) and (4.5) which have been shown to be unambiguously positive if $\omega \in \bar{\Delta}^d$. $\square$

We can see below that the strategy of inducing a stationarizing transformation of the original system proves particularly useful in the case of the decentralized economy. As a matter of fact, the analysis in this lowered dimension enables us to infer the fundamental properties of the transition towards the BGP without having to resort to complicated mathematical arguments in higher dimensions.

4.3.2   The Local Stability Properties of the Fixed Point in $\mathbb{R}^3$

As already discussed in Chapter 2, the local stability analysis exploits the Hartman-Grobman theorem[38] on the topological equivalence, in the neighborhood of the steady-state, between linearized and full dynamics. In particular, the Hartman-Grobman theorem proves that the full dynamics in (4.12i) is topologically equivalent, in the neighborhood of the fixed point, to the associated linearized dynamics:

$$(4.13) \qquad \begin{bmatrix} \dot{p}_t \\ \dot{u}_t \\ \dot{m}_t \end{bmatrix} = J^* \left(p^*, u^*, m^* \right) \begin{bmatrix} p_t - p^* \\ u_t - u^* \\ m_t - m^* \end{bmatrix}$$

where $J(x^*)$ is the Jacobian matrix, evaluated at the steady-state. When governed by the flow of the linearized system (4.13), the motion is much easier to treat than in the original full setting (4.12i). The analysis, however, has the drawback of being only valid in a small neighborhood of the steady-state.

We start the discussion by determining the form of the Jacobian associated with the decentralized dynamics. Recalling that if $\omega \in \bar{\Delta}^d$, $\eta = \frac{\alpha - \gamma}{\alpha}$, we are able to show that:

Lemma 4.1 *The Jacobian matrix associated with the linearized decentralized dynamics is:*

$$J^* = \begin{bmatrix} J_{11}^* & \frac{p^*}{u^*}\left(B\psi u^* - J_{11}^*\right) & -p^* \\ 0 & B\eta u^* & -u^* \\ \phi\frac{J_{11}^* m^*}{p^*} & -\phi\frac{J_{11}^* m^*}{u^*} & m^* \end{bmatrix}$$

where:

(4.14) $J_{11}^* = -\frac{1-\alpha}{\alpha} \frac{\gamma\rho - B\sigma(1-\alpha+\gamma)}{\gamma - \sigma(1-\alpha+\gamma)} < 0$

Proof J^* in proposition has the same form as in equation (2.16). The value of J_{11}^* can be obtained by substituting in the general expression in (2.17) the BGP value of the growth rate of the market economy. The sign of J_{11}^* is negative if $\omega \in \bar{\Delta}^d$. $\square$

As already discussed in Chapter 2, the characteristic equation associated with J^* cannot be factorized (in general terms).[39] Therefore, unless we study special regions of the parameter space, we cannot determine the signs and forms of the eigenvalues in qualitative terms. The Routh-Hurvitz criterion is a precious tool in cases like these. In fact, we know that the number of roots of the Jacobian with negative real parts will be equal to the number of sign variations in the scheme:

$$-1; \; Tr; \; G = -N + Det/Tr; \; Det$$

where Tr, N and Det are, respectively, the trace, sum of principal minors and determinant of J^*. In our specific case, we preliminarily show the following:

Lemma 4.2 *Let ω either belong to $\bar{\Delta}_a^d$ or $\bar{\Delta}_b^d$. Then Tr is positive when $\gamma < 2\alpha$ and negative when $\gamma > 2\alpha$. N is negative when $\gamma > \alpha$. Det is always negative if $\omega \in \bar{\Delta}_a^d$ and always positive if $\omega \in \bar{\Delta}_b^d$.*

Proof The expressions for Tr, N and Det are respectively $Tr = J_{11}^* + B\eta u^* + m^* = B\frac{(2\alpha-\gamma)}{\alpha}u^*$, $Det = J_{11}^* u^* m^* Q$ (where $Q = \frac{\sigma(1-\alpha+\gamma)-\gamma}{\sigma(1-\alpha)}$) and $N = J_{11}^* m^* + \frac{(\alpha-\gamma)}{\alpha}(Bu^*)^2$. The signs of Det and Tr are easily evaluated under both $\bar{\Delta}_a^d$ and $\bar{\Delta}_b^d$. The same applies for N in cases where $\gamma > \alpha$. $\square$

With these results in hand, we are now ready to prove the main proposition:

Proposition 4.9 *Recall Lemmas 4.1 and 4.2. First let $\omega \in \bar{\Delta}_a^d$. Then J^* has one eigenvalue with a negative real part and two eigenvalues with positive real parts. The equilibrium is locally unique. Let, conversely, $\omega \in \bar{\Delta}_b^d$. Then:*

a) *if $\gamma \in (\frac{(1-\alpha)(\rho-B)}{B}, \alpha)$, there exist two subsets, $\bar{\Delta}_{b1}^d$ and $\bar{\Delta}_{b2}^d$, such that when $\omega \in \bar{\Delta}_{b1}^d$, J^* has one eigenvalue with a positive real part and two eigenvalues with negative real parts, and when $\omega \in \bar{\Delta}_{b2}^d$, J^* has three eigenvalues with positive real parts. So, there is either a continuum of equilibria converging towards the steady-state or no stable transitional paths at all;*

b) *if $\gamma > \alpha$, J^* has one eigenvalue with a positive real part and two eigenvalues with negative real parts. There is again a continuum of equilibria converging towards the steady-state.*

---

[39]Unless we consider the exogenous growth case, in the special region of the parameter space where $\alpha = \sigma$.

Proof The results in the proposition are obtained by a standard application of the Routh-Hurvitz criterion. The number of sign variations of the scheme -1; Tr; $G(\gamma)$ $= -N + Det/Tr$, Det; is given below:

Values of γ	$\bar{\Delta}_a^d$	$\bar{\Delta}_b^d$
	Number of Variations	Number of Variations
$\gamma > 2\alpha$	2	1
$\alpha < \gamma < 2\alpha$	2	1
$\gamma < \alpha$	2	Either 1 or 3

□

The stability properties associated with a decentralized regime have many interesting implications. Let us start from the $\bar{\Delta}_a^d$ region of the parameter space. Here, the BGP is determinate since, when $\omega \in \bar{\Delta}_a^d$, the result of saddle-path convergence towards the steady-state is preserved. Given the initial conditions, this means that there is only one possible level of the growing variables at each point in time; economies starting with the same endowments are bound to end up with the same asymptotic levels of physical and human capital. Conversely, economies starting with different $k(0)$ and $h(0)$ will continue to preserve this initial difference.

The other regions of the parameter space allow for both indeterminacy and instability. The economic interpretation of the instability result is quite simple: when there are no equilibrium paths converging to the steady-state, the control variables have to be chosen so that the economy starts already at the fixed point. Any perturbation of this position implies (locally) a progressively increasing distance from the steady-state. In terms of the original $\mathbb{R}^4$ dimension, this means that the economy evolves along the BGP from the very beginning.

The possibility of there being a *continuum* of equilibria is most interesting. Since there are an infinite number of equilibrium paths to be followed (each of which starting from different initial positions), the characteristic of the BGP (in terms of the long-run levels of the original non-stationary variables) will essentially depend on the specific history of a generic economic system. Provided that technology and preferences are the same, the very underlying implication of the indeterminacy result is that cultural, institutional and political factors are key variables in selecting one or another particular equilibrium path and therefore the long-run levels of welfare. Indeed, some countries might well end up much better off than others, despite them being initially similar in wealth and endowments.

4.3.3   *A Numerical Investigation of the Characteristics of the Eigenvalues*

As we saw in the preceding sub-section, the Routh-Hurvitz criterion allows to infer the sign pattern of the real parts of the eigenvalues associated with a complicated (linearized) dynamic system. Yet, although it is undoubtedly a powerful tool in local analysis, it is totally mute on the existence and behavior of the imaginary parts of the roots. This missing information is, however, relevant for the analysis. In particular, in terms of the implications for the bifurcation theory, it is interesting to understand whether, for instance, the fixed point in $\mathbb{R}^3$ is a saddle-focus or a saddle-node (when indeterminacy is present). This is not only because the transition can be shown to occur with or without oscillating motion, but also because other interesting mathematical phenomena are associated with a saddle-focus (but not with a saddle-node).

In the specific case of the ULM, the boundaries of the parameter space where the eigenvalues begin to exist in the imaginary axis depend on a large number of parameters and are computationally heavy to identify. However, by exploiting some relationships among the parameters of control, the characteristic equation can be simplified enough to make it possible to numerically draw an (approximate) bi-dimensional map showing a partition of the parameter space where the associated eigenvalues are either real or complex-conjugate. This numerical work also gives a partition of the parameter space where there prevails instability, indeterminacy or uniqueness of the equilibrium.

Notice also that:

Remark *The results discussed here below, numbered as Interesting Results, have been always qualitatively confirmed by extensive numerical simulations.*

Consider first that, through simple algebra, we can show that:

i) $Bu^* = J_{11}^* + m^*$;

ii) $\frac{2\alpha - \gamma}{\alpha} = \eta + 1$.

Therefore, the characteristic equation in (2.18) can be re-written as:

$$(4.15) \qquad -\kappa^3 + (\eta + 1)\left(J_{11}^* + m^*\right)\kappa^2 - \left[J_{11}^* m^* + \eta\left(J_{11}^* + m^*\right)^2\right]\kappa +$$

$$+ J_{11}^* m^*\left(J_{11}^* + m^*\right)Q = 0$$

where $Q = \frac{\sigma(1-\alpha+\gamma)-\gamma}{\sigma(1-\alpha)} = \psi - \frac{\gamma}{\sigma(1-\alpha)}$ is a useful monotonic transformation of σ (varying from $-\infty$ to ψ when $\omega \in \bar{\Delta}^d$, for given values of the other parameters). Now, fixing an arbitrary distance between J_{11}^* and m^*, we try to identify the way the eigenvalues behave for varying $Q(\sigma)$ and η.

Let us first plot the imaginary parts of the eigenvalues in a specific case. As it is possible to see from Figure 4.4, the parameter space where the complex conjugate eigenvalues emerge is tangent to the planes given by the $Q(\sigma) = 0$ and $Q(\sigma) = 1$ intersections.

Consider now the real parts of the eigenvalues in the same parameter space used to create Figure 4.4. To make the picture clearer, we only plot the real parts of the eigenvalues when negative. The crucial information which is possible to visualize from Figure 4.5 is that there is a region on the left of both $Q(\sigma) = 0$ and $\eta = 0$ where none of the real parts of the eigenvalues is negative

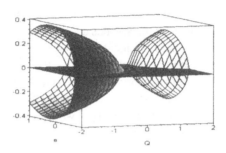

Figure 4.4 The imaginary roots in the space $(Q(\sigma), \eta, Im(\kappa))$

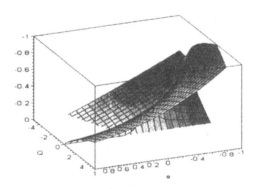

Figure 4.5 Re(κ_i) in the space $(Q(\sigma), \eta, Re(\kappa)\in(-1, 0))$

Putting together the information on the behavior and characteristics of the eigenvalues, we are able to produce an approximate bi-dimensional map (Figure 4.6) where the parameter space is partitioned into regions where there is instability, indeterminacy or uniqueness of the equilibrium both in presence of real and complex conjugate eigenvalues. In Figure 4.6, the RE and CE symbols stand respectively for Real Eigenvalues and Complex Eigenvalues. Recall that $Q(\sigma)$ is equal to zero when $\sigma = \frac{\gamma}{1-\alpha+\gamma}$ [40] and to one when also $\sigma = 1$.

---

[40] This section of the parameter space belongs to $\bar{\Delta}_s^d$, the surface of separation between $\bar{\Delta}_a^d$ and $\bar{\Delta}_b^d$.

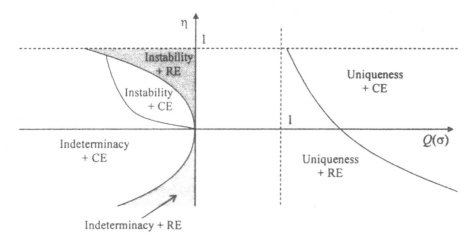

Figure 4.6 The characteristics of the eigenvalues in the $(Q(\sigma), \eta)$ space

Consider, however, that:

Interesting Result 4.1 *The instability regions emerge, other things equal, only for small enough values of $|J_{11}^*|$ with respect to m^*, which, in turn, occurs for sufficiently high values of α and/or for $\gamma\rho$ sufficiently close to $B\sigma\,(1 - \alpha + \gamma)$.*[41]

The observation of the partitioned parameter space in Figure 4.6 provides valuable insights into the wealth of dynamics which can be generated by the decentralized solution of the ULM. Consider, in particular the following:

Interesting Result 4.2 *There exist regions of the parameter space at the left of $Q(\sigma) = 0$ where a small variation of η (given $Q(\sigma)$) determines a change of sign of two roots (in presence of complex-conjugate eigenvalues).*[42]

As we will show in the following sub-section, the singularity theory presents this phenomenon as a pre-requisite for the existence of closed orbits Hopf-bifurcating from the steady-state.

Other results we will find useful in the following sub-sections of this Chapter are the following. Consider first:

Interesting Result 4.3 *The negative eigenvalue can never be larger than m^* in modulus.*

---

[41]Consider furthermore, that the instability region is located in a region of the parameter space where $Q(\sigma)>0$ and $\eta > 0$. This region corresponds to the $\bar{\Delta}_{b2}^d$ set in Proposition 4.9.

[42]The curve separating the instability and indeterminacy area is the projection, in the η and $Q\,(\sigma)$ space, of the $G\,(\gamma) = -N + \frac{Det}{Tr} = 0$ equation. Cf. Lemma 4.6 below.

Observe, in Figure 4.7, the typical behavior of the eigenvalues in the real axis, for a given parameter configuration inside $\bar{\Delta}_a^d$.

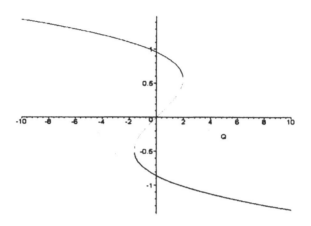

Figure 4.7 The real parts of the eigenvalues in the $(Q(\sigma), \kappa)$ space

Finally, recalling the characteristic polynomial in (4.15) and considering that Q is positive in the region of the parameter space where the steady-state in the $\mathbb{R}^3$–reduced dimension is saddle-path stable we find that:

Interesting Result 4.4 *The negative eigenvalue has a maximum at $Q(\sigma)= 0$. Moreover, it is monotonically decreasing in $Q(\sigma)$.*

4.3.4   *The Economic Forces Governing Transition in the Market Economy*

The extensive numerical simulations in the preceding sub-section have shown that the stability/instability results in the case of decentralized dynamics can be obtained with both real and complex-conjugate eigenvalues.

We can now try to obtain further results on the properties of the transition in the neighborhood of the steady-state.[43] In particular, we would now like to determine the slopes of the functions linking the control and control-like variables of the model to the state of the economy. However, since the explicit form of the eigenvalues is not available, this poses a difficult task.

Proposition 4.9 is helpful here. We know that, when $\omega \in \bar{\Delta}_a^d$ (we are on the right of the $Q(\sigma) = 0$ line in Figure 4.6), we can only have one (real) negative eigenvalue and two eigenvalues with positive real parts.[44] We also know that there exists a sub-region of $\bar{\Delta}_a^d$ where all the eigenvalues are real.

Recall now the functions obtained in (2.19*i*), tying the control and control-like

---

[43]The original material for this sub-section is in [16].

[44]Since the complex conjugate eigenvalues always come in pairs, only the eigenvalues with positive real parts can exist in the imaginary axis.

variables u_t and m_t to the state of the economy in terms of the p_t ratio in case of all-real eigenvalues:

(4.16a) $\frac{u^* - u(0)}{u^*} = \phi \delta_1 \frac{p^* - p(0)}{p^*}$

(4.16b) $\frac{m^* - m(0)}{m^*} = \phi \delta_2 \frac{p^* - p(0)}{p^*}$

where $\delta_1 = \frac{J_{11}^* m^*}{\Gamma(\eta B u^* - \kappa_1)}$ and $\delta_2 = \frac{J_{11}^*}{\Gamma}$. $\Gamma = \frac{J_{11}^* m^* \phi}{B \eta u^* - \kappa_1} - m^* + \kappa_1$, $\eta = \frac{\alpha - \gamma}{\alpha}$ and $\phi = \frac{\alpha - \sigma}{\sigma}$, simplify the notation.

The functions in (4.16i) can be used to infer further information on the behavior of the decentralized economy in the neighborhood of the steady-state in case of saddle-path stability/instability. It is important, in this respect, to point out that, as already discussed in Chapter 2, the equations in (4.16i) cannot be considered as "policy functions" as in the case of the centralized solution of the model; since now we are dealing with a case of decentralization, we will be referring to them as to (modified) *equilibrium functions* linking the control variables to the state of the economy expressed in terms of the p_t variable. The term "modified" applies since the standard way of representing the functions linking the control variables and the state of the economy is through the *level* of the control variable and the *level* of the state variable.

Consider first the case of a small inverse of the intertemporal elasticity of substitution. We can prove the following:

Proposition 4.10 *Let* $\omega \in \bar{\Delta}_a^d$ *with* $\phi > 0$. *The equilibrium functions will then be upward sloping.*

Proof A $\phi > 0$, when $\omega \in \bar{\Delta}_a^d$, implies, by Corollary 4.1, $\gamma < \alpha$ and therefore a positive sign for η and $B \eta u^* - \kappa_1$. This, in turn, entails a negative Γ. Considering that J_{11}^* is always negative, this implies a positive sign for both δ_1 and δ_2. Therefore, since $Sign \frac{u^* - u(0)}{u^*} = Sign \frac{m^* - m(0)}{m^*} = Sign(\phi) > 0$ the result in the proposition is follows. $\square$

The evaluation of the slopes of the equilibrium functions in cases where $\phi < 0$ is much less straightforward. Since now $\omega \in \bar{\Delta}_a^d$, the externality has no upper bound and η might become negative. As a consequence, the signs of $B \eta u^* - \kappa_1$ and Γ are both indeterminate. However, we can still say something on the slopes of the functions linking, in equilibrium, the state of the economy to its control part. To do that, however, we need to recall some of the results obtained in the preceding subsection through extensive numerical simulations. In particular, we need recalling Interesting Result 4.4, by which we have shown that the negative eigenvalue has a maximum at $Q(\sigma) = 0$. This means that if $B \eta u^* - \kappa_1$ is positive at $Q(\sigma) = 0$, it is so for any other value of $Q(\sigma)$ in the positive axis.

Therefore, since the results here below can only be proved in the regions where

Interesting Result 4.4 applies, we define as $\tilde{\Delta}_a^d \in \bar{\Delta}_a^d$ this special parameter configuration.[45]

Now, let ϑ be a positive constant. Taking into account that $(\eta - 1)$ is $< 0 \; \forall \eta \in \bar{\Delta}_a^d$, and making use of $J_{11}^* + m^* = Bu^*$, we have:

Lemma 4.3 *Let $\omega \in \tilde{\Delta}_a^d$. Then, regardless of the size of the externality factor, $B\eta u^* - \kappa_1$ is positive.*

Proof By solving the characteristic equation in (4.15) for $Q(\sigma) = 0$, we find that the negative eigenvalue has the maximum value:

$$\kappa_1(Q(\sigma) = 0) = \tfrac{1}{2} \left\{ Bu^* (\eta + 1) - [(\eta - 1)^2 (Bu^*)^2 - 4J_{11}^* m^*]^{1/2} \right\} =$$

$$= \tfrac{1}{2} \left\{ Bu^* (\eta + 1) + (\eta - 1) Bu^* - 2\vartheta \right\} = B\eta u^* - \vartheta$$

Therefore, $B\eta u^* - \kappa_1(Q(\sigma) = 0) = \vartheta > 0$. $\square$

Notice that, as already explained:

Remark *By Interesting Result 4.4, $B\eta u^* - \kappa_1$ is a fortiori positive for any $Q(\sigma) > 0$.*

The last step is the study of the sign of Γ. Consider first that:

(4.17) $\Gamma = \dfrac{-\kappa_1^2 + \kappa_1(m^* + B\eta u^*) + J_{11}^* m^* \phi - B\eta m^* u^*}{B\eta u^* - \kappa_1}$

is a quadratic expression in κ_1 (with a negative second derivative). Therefore, again for $\omega \in \tilde{\Delta}_a^d$:

Lemma 4.4 Γ *changes sign at* $\bar{\kappa}_{1,2} = \dfrac{m^* + B\eta u^*}{2} \mp \tfrac{1}{2} \left\{ [m^* - B\eta u^*]^2 + 4\phi J_{11}^* m^* \right\}^{1/2}$
$\bar{\kappa}_2$ is always positive and can be discarded. $\bar{\kappa}_1$ is negative only if:

i) $-\dfrac{J_{11}^*}{m^*} > \dfrac{\eta}{\eta - \phi}$ *when $\eta - \phi > 0$*

ii) $-\dfrac{J_{11}^*}{m^*} < \dfrac{\eta}{\eta - \phi}$ *when $\eta - \phi < 0$*

Proof Since, by Lemma 4.3, $B\eta u^* - \kappa_1$ is always positive, we only need to concentrate on the sign change of the numerator of Γ in (4.17). By solving for κ_1, we obtain the roots in the Lemma. $\bar{\kappa}_2$ is always positive and can be discarded. $\bar{\kappa}_1$ is negative if $-\dfrac{J_{11}^*}{m^*} > \dfrac{\eta}{\eta - \phi}$ when $\eta - \phi > 0$ and $-\dfrac{J_{11}^*}{m^*} < \dfrac{\eta}{\eta - \phi}$ when $\eta - \phi < 0$ which, in turn, implies the last part of the proposition. $\square$

---

[45] We have not been able to derive Interesting Result 4.4 analytically. However, since the results obtained in the preceding sub-section have always be confirmed by extensive numerical simulations, we believe that $\tilde{\Delta}_a^d$ coincides with $\bar{\Delta}_a^d$.

Now, considering that $0 < -\frac{J^*_{11}}{m^*} < 1$, we also have:

Lemma 4.5 *Let* $\omega \in \tilde{\Delta}^d_a$. *Then, regardless of the externality,* Γ *is negative.*

Proof The change of sign of Γ occurs inside the relevant parameter space, $\tilde{\Delta}^d_a$ only if it can be shown that $\bar{\kappa}_1$ is lower than $\kappa_1(Q(\sigma) = 0)$ in Lemma 4.3. Notice that $\bar{\kappa}_1 - \kappa_1(Q(\sigma) = 0)$ stays positive for all $-\frac{J^*_{11}}{m^*} > \frac{(\eta+\phi)(1+\phi)}{\eta(1+\phi)-\phi}$. Let us distinguish the proof for cases *i*) and *ii*) of Lemma 4.4:

case *i*) - since in this case $\frac{\eta}{\eta-\phi} > \frac{(\eta+\phi)(1+\phi)}{\eta(1+\phi)-\phi}$, $\bar{\kappa}_1$ is negative only when $\bar{\kappa}_1 - \kappa_1(Q(\sigma) = 0)$ is positive. By Lemma 4.3 this can occur only outside the $\omega \in \tilde{\Delta}^d_a$ region of the parameter space.

case *ii*) - we now have two distinct possibilities, according to whether γ is smaller or larger than σ. In the former case, $\eta(1+\phi) - \phi$ is positive while in the latter is negative. However, since in the former case $(\eta+\phi)(1+\phi)$ is never positive, $\frac{(\eta+\phi)(1+\phi)}{\eta(1+\phi)-\phi} < 0$, $\bar{\kappa}_1 - \kappa_1(Q(\sigma) = 0)$ is always positive. We are again outside the $\omega \in \tilde{\Delta}^d_a$ region of the parameter space. Conversely, if $\eta(1+\phi) - \phi$ is negative, again we have $\frac{\eta}{\eta-\phi} > \frac{(\eta+\phi)(1+\phi)}{\eta(1+\phi)-\phi}$ and we cannot have, at the same time, a change of sign of $\bar{\kappa}_1 - \kappa_1(Q(\sigma) = 0)$ and a negative value of $\bar{\kappa}_1$. $\square$

In Figures 4.8*i*, the numerator of Γ is represented in both cases of negative and positive values of $\bar{\kappa}_1$.

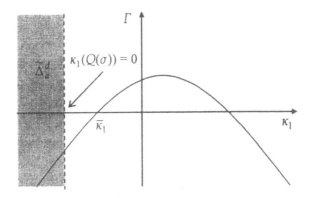

Figure 4.8a The numerator of Γ when $\bar{\kappa}_1$ is negative

We are now ready to prove the main proposition for the case of a large inverse of the intertemporal elasticity of substitution.

Proposition 4.11 *Recall Lemmas* 4.3, 4.4 *and* 4.5 *and let* $\omega \in \tilde{\Delta}^d_a$. *If* $\phi < 0$, *the* *functions in (4.16i), linking in equilibrium the state of the economy to its control part, will be downward sloping.*

Proof Since Γ is negative and $B\eta u^* - \kappa_1$ positive, $\frac{\phi J^*_{11} m^*}{(\eta B u^* - \kappa_1)\Gamma}$ and $\frac{\phi J^*_{11}}{\Gamma}$ are both negative and the result in the proposition can be derived. $\square$

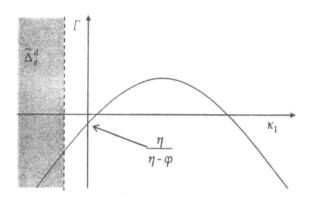

Figure 4.8b The numerator of Γ when $\bar{\kappa}_1$ is positive

Consider that, however, unlike in the efficient case, the ratio between the impact coefficients tying together the state of the economy to its control part will not necessarily be one. As a matter of fact, the elasticity $\frac{\phi J^*_{11} m^*}{\Gamma(B\eta u^* - \kappa_1)}$ can well diverge from $\frac{\phi J^*_{11}}{\Gamma}$. In particular, if $\frac{m^*}{B\eta u^* - \kappa_1} > (<)1$, the impact of a shock on working time can be higher (lower) than the impact on average consumption.

Again recalling the properties of the eigenvalues in the case of decentralized dynamics, the following can be proved:

Corollary 4.3 *Let $\omega \in \bar{\Delta}^d_a$. Then, if $\gamma > \alpha$, a shock altering the state of the economy has a higher impact on working time than on the average consumption.*

Proof Since $-\kappa_1 < m^*$ and η is negative, $B\eta u^* - \kappa_1 < m^*$. The elasticity of impact of a $\frac{p^* - p(0)}{p^*}$ whatsoever is therefore higher for working time. $\square$

As in Chapter 3, let now $D_x = \frac{x^* - x(0)}{x^*}$ represent the deviation of the generic variable x from its steady-state position. Figures 4.9i below show the linear approximations of the equilibrium functions for working time and average consumption in both cases of positive and negative ϕ. The graphs depict the special situation in which the elasticity of impact for u_t is higher than that for m_t. Of course, the two possible orientations are separated by the following critical case:

Corollary 4.4 *When $\alpha = \sigma$, the equilibrium functions linking working time and* *average consumption to the state of the economy are locally horizontal at the zero value.*

Proof From (4.16a) and (4.16b), we can clearly see that if $\phi = 0$, $m^* - m(0) = u^* - u(0) = 0$. $\square$

It becomes now interesting to evaluate the economic implications of Propositions 4.10 and 4.11. They imply that if $\sigma > \alpha$, in presence of a shock reducing physical capital (or increasing human capital), working time rises above its BGP level and so does consumption; therefore, according to Definition 2.1, the BGP value of p_t is mainly restored through the *wage rate effect* (higher work effort). Conversely, if $\sigma < \alpha$, working time falls below its BGP level and cannot contribute to restore k_t. In this case, since consumption is below its BGP level, the BGP value of p_t is restored through higher savings (*consumption-smoothing effect*).

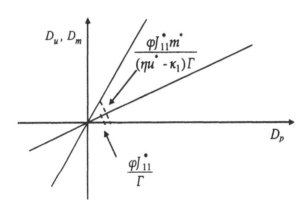

Figure 4.9a Equilibrium functions in case of $\phi > 0$

It is also certainly true that the results in Propositions 4.10 and 4.11 only give an idea of the qualitative behavior of the economy in the $\mathbb{R}^3$ reduced space without unveiling the dynamic evolution of the primitive variables of the model in response to a shock perturbing the state of the economy. Nevertheless, the connection between the signs of the initial values of the variables and ϕ also allows us to examine some implications for the modality by which the variables in the original dimension respond to a shock.

In fact, recalling Definition 2.2, we can prove that:

Proposition 4.12 *Let $\alpha > \sigma$. The decentralized economy belongs to the paradoxical case. The economy belongs to the normal case if $\alpha < \sigma$. If $\alpha = \sigma$, human capital behaves as an exogenous variable.*

Proof Let us prove the case of $\alpha > \sigma$. A shock implying higher (lower) levels of k_t or lower (higher) levels of h_t determines a rise (fall) in the p_t ratio which, in turn, from Proposition 3.10, implies a jump (fall) in $u(0)$. As a consequence, the transitional growth rate of human capital is below (above) its BGP level. Asymptotically, therefore, the normalized levels of both capital stocks are below (above) their initial value, determining a *paradoxical case*. The opposite happens when $\alpha < \sigma$ (*normal case*). When $\alpha = \sigma$, any shock perturbing p_t leaves working time unaffected. The result is that human capital behaves as an exogenous variable, continuing undisturbed in its pre-shock trajectory. $\square$

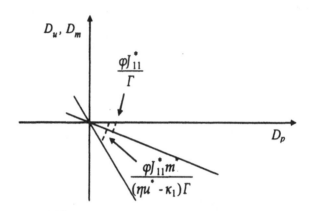

Figure 4.9b Equilibrium functions in case of $\phi < 0$

4.3.5   *The Emergence of Deterministic Cycles*

We have already observed in Interesting Result 4.2 that a structural change in the sign of the real parts of two complex eigenvalues (pre-requisite for the emergence of orbits Hopf-bifurcating from a stationary point) may possibly occur if we cross the surface of separation between the regions with indeterminacy and instability at the left of the $Q(\sigma) = 0$ line in Figure 4.6. From Proposition 4.9, we know that these regions correspond, respectively, to the $\bar{\Delta}_{b1}^d$ and $\bar{\Delta}_{b2}^d$ sets. For notational convenience we will henceforth indicate as $\bar{\Delta}_{Hopf}^d$ the union of these regions of the parameter space.

Before starting the analysis, recall from Lemma 4.2 and Proposition 4.9 that both Tr and Det are positive if $\omega \in \bar{\Delta}_{Hopf}^d$. Therefore, by using the externality as the bifurcation parameter, we can prove the following propedeutical result:

Lemma 4.6 *Let $\omega \in \bar{\Delta}_{Hopf}^d$. Then, there exists at least one value of $\gamma = \bar{\gamma}$, such that J^* has one real eigenvalue (equal to Tr) and a pair of purely imaginary roots (equal to $\pm \operatorname{Im} \sqrt{\frac{Det}{Tr}}$).*

Proof According to Vieta's theorem, J^* has a simple pair of purely imaginary eigenvalues when $G(\gamma) = -N + \frac{Det}{Tr} = 0$. Since $G(\gamma)$ can be made positive or negative by varying γ (cf. Proof of Proposition 4.9), the continuity argument implies that there must exist at least one value $\bar{\gamma}$ such that $G(\gamma) = 0$. Furthermore, by substituting $N = \frac{Det}{Tr}$, we can solve the characteristic equation (4.15) to obtain a positive eigenvalue equal to Tr and two complex-conjugate eigenvalues equal to $\pm \mathrm{Im} \sqrt{\frac{Det}{Tr}}$. $\square$

Moreover:

Lemma 4.7 *The derivative of the real part of the complex conjugate eigenvalues with respect to γ, evaluated at $\gamma = \bar{\gamma}$, is not zero.*

Proof To prove that $\frac{d \,\mathrm{Re}\, \kappa(\gamma)}{d\gamma}$ cannot be zero at the bifurcation point, we follow the strategy developed in Benhabib and Miyao [4] (p. 595) and show that $Sign \frac{d \,\mathrm{Re}\, \kappa(\gamma)}{d\gamma} = Sign \frac{dG(\gamma)}{d\gamma}$. Since $G(\gamma)$ is a four-degree polynomial in the externality factor, changing sign at $\gamma = \bar{\gamma}$ (see proof of Lemma 4.6), the derivative cannot be zero at the bifurcation points. $\square$

We are now in the position to prove the main proposition on the existence of periodic solutions. Since system (4.13i) is smooth, we can state the following:

Proposition 4.13 *There exists a surface of periodic solutions on the centre manifold. At least some of these solutions satisfy the TVC in the original dimension.*

Proof The existence part of the Hopf Bifurcation Theorem (see [29] for references) and Lemmas 4.6 and 4.6, imply that the dynamic system (4.12i) generates undamped oscillations if the externality is in the neighborhood of $\bar{\gamma}$, on the left or on the right. When transposing the results in Proposition to the original system , however, we cannot ignore the TVC. It is important, in fact, to check whether the paths forming periodic orbits can also be accepted as equilibrium trajectories for the original system. We already know that at $\gamma = \bar{\gamma}$ we have the conventional BGP which, as shown in Proposition 1.6, satisfies the TVC. In the case of the periodic orbits, by continuity, we can keep the limits not far from $-Bu^*$ if γ is sufficiently close to $\bar{\gamma}$. $\square$

4.3.6 The Stability Properties of the Orbits

The proof that Hopf cycling can occur when the decentralized motion is restricted to the center manifold opens the doors to a number of other interesting results. Since the Hopf bifurcation theorem tells us that the orbits can arise either on the left or on the right of the critical value of the bifurcation parameter, it is worth establishing which case holds for the ULM.

Consider first the possible cases occurring when the derivative $\frac{d \,\mathrm{Re}\, \kappa(\gamma)}{d\gamma}$ is positive. In this case, the orbits can generally be either attracting or repelling. In the case of an attracting orbit, trajectories on the centre manifold are locally attracted by this orbit, which becomes a limit set. In this so-called *sub-critical case*, the stationary point is an unstable solution meaningless from an economic point of view (unless the initial conditions happen to coincide with the stationary value).

Conversely, if the cycle is unstable in the dynamics of the centre manifold, the steady state is attracting. In this case, defined as *super-critical*, the cycle is economically relevant only if the initial conditions imply that the economy fluctuates right from the beginning. There exist standard analytical procedures which can be used to unveil the stability properties of the orbits in specific cases: in particular, it can be proved that the orbit structure near the bifurcation point (on the vector field restricted to the centre manifold) depends on up-to-third order derivatives on the non-linear terms. Going back to the decentralized dynamics of the ULM, after extensive numerical simulations, we can state the following:

Proposition 4.14 *The closed orbits Hopf-bifurcating from the steady-state can be either sub-critical or super-critical according to whether σ is high or low inside $\omega \in \bar{\Delta}_{Hopf}^d$.*

Proof The study of stability in the emerging orbits on the centre manifold, can be performed by calculating the sign of up-to-third order derivatives of the non-linear part of the system, when written in normal form. The procedure involves a number of algebraically heavy coordinate transformations in the linear part of system (4.13i) and also requires the center manifold to be approximated. The algebra is available in [22]. Since, by numerical simulations, this derivative changes sign according to whether the inverse of the elasticity of intertemporal substitution, σ, approaches its lower or its upper bound inside $\bar{\Delta}_{Hopf}^d$, the periodic solutions may be either attracting or repelling. $\square$

What the numerical simulations show is that it is σ, the inverse of the elasticity of substitution which dictates the direction of the motion on the centre manifolds. This means that for high values of σ, cases of sub-criticality seem to prevail The orbit itself is repelling and a "corridor of stability" exists around the centre-manifold-stable steady state. The region outside the orbit, on the contrary, is unstable and all the trajectories are repelled.

When σ is "small" with respect to its feasible region, we will get the opposite super-critical case, i.e. while the steady state becomes completely unstable and not economically relevant (unless $p(0) = p^*$), the orbits become limit cycles under the dynamics of the centre manifolds. Notice, however, that:

Remark *Given that, under $\omega \in \bar{\Delta}_{Hopf}^d$, the third real root is always positive, the results obtained on the stability of the orbits are only valid on the centre manifold since in $\mathbb{R}^3$ the orbits are always unstable.*

4.4   Transitional Dynamics from the Glocal Point of View

4.4.1   *Restricted Parameter Space and the Laws of Motion*

As discussed on several occasions, the only way of obtaining explicit trajectories in the case of competitive economy (without resorting to the linearization of the dynamics) is by imposing $\alpha = \sigma$. In this case, the system of dynamic laws (4.12*i*) reduces to the following:

$$(4.18a)\qquad \frac{\dot{p}_t}{p_t} = A u_t^{1-\alpha} p_t^{\alpha-1} - m_t - B\psi\left(1 - u_t\right)$$

$$(4.18b)\qquad \frac{\dot{u}_t}{u_t} = B\frac{1-\alpha+\gamma}{\alpha} - m_t + B\frac{\alpha-\gamma}{\alpha}u_t$$

$$(4.18c)\qquad \frac{\dot{m}_t}{m_t} = m_t - \frac{\varrho}{\sigma}$$

The BGP value of working time is now $u^* = 1 - \frac{B-\rho}{B(\alpha-\gamma)}$ and the non-degeneracy of the BGP is guaranteed when the two inequalities $\frac{B-\rho}{B(\alpha-\gamma)} < 1$ (for u^* positive) and $\frac{B-\rho}{B(\alpha-\gamma)} > 0$ (for u^* less than one) are satisfied. In particular, by combining the two inequalities, we see that $u^* \in (0,1)$ if and only if the parameters lie in the following non-connected subsets of $\bar{\Delta}^d$:

$$\bar{\Delta}^d_{a,\sigma=\alpha} \equiv \left\{\omega \in \Delta^d : \sigma = \alpha, \rho \in \left(B\left(1 - \alpha + \gamma\right), B\right), \gamma \in (0, \alpha)\right\}$$

$$\bar{\Delta}^d_{b,\sigma=\alpha} \equiv \left\{\omega \in \Delta^d : \sigma = \alpha, \rho \in \left(B, B\left(1 - \alpha + \gamma\right)\right), \gamma \in (\alpha, \infty)\right\}$$

The surface of separation is now:

$$\bar{\Delta}^d_{s,\sigma=\alpha} \equiv \left\{\omega \in \Delta^d : \rho = B, \gamma = \alpha\right\}$$

It is also important here to recall from Corollary 4.1 that the restriction $\alpha = \sigma$ can be imposed in both the $\bar{\Delta}^d_a$ and $\bar{\Delta}^d_b$ regions of the parameter space.

To simplify the notation, $\bar{\Delta}^d_{\sigma=\alpha} \equiv \bar{\Delta}^d_{a,\sigma=\alpha} \cup \bar{\Delta}^d_{b,\sigma=\alpha}$ will henceforth indicate the region of the parameter space where the motion admits a non-degenerate BGP, under the restriction $\sigma = \alpha$.

4.4.2   *The Solution of the Simplified Differential Equations*

To obtain explicit trajectories solving the dynamic system (4.18*i*) we can preliminarily observe that:[46]

Lemma 4.8 *Let* $\bar{\Delta}^d_{\sigma=\alpha}$. *If so, a solution for the average consumption is* $m_t = \frac{\varrho}{\sigma}$ $\forall t$.

---

[46]The reference for the original material developed for this section is in [19].

Proof By solving the differential equation in system (4.18c) we have the result in the lemma. □

Notice that, regardless of the state of the economy, $m(0) = m_t = \frac{\rho}{\sigma}$. Therefore:

Remark *Lemma 4.8 gives global validity to the results in Corollary 4.4 on the slopes of the equilibrium functions for working time and average consumption in the neighborhood of the steady-state when $\alpha = \sigma$.*

Now, with Lemma 4.8 in hand, positing $\chi = \frac{u^* - u(0)}{u(0)}$ and recalling that $\eta = \frac{\alpha - \gamma}{\alpha}$, we can also prove the following:

Proposition 4.15 Let $\omega \in \bar{\Delta}^d_{s,\sigma = \alpha}$. Then, the fraction of total time dedicated to work evolves according to the logistic equation:

(4.19) $u_t = \frac{u^*}{1 + \chi e^{\bar{\upsilon} \eta u^* t}}$

Any $u(0) \in (0,1)$ converges towards u^*. Conversely, if $\omega \in \bar{\Delta}^d_{a,\sigma = \alpha}$, $u_t = u^* \ \forall t$.

Proof Recall the result in Lemma 4.8. Then the dynamic equation (4.18b) can also be solved to produce an explicit trajectory for u_t. If $\omega \in \bar{\Delta}^d_{a,\sigma = \alpha}$, the externality is small and $\eta > 0$. Therefore, the only way of ensuring the convergence of u_t to u^* is by imposing $u(0) = u^*$. Conversely, when $\omega \in \bar{\Delta}^d_{b,\sigma = \alpha}$, the externality is large ($\eta < 0$) and for any feasible $u(0)$ we will see asymptotic convergence to the steady-state value. □

Proposition 4.15 is rather interesting: if, in the simplified region of the parameter space here under investigation, the externality is large, we have a clear understanding of the indeterminacy results proved for the general case; any $0 < u(0) < 1$ implies logistic convergence towards u^*. Conversely, if the externality is low, we have the conventional exogenous growth case, where there is only one feasible initial value of the control variable u_t which enables the economy to converge towards the steady-state.

Notice also that, given a parameter configuration inside $\bar{\Delta}^d_{b,\sigma = \alpha}$:

Remark *The evolution of the working time variable depends solely on its initial position.*

Now, with the explicit trajectory of working time in hand, we can also solve the differential equation governing the evolution of human capital. We thus have:

Proposition 4.16 *Recall Lemma 4.8 and Proposition 4.15. The law of evolution of human capital has the following form:*

(4.20) $h_t = h(0)e^{\xi_h^* t}\left(\frac{1+\chi e^{B\eta u^* t}}{1+\chi}\right)^{\frac{\alpha}{\alpha-\gamma}}$

Proof With the knowledge that $u_t = \frac{u^*}{1+\chi e^{B\eta u^* t}}$ the result in the proposition is a simple matter of solving the differential equation for human capital. $\square$

As discussed above, if the externality is small, human capital behaves as an exogenous variable; η is positive and, as stated above, χ has to be set to zero. Conversely, when the externality is large, η is negative and any choice of a feasible χ leads to a permanent deviation of the trajectory of human capital from its exogenous growth path. Consider in particular that, recalling the use of the normalized variables in Definition 2.2:

Corollary 4.5 *Let, in presence of indeterminacy,* $\chi = \frac{u^*-u(0)}{u(0)} \neq 0$. *Then, the asymptotic normalized value of human capital,* $\tilde{h}$, *depends on the initial value of working time according to*:

(4.21) $\tilde{h} = h(0)\left(\frac{u(0)}{u^*}\right)^{\frac{\alpha}{\alpha-\gamma}}$

Proof Simply calculating the limit of (4.20) and dividing for the asymptotic growth rate of human capital, we obtain the expression in (4.21). $\square$

Corollary 4.5 will be very useful in the following sub-section where we compare the behavior of two decentralized economies, similar in the parameter configuration, but characterized by an initially-different partition of time between its two uses (production and learning).

Finally, letting $\Xi = A(1-\alpha)h(0)^{1-\alpha+\gamma}u(0)^{\frac{\alpha(1-\alpha+\gamma)}{\alpha-\gamma}}(u^*)^{-\frac{\gamma}{\alpha-\gamma}}$ we can also obtain the law of the evolution of physical capital (and consequently, of consumption):

Proposition 4.17 *Let* $\omega \in \bar{\Delta}^d_{s,\sigma=\alpha}$. *Then, the accumulation of physical capital occurs according to*:

(4.22) $k_t = e^{-\rho/\alpha t}\left[\Xi \int \frac{e^{(1-\alpha)n^* t}}{1+\chi e^{B\eta u^* t}}dt + \_C\right]^{\frac{1}{1-\alpha}}$

where $\_C$ *is a constant of integration. Consumption is equal to* $\frac{\rho}{\alpha}k_t \forall t$.

Proof Substituting (4.19) and (4.20) into (4.1b) the results in the proposition can be obtained. The law for consumption follows from $m_t = \frac{c_t}{k_t} = \frac{\rho}{\alpha}$. $\square$

As was the case for the explicit optimal law of evolution of average consumption in Chapter 3, the explicit solution for physical capital (and consumption) depends on the parameter configuration. In particular, we need to fix the value of $\frac{\gamma}{\gamma-\alpha}$ to be able to solve the integrals in the expressions for physical capital and consumption.

4.4.3   *Indeterminacy* Versus *Exogenous Growth*

Before attempting to obtain further information on the explicit form of the trajectories of physical capital and consumption by assigning values to the parameters, we ought first to clearly distinguish the analysis of the transitional properties of the model in the exogenous growth case, from the study of the infinite equilibrium paths emerging in presence of the indeterminacy phenomenon.

Although both situations are obtained under the same parameter restriction ($\sigma = \alpha$), we have that:

Remark *The exogenous growth case can be generated inside the entire* $\bar{\Delta}^d_{\sigma=\alpha} = \bar{\Delta}^d_{a,\sigma=\alpha} \cup \bar{\Delta}^d_{b,\sigma=\alpha}$ *parameter space. Conversely, the possibility of indeterminacy is feasible only when* $\omega \in \bar{\Delta}^d_{b,\sigma=\alpha}$.

Furthermore, in the exogenous growth case working time always equals its long-run value ($u_t = u^*$, $\forall\, t$) whereas, in the latter there exists a *continuum* of feasible initial conditions of working time such that $u(0) \in (0,1) \neq u^*$. In the light of this, if we are interested in closely examining the implications on the equilibrium exogenous growth case, χ has to be fixed to zero; conversely, if we are interested in the evaluation of the properties of the decentralized economy converging towards the BGP from a different initial value of working time, χ cannot be considered zero.

Of course, the two dynamic possibilities have very different economic implications. To have a first understanding of this, consider two generic economies (economy a and economy b) characterized by the same parameter configuration. Consider, in particular, the ratio between the time paths for human capital:

$$(4.23) \qquad \frac{(h_t)_a}{(h_t)_b} = \frac{h(0)_a}{h(0)_b}\left(\frac{1+\chi_a e^{B\eta u^* t}}{1+\chi_a}\frac{1+\chi_b}{1+\chi_b e^{B\eta u^* t}}\right)^{\frac{\alpha}{\alpha-\gamma}}$$

and let us discuss the implications when the economies both belong to the exogenous growth case or, alternatively, to a situation where indeterminacy prevails.

The exogenous growth case implies the following:

Proposition 4.18 *Let two economies,* a *and* b, *be characterized by the same parameter configuration. Then, the two economies can only diverge in their growth experience if initially endowed with different levels of human capital.*

Proof If the economies belong to the exogenous growth case $u(0) = u^*$. Therefore, $\chi_a = \chi_b = 0$. It is clear that the ratio in (4.23) differs from 1 only if $h(0)_a \neq h(0)_b$. Furthermore, if $h(0)_a = h(0)_b$ the time paths of physical capital (Proposition 4.17) for the two economies coincide and so do the time paths of consumption. $\square$

Conversely, when indeterminacy is present, recalling also Corollary 4.5:

Proposition 4.19 *Given a parameter configuration inside* $\omega \in \bar{\Delta}^d_{b,\sigma=\alpha}$, *economies characterized by the same initial endowment of human capital can still diverge in their growth experience if* $u(0)_a \neq u(0)_b$. *The growth paths associated with a lower* $u(0)$ *lead to asymptotically higher levels of human capital. This, in turn, also implies higher levels of physical capital and consumption.*

Proof It is evident from the expression in (4.21) that when starting from the same $h(0)$, the ratio between two alternative trajectories of human capital differs from one only if $u(0)_b \neq u(0)_a$. In particular, recalling that $\alpha - \gamma < 0$, economy a will enjoy a higher asymptotic level of human capital if $u(0)_a < u(0)_b$. Given the BGP stationarity of the p^* and m^* ratios, a lower $u(0)$ also implies higher asymptotic levels of physical capital and consumption. □

The following graphical analysis, depicting typical time paths generated under the two circumstances of exogenous growth and indeterminacy, makes clear these issues. Consider first Figures 4.10a and 4.10b, comparing typical trajectories of physical capital for two economies initially characterized by the same endowment. The solid lines represent the evolution of physical capital in an (unperturbed) economy in the case of exogenous growth (case of $u(0) = u^*$).

The broken lines, conversely, represent the trajectories of physical capital for economies respectively characterized by a low and high initial fraction of total time spent in working.[47] The values of the parameters for these simulations are detailed in the following sub-section.

The graphs look particularly interesting.

First of all, as it was formally proved in Proposition 4.19, the graphs above show that lower (higher) initial working time imply higher (lower) asymptotic levels of physical capital. Furthermore, they also give some indications of what it can happen to real economies characterized by a different initial partition of time between its two uses *and* levels of human capital.

Let, in particular, country a be initially less endowed in terms of human capital than country b. It then follows that, in presence of indeterminacy:

Corollary 4.6 *Given a common parameter configuration inside* $\omega \in \bar{\Delta}^d_{b,\sigma=\alpha}$, *country a can overtake initially better endowed country b (in terms of human capital, physical capital and consumption levels), provided it happens that:*

$$\frac{u(0)_a^{\frac{\alpha}{\gamma-\alpha}}}{h(0)_a} < \frac{u(0)_b^{\frac{\alpha}{\gamma-\alpha}}}{h(0)_b}.$$

---

[47]In the specific case depicted, the initial values of working time for the broken lines are, respectively, $u(0) = 0.6$ for Figure 4.10a and $u(0) = 0.96$ for Figure 4.10b. Along the exogenous growth case $u(0) = u^* = 5/6$.

Proof The asymptotic value of the ratio in (4.21) between the alternative trajectories of human capital in country a and b is larger than 1 when the threshold in the corollary is trespassed. Again because of the BGP stationarity of the p^* and m^* ratios, physical capital and consumption also have to be asymptotically higher. $\square$

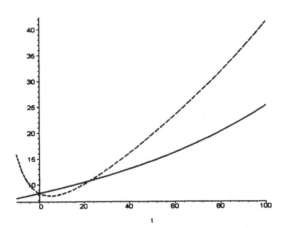

Figure 4.10a Time paths for k_t in presence of indeterminacy ($u(0) < u^*$)

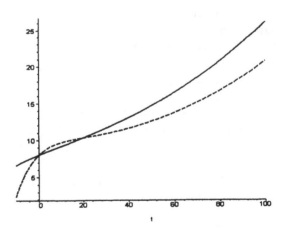

Figure 4.10b Time paths for k_t in presence of indeterminacy ($u(0) > u^*$)

Corollary 4.6 opens the doors to interesting dynamic phenomena such as the overtaking and the falling behind of market economies. In this respect, consider Figures 4.11a and 4.11b, depicting these possibilities in specific cases.[48] The parameter configuration is detailed in the following sub-section. The solid lines represent the

---

[48]The initial values for the broken lines are $h(0) = 0.75$ and $u(0) = 0.5$ in Figure 4.11a and $h(0) = 1.25$ and $u(0) = 0.96$ in Figure 4.11b.

evolution of physical capital in an (unperturbed) economy under conditions of exogenous growth. The broken lines, conversely, represent the trajectories of physical capital for economies, respectively, initially less and better endowed. Notice that the time paths simulated in these Figures only differ from those in the above Figures for their initial condition.

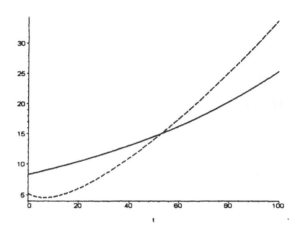

Figure 4.11a A case of overtaking in presence of indeterminacy

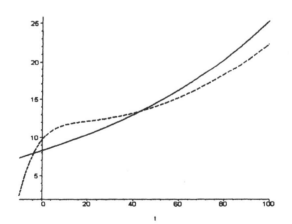

Figure 4.11b A case of falling behind in presence of indeterminacy

The economic interpretation of the two Figures is clear. In Figure 4.11a, an initially less endowed market economy, presenting a relatively low fraction of working time (and, consequently, a relatively high level of time devoted to the learning sector) overtakes, in finite time, an initially better endowed economy, which, conversely, devotes a lower fraction of its total time to learn. The opposite occurs in Figure 4.11b.

4.4.4   The Market Economy Belonging to the Exogenous Growth Case

Let us now investigate more in depth the characteristics of the exogenous growth case. We have, in this case, a substantial simplification of the structure of the differential equations. In particular, as already discussed in Corollary 4.5, $\chi = 0$ and the value of Ξ in (4.22) is now simply:

$$(4.24) \quad \Xi = A\left(1 - \alpha\right) h\left(0\right)^{1-\alpha+\gamma} \left(u^*\right)^{1-\alpha}$$

Therefore, recalling Proposition 4.16 and 4.17, in a market economy finding itself along an exogenous growth case:

Proposition 4.20 *Human capital evolves according to the simple law $h_t = h\left(0\right) e^{\xi_h^* t}$. The law of motion of physical capital can be solved in explicit terms to produce a time path of the form*:

$$(4.25) \quad k_t = e^{-\frac{\rho}{\alpha}t} \left(\Xi \frac{e^{(1-\alpha)(\rho/\alpha+\xi^*)t}}{(1-\alpha)(\rho/\alpha+\xi^*)} + k(0)^{1-\alpha} - \frac{\Xi}{(1-\alpha)(\rho/\alpha+\xi^*)}\right)^{1/(1-\alpha)}$$

where Ξ is as in (4.24). Consumption is $c_t = \frac{\rho}{\alpha} k_t$.

Proof The substantial simplification introduced in the time paths in (4.20) and (4.22) by $\chi = 0$ leads to the results in the proposition. □

The economic implications of the explicit laws in Proposition 4.20 provide a wealth of powerful insights into the asymmetric effects of human and physical capital accumulation (at least in the particular region of the parameter space here under investigation). In particular, we find very interesting to show that, by extracting Ξ and $(1 - \alpha)\left(\rho/\alpha + \xi^*\right) = \left(1 - \alpha\right) n^*$, the explicit laws for physical capital and consumption can be written in the following forms:

$$(4.26a) \quad k_t = \left[\frac{Ah(0)^{1-\alpha+\gamma}(u^*)^{1-\alpha}}{n^*}\right]^{1/(1-\alpha)} e^{\xi^* t} \left(1 + \mu e^{-(1-\alpha)n^* t}\right)^{1/(1-\alpha)}$$

$$(4.26b) \quad c_t = \left[\frac{Ah(0)^{1-\alpha+\gamma}(u^*)^{1-\alpha}}{n^*}\right]^{1/(1-\alpha)} \frac{\rho}{\alpha} e^{\xi^* t} \left(1 + \mu e^{-(1-\alpha)n^* t}\right)^{1/(1-\alpha)}$$

where $\mu = \frac{n^* - n(0)}{n(0)}$. Therefore, quite surprising:

Remark *The analytical formulation of the explicit paths of consumption and physical capital accumulation have exactly the same form of the optimal evolution of consumption and physical capital in equations (3.19a) and (3.19b).*

Of course, needless to say, since u^*, n^* and ξ^* differ in the market economy with respect to the optimal benchmark, c_t and k_t are governed by different control parameters. Despite this, as in the optimal case, the competitive dynamics in the exogenous case may present U-shaped trajectories for consumption and physical capital. We find, in fact:

Corollary 4.7 *Let the economy be characterized by a relative excess of physical capital. Then, if $n(0) < \frac{\ell}{\alpha} = m(0)$, the levels of consumption and physical capital initially decrease, dip to a minimum at $t = -\frac{\ln[\alpha\xi^*/(\rho\mu)]}{(1-\alpha)n^*}$ and then start growing again. A shock decreasing the endowment of physical capital (or increasing human capital) only allows for monotonically increasing levels of consumption.*

Proof Let us prove the corollary for the explicit law of consumption. The time derivative changes sign at $\xi^* = \mu e^{-(1-\alpha)n^* t}[n^* - \xi^*]$. Since $n^* = \frac{\alpha\xi^* + \rho}{\alpha}$, the term inside square brackets becomes $\frac{\ell}{\alpha} = m(0) > 0$. By calculating logarithms, the value of t at which the derivative changes sign can be retrieved. Since the change of sign of the derivatives must occur in positive time, in order to actually observe a reduction in level of consumption, the shock has to be made large enough so that $\alpha\xi^*/(\rho\mu) < 1$. Considering that $\mu = \frac{n^* - n(0)}{n(0)} = \frac{(\alpha\xi^* + \rho)/\alpha}{n(0)} - 1$, this further implies that $n(0) < \frac{\ell}{\alpha}$. $\square$

A further consequence is that, in the light of Definition 2.2:

Corollary 4.8. *The asymptotic values of human capital, physical capital and consumption only depend on $h(0)$ (and not on $k(0)$).*

Proof These results are made evident by the analytical form of equations (4.26a) and (4.26b). $\square$

A Numerical Study of the Exogenous Growth Case Our objective here is to complete the simulation of the transitional behavior of a decentralized economy under conditions of exogenous growth. In order to also allow for the comparisons developed in the preceding sub-section, the parameters are chosen such that trajectories can be simulated both along the exogenous growth case and in presence of indeterminacy. Therefore, we shall concentrate on the case of $\gamma/(\gamma - \alpha) = 2$.[49] To allow for easy-to-solve equations, we also fix $A = 1$, $\alpha = \sigma = 0.25$, $\gamma = 0.5$, $B = 0.04$, $\rho = 25B/24$. With the values for the parameters thus set, the long-run growth rate of the economy is $0.0\bar{1}$. The implied BGP value of the fraction of total time dedicated to work is $5/6$. The BGP value of the weighted ratio between physical and human capital $p^* = \left(\frac{k}{h^\psi}\right)^* = \left(\frac{\rho + \alpha\xi^*}{\alpha A}\right)^{\frac{1}{\alpha-1}} u^*$ is around 8.3.

In reference to the values of the parameters, notice also that:

---

[49] As already remarked in sub-section 4.4.3, although the externality in this case is above the share of physical capital and therefore outside the $\bar{\Delta}^d_{a,\sigma=\alpha}$ region of the parameter space, we can still generate an exogenous growth case, by simply imposing $u(0) = u^*$.

Remark *The qualitative results obtained in this sub-section with the chosen parameter configuration have generalized to any other arbitrary case we have tried.*

We proceed now with a parallel study of the two arbitrary cases of an economy presenting a half and double initial value of the p_t ratio with respect to its BGP level. The unperturbed economy is normalized at $h(0) = 1$ and $k(0) = 8.3$. In order for $m(0) = \frac{\ell}{\alpha} \cong 0.167$, the initial value of consumption (for the unperturbed economy) has to be fixed at $c(0) \cong 1.39$. In all figures below, dotted lines represent the evolution of the unperturbed economy, the broken ones the case with lower $p(0)$, and the solid lines the case with a higher $p(0)$.

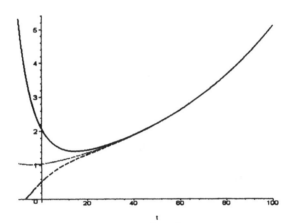

Figure 4.12a Consumption for different $k(0)s$

In Figures 4.12a and 4.12b, the trajectories of consumption and physical capital are simulated (for the above described parameter configuration) in the case of a transition caused by variations in the endowment of physical capital. The plots are rich of economic implications. Notice, in particular, the asymptotic vanishing of any effect of the shock and the convergence of the perturbed economy towards the BGP. Notice also that, in the simplified context of the exogenous case, because of the invariantness of working time, the transition simply restores the pre-shock levels of both (normalized) consumption and physical capital.

What happens to the economy when it is human capital that undergoes a sudden variation? Figures 4.13a and 4.13b depict the trajectories of consumption and physical capital under these alternative conditions. Along the lines of what is proved in Corollary 4.6, the main feature of the graphs is the evidence of a permanent effect; consumption and physical capital start from the outset to diverge from the unperturbed trajectories and to converge towards another BGP, characterized by lower or higher normalized values of the variables.

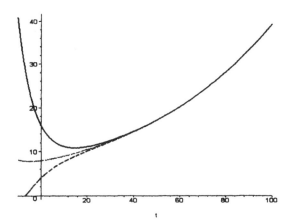

Figure 4.12b Time paths for physical capital starting from different $k(0)s$

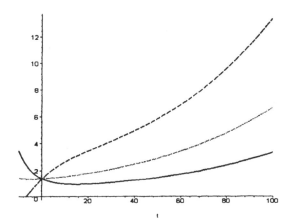

Figure 4.13a Consumption for different $h(0)s$

4.4.5 *A Numerical Analysis of Equilibrium Paths when Indeterminacy is Present*

Let us now turn our attention to the more complicated issue of studying equilibrium paths starting from different initial values of the fraction of total non-leisure time dedicated to work in presence of indeterminacy. In sub-section 4.4.3, when studying the possibility of overtaking and falling behind for market economies, we have already established some features of physical capital and consumption evolving along trajectories like these.

We now give a closer look to the primitive variables of the Uzawa-Lucas economy. Differently than in the less interesting exogenous growth case, we shall also investigate the properties of the adjoint variables and Great Ratios.

Studying indeterminacy in the context of the ULM implies dropping the restriction $\chi = 0$ used in the preceding sub-section. As a consequence, we cannot solve in explicit terms the integral in (4.17) without further restricting the parameter space.

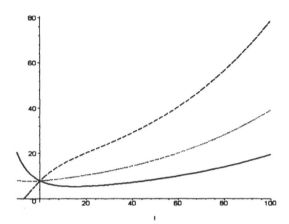

Figure 4.13b Physical capital for different $h(0)$s

To be able to draw information on the behavior of the decentralized economy in relation to the indeterminacy phenomenon, we will simulate two equilibrium paths: one starts at $u(0) = 0.96$; the other at $u(0) = 0.6$. The parameter configuration is as in sub-section 4.4.4 where, to allow for easy-to-solve equations, we have fixed $A = 1$, $\alpha = \sigma = 0.25$, $\gamma = 0.5$, $B = 0.04$, $\rho = 25B/24$. With these values for the parameters, the long-run growth rate of the economy is $0.0\bar{1}$. The implied BGP value of working time is $5/6$. The BGP value of the weighted ratio between physical and human capital is at $p^* \cong 8.3$. Since $u^* = 5/6$, the path with $u(0) = 0.96$ implies $\chi \cong -0.13$; the path with $u(0) = 0.6$ implies $\chi \cong 0.39$. In order to simplify the analysis, the initial state of the economy, in terms of weighted ratio $p_t = \frac{k_t}{h_t^\psi}$, is chosen at its long-run value $p(0) = p^* \cong 8.3$. To this end, the economy is normalized at the values of $h(0) = 1$ and $k(0) \cong 8.3$.

As is usually the case for all the numerical simulations conducted in the book:

Remark *The qualitative results obtained in this sub-section with the chosen parameter configuration have generalized to any other arbitrary values for the parameters and/or initial conditions we have tried.*

Consider first the characteristics of the convergence towards the BGP in the $u(0) = 0.6$ case. The trajectory of the fraction of total non-leisure time dedicated to work (not reported) is monotonic. In Figure 4.14, we depict the behavior of the ratios $p_t = \frac{k_t}{h_t^\psi}$ and $n_t = \frac{\bar{y}_t}{k_t}$.

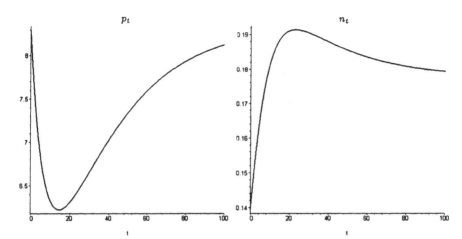

Figure 4.14 A typical time evolution of p_t and n_t when $u(0) < u^*$

Figures 4.15 and 4.16 represent the evolution of the growth rates of $\bar{y}_t$, k_t, c_t and h_t. Given the time paths represented in the Figures, it is important to distinguish the behavior of a decentralized economy starting from a lower-than-BGP value of working time in the short, medium and long run.

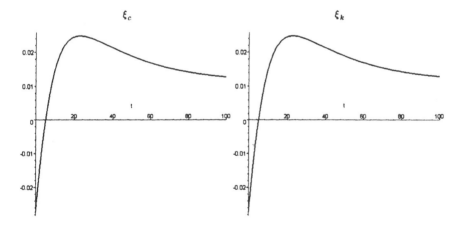

Figure 4.15 The growth rates of c_t and k_t when $u(0) < u^*$

In particular, from the short-run point of view we have:

Interesting Result 4.5 *An economy starting at $u(0) < u^*$ implies an above-BGP growth rate of human capital which, in turn, brings to an above-BGP and increasing growth rate of the economy. Conversely, the short-run growth rate of k_t (and, consequently, c_t) is not only below the BGP level, but even negative.[50] This, in turn,*

---

[50]Consider, however, that negative growth rates of physical capital and consumption are obtained only for large enough deviation of $u(0)$ from its BGP value.

implies the U-shaped behavior of p_t *and* n_t.

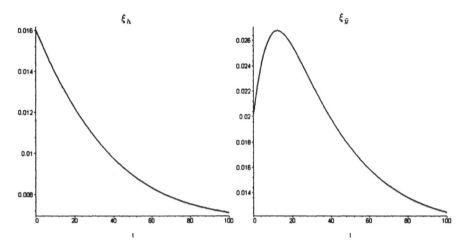

Figure 4.16 The growth rates of h_t and $\bar{y}_t$ when $u(0) < u^*$

Notice that this also implies the following:

Interesting Result 4.6 *The possibility of U-shaped trajectories for consumption and physical capital is preserved when the state of the economy is initially at its BGP level but working time is chosen well below its long-run value.*

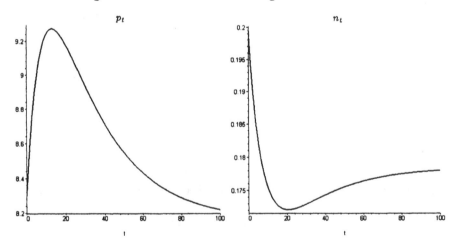

Figure 4.17 A typical time evolution of p_t and n_t when $u(0) < u^*$

Furthermore, in the medium term:

Interesting Result 4.7 *Besides the monotonic behavior of u_t and, consequently h_t, all variables reveal the potential for an over-reaction of their growth rates with respect to the BGP value. The long-run sees the asymptotic convergence of all the* *variables towards the BGP position.*

Notice also that, as proved in Proposition 4.19, all non-stationary variables have to present, asymptotically, higher normalized levels.

Let us now discuss the $u(0) = 0.96$ case. Again the convergence of working time (not reported) is monotonic. As for the $u(0) = 0.6$ case above, we first represent the evolution of the p_t and n_t variables (Figure 4.17). Figures 4.18 and 4.19 depict the growth rates of the economy and of the rest of the primitive variables of the model.

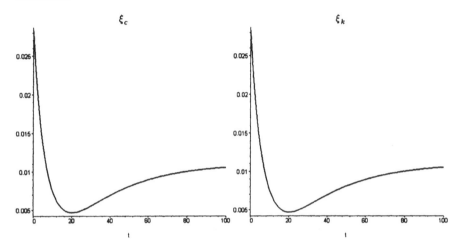

Figure 4.18 Behavior of the growth rates of c_t and k_t when $u(0) < u^*$

Our discussion on the characteristics of the transition must now be reversed *vis-à-vis* the preceding case. It is again useful to distinguish the behavior of the economy in the short, medium and long run. From the short-run point of view:

Interesting Result 4.8 *An economy starting at $u(0) > u^*$ implies a below-BGP growth rate of human capital which, in turn, brings to a below-BGP and decreasing growth rate of the economy. Conversely, the short-run growth rate of k_t (and, consequently, c_t) is well above the BGP level, but decreasing fast. This, in turn, implies the U-shaped behavior of p_t and n_t.*

Interestingly, consider now that:

Remark *Since the growth rates of physical capital and consumption are always positive, we no longer have U-shaped trajectories for these variables.*

As before, the crucial point to be highlighted in the medium term for an economy starting at $u(0) > u^*$ is the following:

Interesting Result 4.9 *Besides the monotonic behavior of u_t and, consequently h_t,* *all variables reveal the potential for an over-reaction of their growth rates with respect to the BGP value. If $u(0)$ is very far away from its BGP values the growth rate of narrow output, of physical capital and consumption almost vanish. The long-run sees the asymptotic convergence towards the BGP position of all the variables.*

As proved in Proposition 4.19, furthermore, all non-stationary variables present asymptotically lower normalized levels.

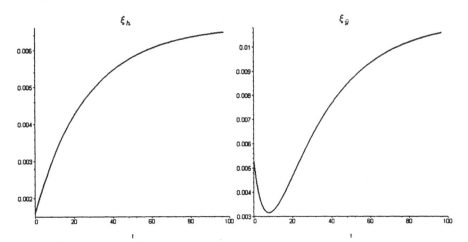

Figure 4.19 Behavior of the growth rates of h_t and $\bar{y}_t$ when $u(0) < u^*$

Summing up, the crucial characteristics obtained for the decentralized economy starting from different initial values of working time concerns the fact that if $u(0)$ is higher than its BGP level, the economy crosses from below its steady-state level (in terms of growth rates). The opposite happens if we start from a lower-than-BGP value of $u(0)$. However, these results have been obtained after assuming that the $p_t = k_t h_t^{-\psi}$ ratio is initially at the BGP value.

What happens if we allow an economy to converge towards the BGP starting from an initial position which is far away from its balanced position in terms of state variables? By letting $p(0)$ vary, through further numerical simulations, we also have the following interesting:

Interesting Result 4.10 *Let $u(0) > u^*$. There will then exist a threshold initial value of $\bar{p}(0)$, such that, if $p(0) > \bar{p}(0)$ any equilibrium path implies monotonic convergence of the primitive variables towards the BGP. Conversely, let $u(0) < u^*$. There is once again a threshold initial value of $\underline{p}(0)$ such that, if $p(0) < \underline{p}(0)$, any equilibrium path implies monotonic convergence towards the BGP.*

Consider also Figure 4.20 where this phenomenon, at least for the growth rate of physical capital, is made evident by the plots of ξ_k, for increasing values of $p(0)$.

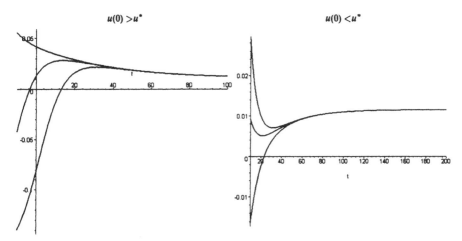

Figure 4.20 The growth rate of k_t for different initial states of the economy

4.4.6 Welfare Considerations in the Exogenous Growth Case

The fact that it is possible to obtain the explicit trajectory of consumption has further important consequences on the information which can be extracted in terms of predictions from the ULM. In this perspective, recall that the explicit law of evolution of consumption in the exogenous case, generated by the decentralized solution in (4.26b), is the same as in the optimal case (equation (3.19a)).

Therefore, from the general form of the welfare integral in (3.22) we can obtain the following result:

Proposition 4.21 *The welfare integral associated with the exogenous growth case in the decentralized economy equals*

$$(4.24) \quad W = \tfrac{1}{(1-\alpha)} \left[-\tfrac{1}{\rho} + \tfrac{1}{\rho} A \frac{\left[(\rho/\alpha) u^* h(0)^\psi \right]^{1-\alpha}}{n^*} \left(\mu + \frac{\rho}{\rho/\alpha - n^*(1-\alpha)} \right) \right]$$

Proof The same arguments used in the proof for Proposition 3.17. $\Box$

Finally, as shown for centralized dynamics:

Corollary 4.8 *Let the economy evolve along an exogenous growth case. Then, sudden increases (decreases) of both physical and human capital always lead to higher (lower) welfare levels.*

Proof By studying the signs of the partial derivatives of W w.r.t the initial values of the state variables it is quite simple to obtain the result in the corollary. $\Box$

Chapter 5

The Inefficiency of the Market Economy and the Design of Optimal Fiscal Policies

5.1   Introduction and Plan of the Chapter

We have observed in several occasions that the presence of an externality implies sub-optimality and therefore inefficiency of the market equilibrium.

In order to determine the exact purport of this assertion in the context of the ULM, the first part of this Chapter provides a critical evaluation of the differences of the decentralized and centralized dynamics obtained in the preceding Chapters of the book. The comparison concerns both the BGP and the transitional dynamics.

The second part of the Chapter changes the perspective of analysis: under the *Path Coincidence* principles, we sketch an outline of the properties of the optimal fiscal policy aimed at reconciling equilibrium and efficient dynamics.

Determining the nature of the inefficiency in the market competitive economy is not an easy task. First of all, we find that the parameter spaces under which the centralized and the decentralized solutions both imply non-degenerate BGP dynamics do not coincide. As a matter of fact, the feasible parameter space in the case of the market economy is wider in the risk-aversion direction. Therefore, to conduct a meaningful analysis, we need to mark first the boundaries of the parameter space where optimal and equilibrium paths can jointly coexist. In this special intersection of the feasible parameter spaces a number of interesting details of the deformation of the market equilibrium with respect to its optimal benchmark emerge.

From the balanced-growth perspective, we show that the growth rate of the market economy is lower than in the centralized case and that the inefficiency increases in proportion to the externality. Other interesting clues can be derived by comparing the long-run optimal and equilibrium growth rates and stationary values of the adjoint variables and *Great Ratios*. In this respect, we find that the decentralized economy experiences lower BGP levels of the average goods production and higher BGP levels of the "weighted" ratio between physical and human capital than the centralized economy. The centralized BGP value of the average consumption is higher only if the inverse of the intertemporal elasticity of substitution is lower than the share of physical capital. Furthermore, the centralized economy has higher BGP levels of the interest and saving rates. Also the ratio between broad and narrow output and the growth rate of wages are higher.

An analysis of the nature of inefficiency in a market economy from the point of view of the transitional dynamics is by no means an easy task, either.

From the local point of view, what we can say is that the stability properties of the fixed point in $\mathbb{R}^3$ show a point of contact between centralized and decentralized dynamics. In the region of the parameter space where optimal and equilibrium non-degenerate dynamics can jointly coexist, we have the common saddle-path stability/instability result. However, since the eigenvalues can also have an imaginary part when the solution is decentralized, convergence towards the fixed point in $\mathbb{R}^3$ can in this case also occur with oscillating motion (a possibility which is excluded, conversely, when resource allocation is efficient). Besides this, in the region of the parameter space where the eigenvalues are all real, the market economy preserves the efficient orientation of the equilibrium trajectories linking the control and control-like variables of the model to the state of the economy (even though the market elasticities are different than in the centralized economy).

Another interesting peculiarity of the market economy is that it tends to adjust locally more slowly than when there exists an efficient system of resource allocation.

The global point of view allows for less general details on the form of the inefficiency. As we have made clear on a number of occasions, the only possibility of jointly obtaining explicit trajectories in both cases of centralized and decentralized dynamics rests on the critical restriction imposing the equality between the intertemporal elasticity of substitution and the share of physical capital. We have also remarked that this restriction implies the exogenous growth case for the Uzawa-Lucas economy.[51] The comparison among explicit paths, in this critical growth case, produces useful insights on the form of the inefficiency from a dynamic point of view. As a critical result, the graphical analysis approach conducted in the Chapter shows that there is always a time threshold such that the market economy initially produces, consumes and invests more than its centralized counterpart and, after the threshold is crossed, it produces, consumes and invests less over the rest of the infinite horizon.

The second part of the Chapter changes the angle of discussion. As already anticipated, an interesting normative issue which arises quite naturally in the context of the ULM concerns the feasibility of inducing the decentralized economy to correct its inefficiency. The problem has been solved, at least partially, by Garcia-Castrillo and Sanso [10]. Using the principles of *Path Coincidence,* these authors identify the characteristics of the fiscal policy capable of providing the correct incentives for the market economy to behave efficiently. What they find is that the return on physical capital has to remain free of taxes. A subsidy relaxing the opportunity cost of learning has also to be introduced. A combination of a tax on wages and a lump-

---

[51]Actually, in the case of decentralized dynamics we also need $u(0) = u^*$.

sum tax provides the resources for the subsidy. The slope of the new policy function, relating the subsidy per unit of goods production to the state of the economy, is shown to depend (again) on the sign of the difference between the inverse of the intertemporal elasticity of substitution and the share of physical capital.

By exploiting the explicit laws governing the efficient economy in Chapter 3, we are able to numerically extend to-the-large some of the results of these authors. In particular, we find that the local orientation of the new policy function, relating the subsidy per unit of goods production to the state of the economy, still holds from the global viewpoint. Furthermore, under the hypothesis of an fixed rate for the tax on wages, we are able to obtain and discuss the explicit time paths for all the relevant fiscal variables of the economy.

Of course, the whole exercise is prone to the usual objections concerning the time consistency of the policy decisions. As we are only interested in determining optimal policy (assuming perfect foresight and a time-consistent Government) we shall not consider this problem, which remains beyond the scope of this Chapter.

The plan of the Chapter is as follows. The second section marks the boundaries of the parameter space regions where the centralized and decentralized solutions of the model both imply non-degenerate dynamics. The third section compares the BGP properties of decentralized and centralized economies.

The fourth section explores the form of the inefficiency when the economy is in transition from the point of view of the local analysis. It complements the fifth, where the principles of global analysis are used to determine the valid-in-the-large dimension of inefficiency.

The final section investigates the design of optimal fiscal policy, from the BGP and transitional viewpoints.

5.2 Centralization *Versus* Decentralization. The Parameter Space

Before starting the discussion, it is important firstly to understand in which regions of the parameter space the ULM can simultaneously determine non-degenerate balanced dynamics in both cases of the centralized and the decentralized solution.[52]

Recall from Proposition 3.1 that the non-degeneracy of the BGP in the case of the centralized solution is achieved when the parameters are inside the following subset of Δ:

$$\bar{\Delta}^c \equiv \left\{ \omega \in \Delta : \rho \in (0, B\psi), \sigma > 1 - \frac{\rho}{B\psi} \right\}$$

Conversely, as proved in Proposition 4.1, there are two non-connected regions of the parameter space where the BGP is non-degenerate in the case of a market economy:

$$\bar{\Delta}^d_a \equiv \left\{ \omega \in \Delta : \rho \in (0, B), \sigma > 1 - \rho/(B\psi) \right\}$$

---

[52]The reference for the original material developed in this section is in [18].

$$\bar{\Delta}_b^d \equiv \left\{ \omega \in \Delta : \rho \in (B, B\psi), \sigma < 1 - \tfrac{\rho}{B\psi}, \gamma \in \left(\tfrac{(1-\alpha)(\rho - B)}{B}, \infty \right) \right\}$$

Overlapping the two regions, we can produce the following partition of the parameter space:

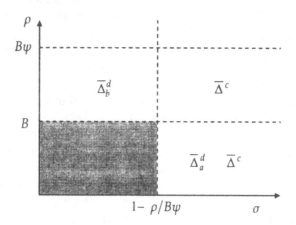

Figure 5.1 The partition of the parameter space in the two solutions

where the shaded area is a region of the parameter space where neither centralized nor decentralized dynamics imply a non-degenerate BGP.

It appears evident that:

Remark *Neither optimal nor equilibrium trajectories can be generated by the ULM when both the discount rate and the inverse of the intertemporal elasticity of substitution are small with respect to their existence range. The feasible parameter space in the case of a decentralized economy is wider in the σ direction.*

The partition of the parameter space in Figure 5.1 is crucial for the rest of the analysis conducted below. In order for it to make sense, in fact, the comparison between the properties of the model under the two solutions must be undertaken in the region of the parameter space where the two different dynamics coexist. We will henceforth indicate this special region of the parameter space as $\tilde{\Delta} \equiv \bar{\Delta}^d \cap \bar{\Delta}^c$. As a consequence, $\tilde{\Delta}$ is defined such that:

$$(5.1) \qquad \tilde{\Delta} \equiv \{ \omega \in \Delta : \rho \in (0, B), \sigma > 1 - \rho/(B\psi) \}$$

For the sake of a simple representation, throughout the Chapter, we will be distinguishing the centralized outcomes of the representative-agent utility-maximization problems from their decentralized counterparts by using the symbols c and d at the apex or foot of the variables.

5.3   The Inefficiency and the BGP

5.3.1   *The Inefficiency and the BGP Growth Rate of the Economy*

To simplify our analysis, let us now recall the expressions in (3.2) and (4.2) where the BGP value of working time is obtained under the two centralized and decentralized, perspectives:

$$u_c^* = 1 - \frac{(1-\alpha)(B-\rho)+B\gamma}{B\sigma(1-\alpha+\gamma)}$$

$$u_d^* = 1 - \frac{(1-\alpha)(B-\rho)}{B[\sigma(1-\alpha+\gamma)-\gamma]}$$

Taking the difference, after carrying out a little algebra, we arrive at:

$$(5.2) \qquad u_d^* - u_c^* = \frac{\gamma}{\sigma[\sigma(1-\alpha+\gamma)-\gamma]}\left[\sigma - 1 + \frac{\rho}{B\psi}\right]$$

Therefore, we can prove the following:

Lemma 5.1 *Let $\omega \in \tilde{\Delta}$. Then, along the BGP, the fraction of total non-leisure time dedicated to work is higher in the market economy for all possible parameter configurations.*

Proof Consider the definition of $\tilde{\Delta}$. Since the right hand side of expression (5.2) is always positive if $\omega \in \tilde{\Delta}$, the result in the proposition follows. $\square$

We can now reach the following crucial result:

Proposition 5.1 *Recall Lemma 5.1. The growth rate of the centralized economy is always higher than in case of decentralization. The inefficiency is measured by the following expression*:

$$(5.3) \qquad \xi_c^* - \xi_d^* = B\psi\left(u_d^* - u_c^*\right) > 0$$

Proof The difference between the optimal growth rate, $\xi_c^* = B\psi(1 - u_c^*)$, and its equilibrium counterpart, $\xi_d^* = B\psi(1 - u_d^*)$, can be put as in (5.3). Since, by Lemma 5.1, $(u_d^* - u_c^*) > 0$ the result in the proposition is implied. $\square$

As expected, the centralized solution of the model implies that an efficient economy develops higher growth rates. Consider, in Figures 5.2a and 5.2b, the plots of the distortion with respect to the externality. The two plots are justified because the second derivative of ξ_d^* with respect to the externality changes sign according to whether σ is larger or smaller than 1. Only when the externality is set to zero do the centralized and decentralized economy growth rates coincide.

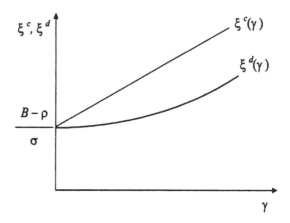

Figure 5.2a Optimal and equilibrium growth rates w.r.t. γ ($\sigma < 1$)

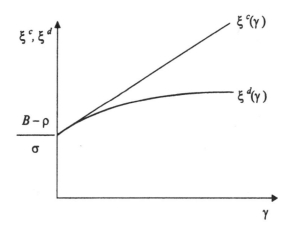

Figure 5.2b Optimal and equilibrium growth rates w.r.t. γ ($\sigma > 1$)

We will show in the numerical simulations below that it suffices a small external-ity to create a large divarication of the market-economy growth rate from its efficient benchmark. Of course, given Proposition 5.1, the following is also implied.

Corollary 5.1 *The result in Proposition 5.1 extends to the BGP growth rates of all the non-stationary original variables of the ULM, namely consumption, physical capital and human capital.*

Proof Recall Lemma 1.1 unveiling, for both the centralized and market economies, the long-run relationships among the growth rates of the original variables of the model. □

5.3.2   *The Inefficiency and the* Great Ratios

To evaluate the impact of the inefficiency on the BGP values of the *Great Ratios*, we subtract the centralized-economy stationary values undertaken by m_t, n_t and p_t from their equilibrium counterparts. We find that:

(5.4) $m_c^* - m_d^* = \frac{\alpha - \sigma}{\alpha} (\xi_c^* - \xi_d^*)$

(5.5) $n_c^* - n_d^* = \frac{\sigma}{\alpha} (\xi_c^* - \xi_d^*) > 0$

(5.6) $\frac{p_c^*}{p_d^*} = \left(\frac{\rho + \sigma \xi_d^*}{\rho + \sigma \xi_c^*}\right)^{1/(1-\alpha)} \frac{u_c^*}{u_d^*} < 1$

As a consequence, taking into consideration Proposition 5.1, we have:

Proposition 5.2 *When* $\omega \in \tilde{\Delta}$ *the centralized economy will experience higher BGP levels of the* n^* *ratio and lower BGP levels of the* p^* *ratio than its market counterparts. The centralized BGP value of* m^* *is higher only if the inverse of the intertemporal elasticity of substitution is lower than the share of physical capital.*

Proof Recalling the formulation of the Great Ratios in (2.2), (2.3) and (2.4), the differences in (5.4), (5.5) and (5.6) can be easily reconstructed. Under Lemma 5.1 and Proposition 5.1, the sign evaluation of the expressions leads us to the results in the proposition. $\square$

It is useful to point out that:

Remark *When* $\alpha = \sigma$, *the centralized and decentralized BGP values of the average consumption are the same.*

5.3.3   *The Inefficiency and the* Adjoint Variables

Further interesting information on the inefficient dimension of the market economy evolving along the BGP comes from a comparison of the stationary values and growth rates of the adjoint variables. Simple algebra shows that the inefficiency implies the following:

(5.7) $\left(\frac{y^T}{\bar{y}}\right)_c^* - \left(\frac{y^T}{\bar{y}}\right)_d^* = \frac{(u_d^* - u_c^*)(1-\alpha)}{u_d^* u_c^*} > 0$

(5.8) $r_c^* - r_d^* = \sigma (\xi_c^* - \xi_d^*) > 0$

(5.9) $\left(\frac{\dot{w}}{w}\right)_c^* - \left(\frac{\dot{w}}{w}\right)_d^* = \frac{\gamma}{(1-\alpha+\gamma)} (\xi_c^* - \xi_d^*) > 0$

(5.10) $s_c^* - s_d^* = \frac{\alpha \rho}{(\rho + \sigma \xi_c^*)(\rho + \sigma \xi_d^*)} (\xi_c^* - \xi_d^*) > 0$

Therefore:

Proposition 5.3 *When* $\omega \in \tilde{\Delta}$ *the centralized economy will experience higher BGP levels of the interest and saving rate. The ratio between broad and narrow output and the growth rate of wages will also be higher.*

Proof To obtain (5.7), recall the expression for the $\frac{y^T}{\bar{y}}$ ratio in Corollary 2.1. The expressions in (5.8), (5.9) and (5.10) can be respectively obtained using the centralized and decentralized formulations of (2.9), (2.10) and (2.12). The sign evaluations, recalling Lemma 5.1 and Proposition 5.1, lead to the results in the proposition. $\square$

5.4   Comparing Transitional Dynamics from the Local Point of View

5.4.1   *The Inefficiency and the Stability Properties in* $\mathbb{R}^3$

In the preceding Chapters, we have determined, starting from the local point of view, which kind of stability properties of the BGP we can expect from the optimal and the market economies. In particular, we have shown that the Jacobian matrix associated with the $\mathbb{R}^3$ transformed dynamic system generated by the centralized solution of the ULM has a fixed one-negative-two-positive structure of eigenvalues; thus the saddle-path stability/instability result is the only possible outcome.

Conversely, since in a market economy the representative agent is unable to take into account the externality, we obtain qualitative deviations from this saddle-path stability/instability result. In particular, we have shown that if the parameters belong to the $\bar{\Delta}_b^d$ region, the presence of an externality creates room for the emergence of a *continuum* of equilibria. In mathematical terms, this means that there exist regions in the parameter space where the conditions for the emergence (in $\mathbb{R}^3$) of a saddle-node or a saddle-focus can be determined.[53]

As proved in Chapter 4, furthermore, the case of the saddle-focus can be made even more complicated by considering that, as the externality crosses the critical value $\bar{\gamma}$, either from the right or from the left, the steady state is surrounded by a one-dimensional object which has an intersection with the two-dimensional plane determined by the initial condition on the variable associated with the real eigenvalue.

If the parameters belong to the $\tilde{\Delta} \equiv \bar{\Delta}^d \cap \bar{\Delta}^c = \bar{\Delta}_a^d$ region of the parameter space, namely in the special case in which both centralized and decentralized dynamics can coexist, things are much easier to describe. In this case, both centralized and decentralized dynamics give a saddle-path stability/instability result. There exists a one-dimensional local manifold consisting of the steady state and of all so-

---

[53] We have also shown that there is the possibility of instability. This case implies that no transition is possible and that the initial conditions for the control variables have to be chosen so that the economy finds itself moving along the BGP from the very beginning.

lutions converging towards the steady state. There remains, however, the crucial difference that the eigenvalues, in the case of optimal dynamics, are bound to stay in the real axis. According to the numerical work done in sub-section 4.3.3, this does not happen in the case of decentralization. In other words, while optimal dynamics cannot occur (locally) with sinusoidal motion, inefficiency in a market economy can produce oscillations.

Since, in general terms, the characteristic equation in the case of the market solution cannot be factorized, other local details of the inefficiency in the market economy are difficult to obtain. In particular, a qualitative treatment of the impact of the inefficiency on values such as the local speed of convergence or the response elasticities of the control variables to shocks perturbing the state of the economy mainly remains out of reach. Nevertheless, in order to have an idea of these issues, as in many other occasions in the book, we shall now proceed to combine the available information with the results of extensive numerical study.

5.4.2 The Speeds of Adjustment

Let us compare the local approximation of the speeds of adjustment associated with decentralized and centralized economy when the parameters belong to the $\tilde{\Delta} \equiv \bar{\Delta}^d \cap \bar{\Delta}^c = \bar{\Delta}^d_a$ region of the parameter space. We need here the negative eigenvalues governing the convergence towards the steady-state. In this respect, we know from Proposition 3.8 that the negative eigenvalue, in the case of a centralized solution, is a technical coefficient fixed at:

$$\kappa_1 = (J_{11}^*)^c = -(1-\alpha)\, n_c^* = -B \frac{(1-\alpha+\gamma)}{\alpha}$$

Conversely, we have proved that the negative eigenvalue governing the (linearized) decentralized dynamics in the case of saddle-path stability cannot be qualitatively retrieved without further parameter restrictions.

The empirical regularities found in sub-section 4.3.3 are of great help here. Recalling that we defined as $\tilde{\Delta} \in \bar{\Delta}^d$ the restricted parameter space where those empirical regularities are actually confirmed, we can, firstly, show the following:

Proposition 5.4 *Let $\omega \in \tilde{\Delta}$. Then, if $\gamma > \alpha$, the market economy experiences a lower speed of adjustment than its centralized counterpart.*

Proof Interesting Result 4.3 in sub-section 4.2.3 shows that, in the case of a decentralized regime, the negative eigenvalue associated with the Jacobian of the linearized dynamics cannot be larger in modulus than m^*. Therefore, we can compare $-(J_{11}^*)^c = -B \frac{(1-\alpha+\gamma)}{\alpha}$ and the decentralized value of m_d^* in (4.5). Since we have always found that, if $\gamma > \alpha$ (inside $\omega \in \tilde{\Delta}$), $(J_{11}^*)^c$ is surely larger in modulus than m_d^*, the result in proposition follows. $\square$

The case with $\gamma < \alpha$ is more difficult to prove. However, with the help of extensive numerical simulations, we find the following:

Interesting Result 5.1 *Efficient economies with a small externality also have a higher local speed of adjustment than market economies characterized by the same parameter choices.*

5.4.3   The Slopes of the Functions Linking Controls to States

Another interesting feature worth investigating is the different reaction the centralized economy shows with respect to its decentralized counterpart when a shock perturbs the BGP. To undertake this kind of analysis, we first recall, for the sake of a simple discussion, the general formulation of the functions in (2.19a) and (2.19b), linking the initial values of the control and control-like variables to the state of the economy:

(5.11a) $\dfrac{u^*-u(0)}{u^*} = \phi\delta_1 \dfrac{p^*-p(0)}{p^*}$

(5.11b) $\dfrac{m^*-m(0)}{m^*} = \phi\delta_2 \dfrac{p^*-p(0)}{p^*}$

In (5.11i), $\delta_1 = \dfrac{J^*_{11}m^*}{\Gamma(B\eta u^*-\kappa_1)}$, $\delta_2 = \dfrac{J^*_{11}}{\Gamma}$ and $\Gamma = \left(\dfrac{J^*_{11}m^*\phi}{B\eta u^*-\kappa_1} - m^* + \kappa_1\right)$.

In case of optimal paths, we have proven in Lemma 3.1, that, since $\eta = \psi$ and $\kappa_1 = J^*_{11} = -B\dfrac{(1-\alpha+\gamma)}{\alpha}$, $B\eta u^*-\kappa_1 = B\psi u^*+B\dfrac{(1-\alpha+\gamma)}{\alpha} = m^*$. Therefore, given a deviation of the state of the economy from its ordered position of size $\dfrac{p^*-p(0)}{p^*}$, we find that $\delta_1 = \delta_2 = \delta = \dfrac{J^*_{11}}{\Gamma}$, where Γ is simply $\dfrac{\alpha}{\sigma}J^*_{11} - m^* < 0$. Therefore, it was easy to prove Proposition 3.9, saying that the policy functions are locally upward or downward sloping according to whether ϕ is positive or negative.

In the case of the market economy things are a lot more difficult. First of all, the eigenvalues are not necessarily real and more than one of them can be negative. Therefore, we need to restrict the parameter space to the special region where all the roots of the Jacobian associated with the decentralized dynamics are real with only one of them negative.

Several steps were then required to obtain the signs of δ_1 and δ_2. Later, after a number of preliminary results, we have been able to prove Propositions 4.10 and 4.11 telling us that if $\omega \in \tilde{\Delta}$, the optimal orientation of the functions is preserved along equilibrium paths. However, since we do not know the explicit value of the negative eigenvalue, we cannot measure the effect on the control-like variables of deviations in the state of the economy from its balanced position. What we have been able to say is that δ_1 diverges from δ_2, so that the response of the decentralized economy to shocks perturbing its balanced evolution is more intense for a control variable than for the other. In particular, the elasticity of working time is higher (lower) than the elasticity of average consumption if $\dfrac{m^*}{B\eta u^*-\kappa_1} > (<)1$.

5.5 Optimal and Equilibrium Off-balanced Paths from the Global Point of View

A possibility of deriving valid-in-the-large results on the different behavior of the centralized and decentralized economies evolving along off-balanced trajectories is offered by the exogenous growth case. As discussed in both Chapters 3 and 4, this growth case implies a substantial simplification and allows for the closed-form solution of both the centralized and decentralized dynamics.

Once explicit paths for the variables of the model are available, by comparing them through analytical and graphical methods, it becomes easy to determine further details on the dimension of the inefficiency with respect to those obtained by the local analysis. There is, however, a cost to be paid; to generate an exogenous growth case, the inverse of the intertemporal elasticity of substitution has to be fixed at low levels in order to match the share of physical capital.[54]

To proceed in this direction, let us first, for the sake of a simple discussion, mark the boundaries of the relevant parameter space. We can define as:

$$\tilde{\Delta}_{\sigma=\alpha} \equiv \left\{ \omega \in \tilde{\Delta} : \sigma = \alpha, \rho \in [B(1 - \alpha + \gamma), B], \gamma \in (0, \alpha) \right\}$$

the region of the parameter space where centralized and decentralized dynamics jointly produce non-degenerate results when $\sigma = \alpha$. Notice that $\tilde{\Delta}_{\sigma=\alpha}$ is inside $\bar{\Delta}^c$ and coincides with $\bar{\Delta}^d_{a,\sigma=\alpha}$ above. Given the discussion in sub-section 4.4.2, this also implies that:

Remark *If $\omega \in \tilde{\Delta}_{\sigma=\alpha}$ the decentralized dynamics cannot produce the indeterminacy result.*

5.5.1 *Optimal and Equilibrium Exogenous Growth*

We start the analysis by considering the unperturbed economy evolving along the BGP. Only later, we will be considering the different optimal and equilibrium responses to shocks altering the state of the economy.

The Case of the Unperturbed Economy The study of the unperturbed-economy case corresponds, in the $\mathbb{R}^3$–reduced dimension, to the BGP analysis. Therefore, simply equating the share of physical capital to the inverse of the intertemporal elasticity of substitution in the equations developed in section 5.3, we would be able to retrieve a large number of (less general) specific results applying to this particular economy.

However, since now we are able to solve the differential equations, we can investigate the characteristics of the inefficiency from the original-dimension point of view. Consider also that this kind of analysis produces valid-in-the-large results. To this issues we shall concentrate in this sub-section.

---

[54]The reference for the original material developed in this section is in [19].

We start by deriving some information on the state of the centralized economy *vis-à-vis* its market counterpart. We have that, given the parameter configuration:

Lemma 5.2 *Let the centralized and decentralized economies evolve along the BGP. Then, the centralized economy always presents a lower endowment of physical capital per unit of human capital.*

Proof By equation (5.6), we have that $p_c^* = p(0)_c < p_d^* = p(0)_d$. Since we are along the BGP, this remains true $\forall\, t$. $\square$

Therefore, recalling equation (5.4), Lemma 4.8 and Corollary 3.9, we can prove the following:

Proposition 5.5 *Let $\omega \in \tilde{\Delta}_{\alpha=\sigma}$. Let furthermore both economies be normalized at the same level of human capital. Then, the centralized economy is characterized by a lower initial value of consumption and physical capital than the decentralized economy. Conversely, if the economy is normalized at the same level of physical capital, the initial value of consumption is the same for the two economies, but human capital has to be initially higher.*

Proof Let us prove first the case with the same initial value of human capital. By Lemma 5.2, this implies that since $p_c^* = p(0)_c = \frac{k(0)_c}{h(0)_c^\psi} < p_d^* = p(0)_d = \frac{k(0)_d}{h(0)_d^\psi}$, it has to be that $k(0)_c < k(0)_d$. Furthermore, since by equation (5.4), $m_c^* = m_d^* = \frac{\ell}{\sigma}$, we have that $c(0)_c < c(0)_d$. Conversely, if $k(0)_c = k(0)_d$, then $c(0)_c = c(0)_d$ and $h(0)_c > h(0)_d$. $\square$

Let us now consider the case when both the centralized and market economies are normalized at the same level of human capital. Letting time to go by, we also have the following interesting:

Proposition 5.6 *Let $\omega \in \tilde{\Delta}_{\alpha=\sigma}$. Then, there exists a finite $t = \bar{t} = -\ln[\frac{p_d^*}{p_c^*}]/(\xi_c^* - \xi_d^*)$ such that if $t < \bar{t}$, the market economy initially consumes and invests more than its centralized counterparts and if $t > \bar{t}$, it consumes and invests less.*

Proof Let us consider equations (3.19b) and (4.26b) to form the ratio $\frac{c_t^c}{c_t^d}$ when $h(0)_c = h(0)_d$. If $\mu = 0$ the ratio simplifies to $\frac{c_t^c}{c_t^d} = \frac{e^{\xi_c^* t} u_c^*}{e^{\xi_d^* t} u_d^*} \left(\frac{n_d^*}{n_c^*} \right)^{\frac{1}{1-\alpha}}$. This ratio is less than one when $t = 0$ and goes to infinity as $t \to \infty$. A simple continuity argument implies the result in proposition. The threshold value of t can be retrieved by equating to one the ratio of the two time paths of consumption and solving. $\square$

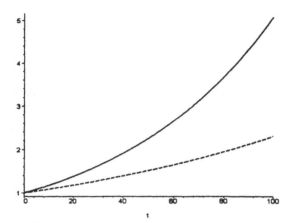

Figure 5.3 Optimal and equilibrium BGP trajectories for h_t when $\alpha = \sigma$

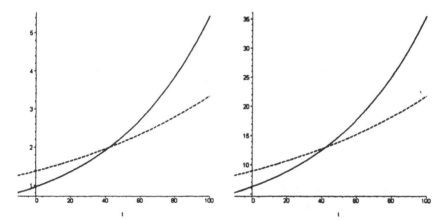

Figure 5.4 Optimal and equilibrium BGP trajectories for c_t and k_t when $\alpha = \sigma$

We proceed now to a graphical analysis depicting typical time paths of consumption, physical capital and human capital in the case of an economy belonging to the exogenous growth case.

In order for the BGP-constant values of working time not to diverge too much, the parameters are chosen so that $A = 1$, $\alpha = \sigma = 1/4$, $B = 0.04$, $\rho = 23/24B$ and $\gamma = 0.05$. With this parameter configuration, the growth rates of the centralized and decentralized economy are respectively $\xi_c^* \cong 0.0173$ and $\xi_d^* \cong 0.0088$. Both economies are normalized at an initial value of human capital equal to one ($h(0) = 1$).

Figure 5.3 depicts the all-time diverging optimal and equilibrium paths of human capital. Notice the rapid divarication of the two economies even in presence of a small distorting factor.

Figure 5.4, depicting the optimal and equilibrium trajectories of consumption and physical capital for the chosen parameter configuration, makes evident the predictions in Propositions 5.5 and 5.6.

The Case of the Perturbed Economy   More interesting is the comparison of optimal and equilibrium paths when a shock perturbs the state of an economy belonging to the exogenous growth case. If both economies are characterized by the same initial endowment of human capital and parameter configuration, we have the following extension of Propositions 5.5 and 5.6:

Proposition 5.7 *Let $\omega \in \tilde{\Delta}_{\alpha=\sigma}$. Let furthermore both economies undergo a shock in the respective endowments of physical capital implying the same $\mu = \frac{n^*}{n(0)} - 1$. Then, the centralized economy responds with a lower initial value of consumption and physical capital than the decentralized economy. Conversely, if the economy is normalized at the same level of physical capital, $c(0)$ is the same for the two economies, but human capital has to be initially higher. There exists a finite $\bar{t}$ such that if $t < \bar{t}$, the market economy initially consumes and invests more in transition than its centralized counterparts and if $t > \bar{t}$, it consumes and invests less.*

Proof Let us again consider equations (3.19b) and (4.26b) to form the ratio $\frac{c_t^c}{c_t^d}$ when $h(0)_c = h(0)_d$. We have $\frac{c_t^c}{c_t^d} = \frac{e^{\xi_c^* t} u_c^*}{e^{\xi_d^* t} u_d^*} \left(\frac{n_d^*}{n_c^*} \frac{1 + \mu e^{-(1-\alpha)n_c^* t}}{1 + \mu e^{-(1-\alpha)n_d^* t}} \right)^{\frac{1}{1-\alpha}}$. Since, at time zero, the ratio is less than one, but it goes to infinity as $t \to \infty$, a continuity argument implies the result in the proposition. The value $\bar{t}$ can be easily obtained solving for t the ratio between the two time paths in specific circumstances. $\square$

We propose now a graphical analysis of the typical behavior of off-balanced optimal and equilibrium paths for an economy belonging to the exogenous case. The simulations depict the behavior of both the primitive and adjoint variables of the Uzawa-Lucas economy. The parameter configuration is as above: $A = 1$, $\alpha = \sigma = 1/4$, $B = 0.04$, $\rho = 23/24B$ and $\gamma = 0.05$. The BGP growth rates of the centralized and decentralized economy are respectively $\xi_c^* \cong 0.0173$ and $\xi_d^* \cong 0.0088$. In addition, as in all the simulations conducted in Chapters 3 and 4, μ is alternatively fixed at 1 and -1/3.

The solid lines always represent the efficient trajectory of a particular variable, while the broken lines are trajectories generated in decentralized economies for the same parameter configuration.

Consider first Figures 5.5a and 5.5b depicting optimal and equilibrium paths for consumption when the economy is in transition. As proved in Proposition 5.7, in both cases of a positive and negative value for μ, there is an initial period in which the market economy consumes more, even if it has the same endowment of human capital as its efficient counterpart.

After t periods, the market economy starts to consume less.

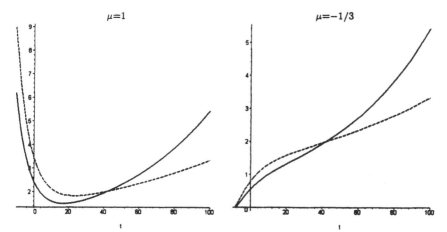

Figure 5.5a Optimal and equilibrium paths of c_t when $\alpha = \sigma$

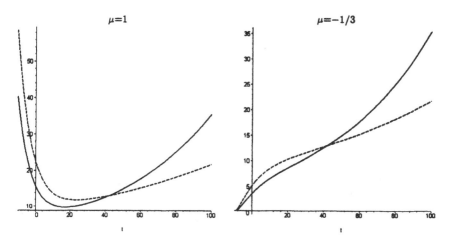

Figure 5.5b Optimal and equilibrium paths of k_t when $\alpha = \sigma$

The plots for physical capital simply mimic the behavior of consumption, though on a different scale. Notice also the quite similar behavior of goods production, in Figure 5.6.

The evolution of the other adjoint variables follows the laws obtained in section 2.2. The following Figures represent the behavior of these variables in terms of growth rates (recall that u_t and, consequently $\frac{y_t^T}{y_t}$ are both constant at their BGP value). Summing up the information contained in the Figures, we can say that:

Interesting Result 5.2 *A market economy with the same initial value of human capital as its efficient counterpart has initially-higher levels of the BGP growing variables k_t, c_t, y_t, and w_t,[55] but always presents lower values of r_t and s_t.*

---

[55]Consider that, if we normalize the economies at the same initial value of physical capital, then we

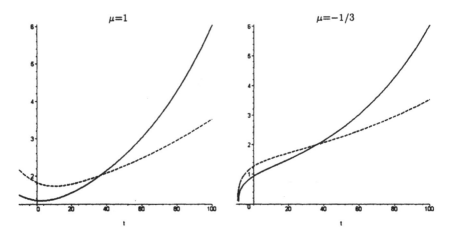

Figure 5.6 Optimal and equilibrium paths of goods production when $\alpha = \sigma$

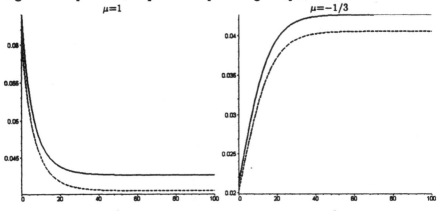

Figure 5.7 Optimal and equilibrium paths of the interest rate when $\alpha = \sigma$

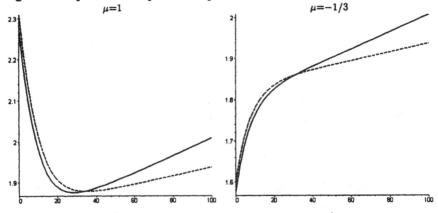

Figure 5.8 Optimal and equilibrium paths of the level of wages when $\alpha = \sigma$

would only observe intersections in the optimal and competitive paths of human capital.

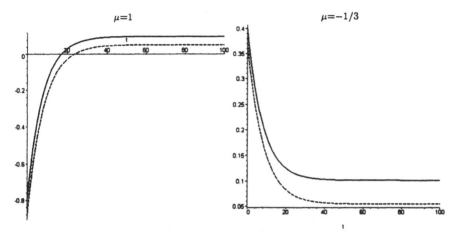

Figure 5.9 Optimal and equilibrium paths of savings when $\alpha = \sigma$

5.5.2 *Welfare when the Economy Belongs to the Exogenous Growth Case*

It is a useful goal to be able to understand what the impact of inefficiency on the welfare levels of the market economy might be. To this end, we will proceed here to compare the expressions for the welfare integrals obtained in the last sections of Chapter 3 and Chapter 4, respectively for centralized and decentralized economies. This can only be done in the intersection of the parameter space where the welfare integrals can be both solved, namely when $\alpha = \sigma$, and both economies belong to the exogenous growth case. To simplify the discussion, we only take into account the case of centralized and decentralized economies characterized by the same initial value of physical capital.

Let us first recall the welfare integral for the optimal exogenous growth case from equation (3.22):

$$(5.12) \qquad W^c = \frac{1}{(1-\alpha)}\left[-\frac{1}{\rho} + \frac{1}{\rho}\frac{\left[(\rho/\alpha)k(0)^\psi\right]^{1-\alpha}}{1+\mu}\left(\mu + \frac{\rho}{\rho/\alpha - n_c^*(1-\alpha)}\right)\right]$$

The analog which we obtain when, conversely, agents are left to their optimizing behavior in a market economy characterized by the same initial level of physical capital is:

$$(5.13) \qquad W^d = \frac{1}{(1-\alpha)}\left[-\frac{1}{\rho} + \frac{1}{\rho}\frac{\left[(\rho/\alpha)k(0)^\psi\right]^{1-\alpha}}{1+\mu}\left(\mu + \frac{\rho}{\rho/\alpha - n_d^*(1-\alpha)}\right)\right]$$

The difference between (5.12) and (5.13), evaluated at $\mu = 0$ (the unperturbed case), can be put in the form:

$$(5.14) \qquad W^c - W^d = \frac{1}{(1-\alpha)}\left[\frac{\rho}{\alpha}k(0)^\psi\right]^{1-\alpha}\left(\frac{(1-\alpha)(n_c^* - n_d^*)}{[\rho/\alpha - n_c^*(1-\alpha)][\rho/\alpha - n_d^*(1-\alpha)]}\right)$$

Therefore, recalling that $\rho/\alpha - n_c^*(1-\alpha)$ and $\rho/\alpha - n_d^*(1-\alpha)$ are both positive when $\omega \in \tilde{\Delta}_{\alpha=\sigma}$, and since we know from (5.5) that $n_c^* - n_d^* > 0$:

Proposition 5.8 *Let $\omega \in \tilde{\Delta}_{\alpha=\sigma}$. Then $W^c - W^d > 0$*

Proof Since $\rho/\alpha - n_c^*(1-\alpha)$ and $\rho/\alpha - n_d^*(1-\alpha)$ are both positive when $\omega \in \tilde{\Delta}_{\alpha=\sigma}$, and since we know from (5.5) that $n_c^* - n_d^* > 0$, the result in the proposition is easily obtained. $\square$

5.6 The Desirability of Public Policies

As discussed in the introduction to this book, welfare-improving Government interventions in a decentralized economy are not justified when the externality is set to zero. As a matter of fact, in this case, the optimization conducted from a decentralized point of view leads to a Pareto-optimal allocation of resources.

On the contrary, when an externality is present, the competitive equilibrium is sub-optimal. As shown in Proposition 1.2, the first-order conditions associated with problems $\mathbf{P}^c$ and $\mathbf{P}^d$ differ in the valuation of human capital. In particular, when the decentralized solution is considered, the istantaneous growth rate of the shadow price of human capital accumulation is constant and equal to the value of $\rho - B$. It is lower and equal to $\rho - B - B\frac{\gamma}{1-\alpha}u_t$ in the case of the centralized solution. The entire contents of Chapters 3 and 4 were indeed dedicated to the exploration of the properties of the economy under the two alternative valuations of human capital.

Furthermore, in the first part of this Chapter, we have compared the decentralized and centralized economies to determine the multidimensional form of the inefficiency, at least in the parameter space where the resulting motion is jointly non-degenerate. In particular, we have proved a critical result showing that, asymptotically, the fraction of total non-leisure time devoted to work is higher under a decentralized regime, while the growth rate of narrow output is always lower.

In the light of this, an issue which naturally begs attention concerns the actions which might be taken by the Government to induce agents to dedicate more time to the educational sector in order that the sub-optimality of equilibrium paths can somehow be corrected.[56] This is clearly a complicated task to undertake; only Garcia-Castrillo and Sanso [10], to our knowledge, have produced some partial results on this issue, mainly referring to the market economy evolving along the BGP.

Following in the footsteps of these authors, the first part of this section makes use of the *Path-Coincidence* criterion, so as to determine the characteristics of a fiscal policy capable of providing the correct incentives in order that the market economy behaves efficiently.

---

[56] A taxed version of the Uzawa-Lucas economy has also been used in literature to evaluate, with different objectives, the impact of taxation. Cf. Ortigueira [24].

The second part exploits the critical advantage we have on Garcia-Castrillo and Sanso: we know, in fact, that given the parameter configuration it is possible to find the explicit trajectories of all the variables of the efficient economy. As a consequence, the principles of Path-Coincidence can also be applied in transition.[57]

A set of four policy instruments shall be considered henceforth: a tax on the returns of both physical and (skilled) labour, τ_k and τ_w, a lump-sum tax T and a subsidy on the fraction of total time dedicated to learning, S_t. The Government has, at each point in time, to equate expenditure and revenues. To simplify the analysis, τ_k and τ_w are considered fixed along both the BGP and in transition. Furthermore, to make the problem manageable from an analytical point of view, we will be assuming the presence of a time-consistent Government.

5.6.1 *The Optimization Problem in Presence of Interventions*

Given the instruments for fiscal policy intervention, the decentralized constraint to the accumulation of physical capital in Definition 1.4, becomes:

$$(5.15) \qquad \dot{k}_t = (1 - \tau_k)\, r_t k_t + (1 - \tau_w)\, w_t\, (uh)_t - T_t + (1 - u_t)\, S_t - c_t$$

The maximization problem can be tackled again by means of the Maximum Principle. Being the other constraint unaffected, the present-value Hamiltonian becomes:

$$(5.16) \qquad H^\tau = \frac{c_t^{1-\sigma}-1}{1-\sigma} + \lambda_{1t} \left[(1 - \tau_k)\, r_t k_t + (1 - \tau_w)\, w_t\, (uh)_t - c_t - T_t \right] +$$

$$+ \lambda_{1t} \left[(1 - u_t)\, S_t \right] + \lambda_{2t} \left[B h_t\, (1 - u_t) \right]$$

where λ_{1t} and λ_{2t} are again co-state variables.

Since u_t and c_t are control variables and k_t and h_t are state variables, the solution candidates proposed by the Maximum Principle in the case of the taxed decentralized economy are:

$$(5.17a) \qquad H_c^\tau = 0 \Longrightarrow c_t^{-\sigma} = \lambda_{1t}$$

$$(5.17b) \qquad H_u^\tau = 0 \Longrightarrow (1 - \tau_w)\, w_t h_t \lambda_{1t} - S_t = B h_t \lambda_{2t}$$

$$(5.17c) \qquad H_{\lambda_1}^\tau = \dot{k}_t \Longrightarrow \dot{k}_t = (1 - \tau_k)\, r_t k_t + (1 - \tau_w)\, w_t\, (uh)_t - c_t - T_t +$$

$$+ (1 - u_t)\, S_t$$

$$(5.17d) \qquad H_{\lambda_2}^\tau = \dot{h}_t \Longrightarrow \dot{h}_t = B h_t\, (1 - u_t)$$

$$(5.17e) \qquad H_k^\tau = \rho \lambda_{1t} - \dot{\lambda}_{1t} \Longrightarrow \dot{\lambda}_{1t} = -(1 - \tau_k)\, r_t \lambda_{1t} + \rho \lambda_{1t}$$

---

[57]The reference for the original material developed in this section is in [17].

(5.17f) $H_h^T = \rho\lambda_{2t} - \dot{\lambda}_{2t} \Longrightarrow \dot{\lambda}_{2t} = -\lambda_{1t}(1 - \tau_w)w_t u_t - \lambda_{2t}[B(1 - u_t)] +$

$+\rho\lambda_{2t}$

Recalling that $\alpha\frac{\bar{y}_t}{k_t} = r_t$, that $(1 - \alpha)\frac{\bar{y}_t}{(uh)_t} = w_t$ and that $\bar{y}_t = Ak_t^\alpha u_t^{1-\alpha}h_t^{1-\alpha+\gamma}$, the FOCs become:

(5.18a) $c_t^{-\sigma} = \lambda_{1t}$

(5.18b) $(1 - \tau_w)(1 - \alpha)\frac{\bar{y}_t}{u_t}\lambda_{1t} - S_t = Bh_t\lambda_{2t}$

(5.18c) $\dot{k}_t = \alpha(1 - \tau_k)\bar{y}_t + (1 - \alpha)(1 - \tau_w)\bar{y}_t - c_t - T_t + (1 - u_t)S_t$

(5.18d) $\dot{h}_t = Bh_t(1 - u_t)$

(5.18e) $\dot{\lambda}_{1t} = -\alpha(1 - \tau_k)\frac{\bar{y}_t}{k_t}\lambda_{1t} + \rho\lambda_{1t}$

(5.18f) $\dot{\lambda}_{2t} = -\lambda_{1t}(1 - \tau_w)(1 - \alpha)\frac{\bar{y}_t}{h_t} - \lambda_{2t}[B(1 - u_t)] + \rho\lambda_{2t}$

Let us now use the equilibrium/duality conditions (5.18a) and (5.18b) to compact the FOCs in a four-dimensional system of first-order differential equations in the states and controls. The result is the following:

(5.19a) $\xi_c = \frac{\alpha}{\sigma}(1 - \tau_k)\frac{\bar{y}_t}{k_t} - \frac{\rho}{\sigma}$

(5.19b) $\xi_k = \frac{1}{k_t}[\bar{y}_t[\alpha(1 - \tau_k) + (1 - \alpha)(1 - \tau_w)] - c_t - T_t + (1 - u_t)S_t]$

(5.19c) $\xi_h = B(1 - u_t)$

(5.19d) $\xi_u = \tau_k\frac{\bar{y}_t}{k_t} - \frac{c_t}{k_t} + \frac{B(1-\alpha+\gamma)}{\alpha} + B\frac{\alpha-\gamma}{\alpha}u_t +$

$+\frac{u_t}{(1-\alpha)(1-\tau_w)}\left[(1 - \tau_k)\frac{S_t}{k_t} - \frac{\dot{S}_t}{\alpha\bar{y}_t}\right]$

Now, since the Government budget constraint implies that:

(5.20) $\alpha\tau_k\bar{y}_t + (1 - \alpha)\tau_w\bar{y}_t + T_t = (1 - u_t)S_t$

the equation for the growth rate of k_t in (5.19b) simplifies and becomes the usual $\xi_k = \frac{\bar{y}_t}{k_t} + \frac{c_t}{k_t}$ condition.

5.6.2   *Some General Characteristics of Optimal Fiscal Policy*

Let us now compare the motion in a taxed market economy with the optimal laws of evolution of the variables in system (3.1i). Following the principles of Path Coincidence, we first observe that:

Proposition 5.9 *The optimal fiscal policy has to leave the return on physical capital free of taxes.*

Proof The only way to make (5.19a) and (3.1a) coincide is to impose $\tau_k = 0$. $\square$

Therefore, we are left in a situation where the only law of motion to differ from its efficient counterpart is that governing the growth rate of working time. By considering that, by Proposition 5.9, $\tau_k = 0$, this law reduces to:

$$(5.21a) \qquad \xi_u = -\frac{c_t}{k_t} + \frac{B(1-\alpha+\gamma)}{\alpha} + B\frac{\alpha-\gamma}{\alpha}u_t + \frac{u_t}{(1-\alpha)(1-\tau_w)}\left[\frac{S_t}{k_t} - \frac{\dot{S}_t}{\alpha y_t}\right]$$

This means that we need to choose S_t, $\dot{S}_t$ and τ_w such that equation (5.21a) above and equation (3.1d), we report here for the sake of a simple discussion:

$$(5.21b) \qquad \xi_u = \frac{\dot{u}_t}{u_t} = \frac{B(1-\alpha+\gamma)}{\alpha} - \frac{c_t}{k_t} + B\psi u_t$$

coincide for all t. Let us equate (5.21a) and (5.21b). After conducting a little algebra, it is easy to show that the two paths coincide if:

$$(5.22) \qquad \frac{S_t}{\bar{y}_t}\left[\alpha n_t - \frac{\dot{S}_t}{S_t}\right] = B\gamma(1 - \tau_w)$$

where $n_t = \frac{\bar{y}_t}{k_t}$ is the optimal level, at time t, of the average goods production. We will use equation (5.22) to study further implications on the design of optimal fiscal policy along the BGP and in transition.

5.6.3   The Optimal Fiscal Policy Along the BGP

In this sub-section, we basically replicate the main results obtained by Garcia-Castrillo and Sanso [10] for the economy evolving along the BGP.

Let us first prove the following:

Proposition 5.10 *Let the economy evolve along a non-degenerate BGP. The growth rate of the subsidy is constant and equal to the efficient growth rate of the economy. The ratio* $\left(\frac{S}{\bar{y}}\right)^*$ *is constant at the value:*

$$(5.23) \qquad \left(\frac{S}{\bar{y}}\right)^* = \gamma\frac{1-\tau_w}{\psi u^*} > 0$$

Proof Since $B\gamma(1 - \tau_w)$ in equation (5.22) is a positive constant, the growth rate of the subsidy $\xi_S^* \equiv \frac{\dot{S}_t}{S_t}$ cannot indefinitely grow or decrease (provided we are interested in a situation where $\frac{S_t}{\bar{y}_t}$ neither vanishes nor explodes). A constant value for ξ_S^* also implies a constant value for $\left(\frac{S}{\bar{y}}\right)^*$ and therefore the equivalence $\xi_S^* = \xi^* = B\psi\left(1 - u^*\right)$. By substituting the efficient BGP value of average goods production from (3.9), we can obtain the stationary value of the subsidy per unit of goods production in (5.23). $\square$

The form of equation (5.23) has important implications; as it appears evident, the subsidy S_t, is not unique, but depends on τ_w. Therefore:

Proposition 5.11 *Let the economy evolve along a non-degenerate BGP. Given the level of goods production and the parameter configuration, the amount of subsidy required for a decentralized economy to behave as a centralized economy is negatively linked to the level of wage taxation.*

Proof The result in the proposition is a consequence of the form of equation (5.23). $\square$

Now, recalling that we have also hypothesized the existence of a non-distortionary tax in the form of the lump-sum tax T, we can divide the budget constraint in (5.20) by $\bar{y}_t$. After conducting a little algebra (recall that $\tau_k = 0$), and restricting attention to the BGP, we find that the balanced constraint can be written as:

$$(5.24) \qquad \left(\frac{T}{\bar{y}}\right)^* = \gamma\frac{1-u^*}{\psi u^*} - \frac{\gamma+(1-\alpha)u^*}{\psi u^*}\tau_w$$

Thus, along the BGP:

Corollary 5.3 *There exists a continuum of combinations of T and τ_w which can finance the optimal fiscal policy.*

Proof The result in the proposition is a consequence of the form of equation (5.24). $\square$

Given (5.24), we can determine further interesting details on the optimal design of fiscal policy along the BGP. Consider first that the extent of Government intervention (hereafter Government size) is $\Sigma_t = (1-\alpha)\tau_w + T_t/\bar{y}_t$ when $T_t \gtreqqless 0$ and $\Sigma_t = (1-\alpha)\tau_w - T_t/\bar{y}_t$ when $T_t < 0$. The need for $\Sigma^* < 1$ along the BGP implies that:

Proposition 5.12 *Let the economy evolve along a non-degenerate BGP. There will then exist a minimum value of τ_w, $\tau_{w,\min} = 1 - \frac{\psi u^*}{\gamma(1-u^*)}$, such that only if $\tau_w > \tau_{w,\min}$ will the fiscal policy be feasible. If $u^* > \frac{\gamma}{\gamma+\psi}(< 1)$, $\tau_{w,\min} < 0$ and wage taxation can be set to zero.*

Proof By definition, the Government size equals the amount of the subsidy per unit of goods production, namely $\Sigma_t = (1 - u_t)\, S_t/\bar{y}_t$. Restricting attention to the BGP, and recalling (5.23), the need for $\Sigma^* < 1$ implies the results in the proposition. □

The content of Proposition 5.12 is represented in Figures 5.9a and 5.9b,[58] illustrating the two cases of $\tau_{w,\min} > 0$ and $\tau_{w,\min} < 0$. Since $(T/\bar{y})^*$ (from 5.24) has a maximum value of one, τ_w cannot be set to zero in the first case. Conversely, this can happen when $\tau_{w,\min} < 0$ and the fiscal policy is entirely financed with the lump-sum tax.

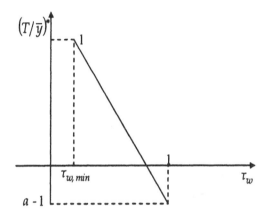

Figure 5.10a **The minimum value of τ_w when $\tau_{w,\min} > 0$**

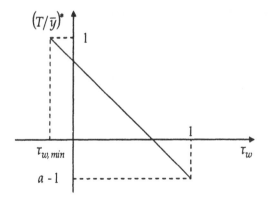

Figure 5.10b **The minimum value of τ_w when $\tau_{w,\min} < 0$**

Nearing the end of this sub-section, consider also that in Figures 5.9a and 5.9b it

[58]Reprinted from Review of Economic Dynamics, Vol. 3, N° 4, Garcia-Castrillo and Sanso, Human Capital and Optimal Policy in a Lucas-Type Model", 757-770, Copyright 2000, with permission from Elsevier.

appears that there is a value of τ_w at which point $(T/\bar{y})^* = 0$. Given the definition of Government size, the following is therefore true:

Corollary 5.4 *The combination of T and τ_w which minimizes Σ along the BGP, requires $(T/\bar{y})^* = 0$. When the size of the Government is minimized, the value of the wage tax rate is*:

$$\tau_w^* = 0 < \gamma \frac{1-u^*}{\gamma+(1-\alpha)u^*} < 1$$

Proof By imposing $(T/\bar{y})^* = 0$ in (5.24), we can obtain the value of the tax rate on wages in corollary. $\square$

5.6.4   *Fiscal Policy in Transition: the Case of a Small Coefficient of Risk Aversion*

It is without doubt much more complicated to figure out the characteristics of the optimal fiscal intervention when the economy is along off-balanced paths.[59] However, the availability of optimal transitional paths for the average goods production, physical capital and working time is of particular help and gives us a critical advantage on Garcia-Castrillo and Sanso [10].

Consider, once more, equation (5.22). Since we know, from Chapter 3, that we can obtain the explicit trajectories of n_t and $\bar{y}_t$ for a given parameter configuration, we can try to solve numerically the equation for $\dot{S}_t$. By considering the parameter choices in the simulations of sub-section 3.4.5 and the alternative values of 1 and -1/3 for $\mu = \frac{n^* - n(0)}{n(0)}$, we can try to determine the optimal design of the fiscal policy in transition. As in many other occasions in the book:

Remark *The numerical results discussed in this section have always been confirmed by extensive numerical experimentation conducted in all regions of the feasible parameter space.*

Let us start the discussion by considering the case of $\sigma < \alpha$. As already discussed, the steady-state level of the subsidy S_t per unit of goods production depends on the level of τ_w. Consider Figure 5.11 where the surface of possible time evolutions of the subsidy is depicted for all (positive) values of τ_w. What appears evident from the Figure is that the inverse relationship between the level of the subsidy and the value of the tax rate on the return of human capital also binds in transition. This means that, at each point in time:

Interesting Result 5.3 *Higher values of τ_w always imply, all conditions being equal, lower levels of the subsidy.*

---

[59] A proof that the taxed decentralized economy following the optimal fiscal policy is saddle-path stable is given in Garcia-Castrillo and Sanso [10]. In this sub-section and in the following we will be showing that, from the global point of view as well, there only exists one trajectory which implies an asymptotic positive and finite value of $\frac{S_t}{\bar{y}_t}$.

$\mu=1$ $\mu=-1/3$

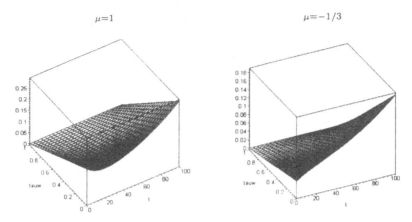

Figure 5.11 The time evolution of S_t for all feasible values of τ_w

In order to infer further details on the properties of optimal fiscal policy in transition when σ is small, let us consider the particular case of $\tau_w = 1/5$. Next Figures contains the time evolution of the subsidy when the imbalances are such that μ is respectively equal to 1 and -1/3.[60] Consider that, given the sign of the slope of the policy function for the average goods production numerically obtained in Interesting Result 3.5, a positive $\mu = \frac{n^*-n(0)}{n(0)}$ implies low $n(0)$ values and therefore high $p(0) = \frac{k(0)}{h(0)^\psi}$ values.

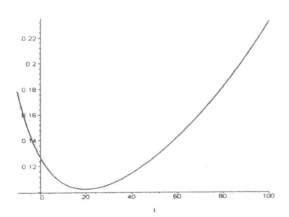

Figure 5.12a The subsidy in transition in case of high $p(0)$ values ($\mu = 1$)

Therefore, it is highly interesting to observe that:

---

[60]When solving equation (5.22), the constant of integration must be accurately chosen so that the subsidy follows the only possible feasible optimal path.

Interesting Result 5.4 *When the economy presents a large relative excess of physical capital, the subsidy will initially decrease in transition and then start again to grow. An economy having a relative excess of human capital only allows for monotonically increasing levels of the subsidy in transition.*

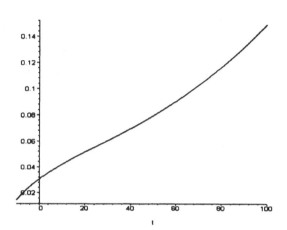

Figure 5.12b The subsidy in transition in case of low $p(0)$ values ($\mu = -1/3$)

Figure 5.13 traces the growth rates of the subsidy (broken lines) and of goods production (growth rate of the narrow economy) in transition for both cases of a positive and negative μ. Notice that the growth rate of the subsidy is always above the growth rate of the economy if $\mu = 1$. The contrary happens when $\mu = -1/3$. Therefore, as depicted in Figure 5.14, the ratio $S_t/\bar{y}_t$ is monotonically growing (decreasing) in transition when $\mu = 1$ ($\mu = -1/3$).

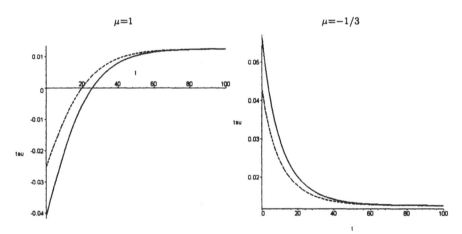

Figure 5.13 Off-balanced trajectories of ξ_S and $\xi_{\bar{y}}$ when $\sigma < \alpha$

Therefore, recalling Interesting Result 3.5 showing that the policy function for the average goods production is always negatively-sloped, this further implies:

Interesting Result 5.5 *The policy function $\frac{S_t}{\bar{y}_t}(p_t)$ is globally downward sloping if the inverse of the intertemporal elasticity of substitution is small with respect to the share of physical capital*

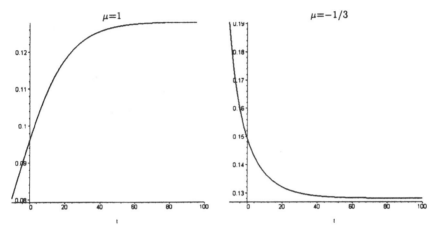

Figure 5.14 **The time evolution of $S_t/\bar{y}_t$ when $\sigma < \alpha$**

Notice that, very interestingly:

Remark *The numerical result above found implies an inverted-sign slope w.r.t what was found for the other policy functions $u_t(p_t)$ and $m_t(p_t)$.*

We shall end this sub-section by plotting the time evolution of the Government size Σ for the specific values used in this simulation:

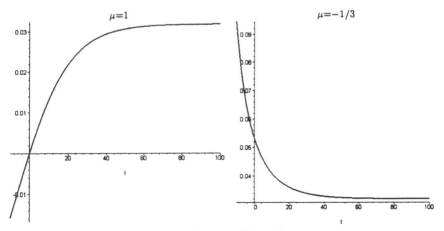

Figure 5.15 **The Government size in transition when $\sigma < \alpha$**

Considering that a positive (negative) value of μ is associated with an excess of physical capital (human capital) it is evident from Figure 5.15 that the numerical simulations (in case of a low σ) depict a situation where:

Interesting Result 5.6 *Shocks implying an excess of physical capital (human capital) lead to a transitionally lower-than-BGP (higher-than-BGP) Government size.*

5.6.5   Fiscal Policy in Transition: the Case of a Large Coefficient of Risk Aversion

Since the arbitrary constant associated with the solution of the differential equation for S_t now depends on τ_w, we cannot show the behavior of the subsidy for all feasible values of $\tau_w \in (0,1)$. Therefore, we shall simply fix $\tau_w = 1/5$ as in the above sub-section and proceed to study the behavior of the economy in transition. The parameter configuration is as above.

In Figures 5.16a and 5.16b, we first show the time evolution of S_t after a shock alternatively raising or decreasing the economy's endowment of physical capital.

As it is evident from the graphs, also in the case of a large σ:

Interesting Result 5.7 *When the economy presents a large relative excess of physical capital, the subsidy will initially decrease in transition and then start again to grow. An economy having a relative excess of human capital only allows for monotonically increasing levels of the subsidy in transition.*

However, comparing the graphs in Figures 5.12a and 5.16a, the following must be considered:

Remark *When the taxed economy experience a large excess of physical capital, higher σ reduce the decreasing period of the subsidy.*

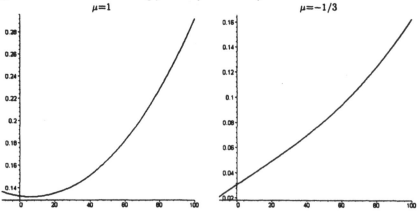

Figure 5.16 The level of the subsidy in transition

The growth rates of the subsidy and goods production with this specific parameter configuration are represented in Figure 5.17. The evolution of the ratio $S_t/\bar{y}_t$ is shown in Figure 5.18.

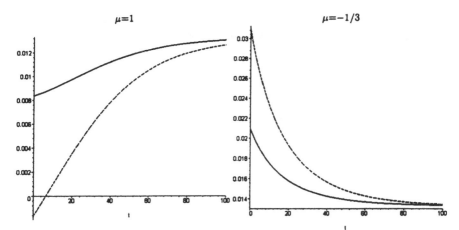

Figure 5.17 The growth rates of the subsidy and of the economy in transition

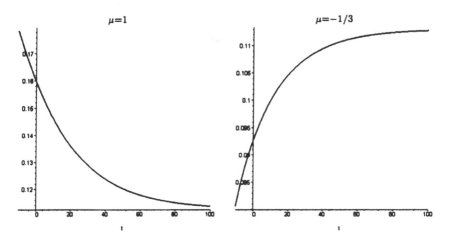

Figure 5.18 The time evolution of $S_t/\bar{y}_t$ in transition when $\sigma > \alpha$

As it can be seen by a comparison of Figures 5.14 and 5.18, the change of sign in $\alpha - \sigma$ leads to a change of sign in the slope of the policy function $\frac{S_t}{\bar{y}_t}(p_t)$. As a matter of fact, we find that:

Interesting Result 5.8 *The policy function $\frac{S_t}{\bar{y}_t}(p_t)$ is globally downward sloping if the inverse of the intertemporal elasticity of substitution is large with respect to the share of physical capital.*

Consider now, in Figure 5.19, the convergence of Government size to its long-run position after a shock altering the BGP.

Contrarily to what happens when the inverse of the intertemporal elasticity of substitution is small, now we have that:

Interesting Result 5.9 *Shocks implying an excess of physical capital (human capital) lead to a transitionally higher-than-BGP (lower-than-BGP) Government size.*

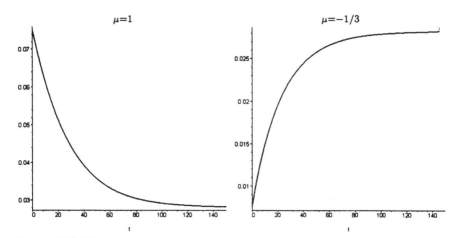

Figure 5.19 The Government size in transition when $\sigma > \alpha$

Bibliography

[1] Asada T. *et al.* (1998), "Endogenous Growth and the Balanced Growth Equilibrium", *Research in Economics*, **52**, pp. 191-212.

[2] Barro R. and Sala-i-Martin X. (1995), *Economic Growth*, Mc-Graw Hill, New York.

[3] Becker G. S. (1964), *Human Capital*, Columbia University Press for the National Bureau of Economic Research, New York.

[4] Benhabib J. and Myiao T. (1981), "Some New Results on the Dynamics of the Generalized Tobin Model", *International Economic Review*, **22**, pp. 589-96.

[5] Benhabib J. and Perli R. (1994), "Uniqueness and Indeterminacy: on the Dynamics of Endogenous Growth", *Journal of Economic Theory*, **63**, pp. 113-142.

[6] Bond E. W., *et al.* (1996), "A General Two-sector Model of Endogenous Growth with Human and Physical Capital: Balanced Growth and Transitional Dynamics", *Journal of Economic Theory*, **68**, pp. 149-173.

[7] Caballè J. and Santos M. (1993), "On Endogenous Growth with Physical and Human Capital", *Journal of Political Economy*, **101**, pp. 1042-1067.

[8] Chamley C. (1993), "Externalities and Dynamics in Models of 'Learning or Doing'", *International Economic Review*, **34**, pp. 583-609.

[9] Faig M. (1993), "A Simple Economy with Human Capital: Transitional Dynamics, Technology Shocks and Fiscal Policy", *Journal of Macroeconomics*, **101**, pp. 1042-1067.

[10] Garcia-Castrillo P. and Sanso M. (2000), "Human Capital and Optimal Policy in a Lucas-Type Model", *Review of Economic Dynamics*, **3**, pp. 757-770.

[11] Ladron-de-Guevara A. *et al.* (1997), "Equilibrium Dynamics in Two-Sector Models of Endogenous Growth," *Journal of Economic Dynamics and Control*, **21**, pp. 115-143.

[12] Lucas R. (1988), "On the Mechanics of Economic Development", *Journal of Monetary Economics*, **22**, pp. 3-42.

[13] Mattana P. (2003), "Global Logistic Growth in Two-Sector Capital Accumulation Models", Working Paper n° 21, Department of Economics, University of Cagliari.

[14] Mattana P. (2003), "A Global Characterization of the Optimal Solution of the Uzawa-Lucas Model", Working Paper n° 23, Department of Economics, University of Cagliari.

[15] Mattana P. (2003), "Optimal Trajectories of Consumption and Physical Capital in Presence of Learning", Working Paper n° 24, Department of Economics, University of Cagliari.

[16] Mattana P. (2003), "The Slopes of the Equilibrium Functions Linking Control and State Variables in the Uzawa-Lucas Model", Working Paper n° 25, Department of Economics, University of Cagliari.

[17] Mattana P. (2003), "The Global Properties of the Optimal Fiscal Policy in Presence of a Learning Sector", Working Paper n° 26, Department of Economics, University of Cagliari.

[18] Mattana P. (2003), "The BGP Deformation of the Market Economy in Presence of a Learning Sector", Working Paper n° 27, Department of Economics, University of Cagliari.

[19] Mattana P. (2003), "Mattana P., 2003, "Equilibrium and Optimal Exogenous Growth in the Uzawa-Lucas Model", Working Paper n° 28, Department of Economics, University of Cagliari.", Working Paper n° 28, Department of Economics, University of Cagliari.

[20] Mattana P. (2003), "Some Local Properties of the Centralized Solution of the Uzawa-Lucas Model", Working Paper n° 31, Department of Economics, University of Cagliari.

[21] Mattana P. (2004), "Fiscal Policy and Reconciliation of Optimal and Equilibrium Transitional Growth Paths", Working Paper n° 35, Department of Economics, University of Cagliari.

[22] Mattana P. and Venturi B. (1999), "Existence and Stability of Periodic Solutions in the Dynamics of Endogenous Growth", *International Review of Economics and Business*, **46**, pp. 259-284.

[23] Mulligan C. B. and Sala-i-Martin X. (1993), "Transitional Dynamics in Two-Sector Models of Endogenous Growth", *Quarterly Journal of Economics*, **108**, pp. 739-773.

[24] Ortigueira S. (1998), "Fiscal Policy in an Endogenous Growth Model with Human Capital Accumulation", *Journal of Monetary Economics*, **42**, pp. 323-355.

[25] Piras R. (1997), "On Lucas's Model of Endogenous Growth", *Economic Notes*, **26**, pp. 111-134.

[26] Romer P. (1990), "Endogenous Technical Change", *Journal of Political Economy*, **98**, pp. 71-102.

[27] Ruiz-Tamarit J. R. (2002), "Multiplicity, Overtaking and Convergence in the Lucas Two-Sector Growth Model", Working Paper n° 17, FEDEA, University of Valencia.

[28] Uzawa H. (1965), "Optimal Technical Change in an Aggregative Model of Economic Growth", *International Economic Review*, **6**, pp. 18-31.

[29] Wiggins S. (1990), *Introduction to Applied Nonlinear Dynamical Systems and Chaos*, Springer-Verlag. New York.

[30] Xie D. (1994), "Divergence in Economic Performance: Transitional Dynamics with Multiple Equilibria", *Journal of Economic Theory*, **63**, pp. 97-112.

Index